Winning the West for Christ

Winning the West for Christ

Sheldon Jackson and Presbyterianism
on the Rocky Mountain Frontier,
1869–1880

NORMAN J. BENDER

University of New Mexico Press
Albuquerque

Library of Congress Cataloging-in-Publication Data

Bender, Norman J., 1927–
　Winning the West for Christ: Sheldon Jackson and
Presbyterianism on the Rocky Mountain frontier, 1869–1880 /
Norman J. Bender. — 1st ed.
　　p.　cm.
　Includes bibliographical references (p.) and index.
　ISBN 0–8263–1670–0
　1. Jackson, Sheldon, 1834–1909. 2. Presbyterian Church—West
(U.S.)—Clergy—Biography. 3. Missionaries—West (U.S.)—
Biography. 4. Presbyterian Church—Missions—West (U.S.)
5. West (U.S.)—Church history—19th century.　I. Title.
BX9225.J25B46　1996
266´.51—dc20　　　　　　　　　　　　　　　　　　96–4421
　　　　　　　　　　　　　　　　　　　　　　　　　CIP

For
Norman Carl,
Mark and Elizabeth,
and my very good friends Christopher and Jessica

Contents

Illustrations

Preface

*The Home Missionary work is like that of an army of occupation.
We send a few men to the frontier; they enter all the new States
and Territories; they explore the country thoroughly; they go down
into the valleys and up the mountain sides, and if they find no
insuperable obstacles, they take possession of the most eligible points,
fortify themselves, and send back for reinforcements.*
—*Rocky Mountain Presbyterian*, MAY 1876

In 1990 the Presbyterian Church in the United States of
America authorized publication of a new hymnal. Repelled, perhaps, by
the militant language employed in the famous old hymn *Onward Christian
Soldiers*, the publication committee decided to reject the hymn; it does not
appear in the new volume.

Sheldon Jackson would not have approved!

Jackson's career as self-styled superintendent of Presbyterian mission
work in the Rocky Mountain West during the 1870s serves admirably as a
basis for examining the many controversial issues raised by the irresistible
drive for post-Civil War settlement of the West.[1] The response to these
challenges by a great Protestant denomination, determined to place its
standard on the highest peaks of what was regarded as a vast and sinful
land, is well characterized by the theme of the church militant embark-
ing to win the West for Christ. A colleague who witnessed many of
Jackson's exploits certainly conveyed that impression when he wrote
about the progression westward of the Blue Banner, historic symbol of
the Presbyterian Church:

> So in this crisis hour of our home mission advance, when the line was
> wavering and halting in the face of a great opportunity, this veteran
> of the ranks seized the standard of the Cross, beneath which was a
> fluttering pennant of blue, advanced it swiftly to the front, and, plant-
> ing it far in advance of the line, called upon the Presbyterian hosts to
> bring their men up to it.[2]

As they reflected on the awesome task before them, Jackson and the
missionaries he supervised never doubted that they were locked into the

age-old struggle of good versus evil. Many indeed were the challenges perceived by the advancing vanguard of the Presbyterian host. Accepting an
assignment on a remote western skirmish line, the home missionary anticipated encounters with rival denominations, with the heathen religious
practices of the native inhabitants, and with the whole gamut of sinful conduct attributed to lives devoid of restraining religious influences. In the
arsenal of weapons employed by the Presbyterians to defeat their foes, the
lessons of the Bible, as they interpreted them, were, of course, foremost.
As vehicles for making practical applications of the written word, missionaries organized churches, erected houses of worship, and conducted both
Sabbath schools and day schools. As might be expected, some of these
endeavors to spread the Word flourished in favorable locations under the
leadership of talented and dedicated individuals. Others withered and died,
when expectations failed to materialize and discouraged missionaries abandoned the field. No matter the outcome, these churches must be recognized for their important role in attempting to mold what they perceived
as a spiritually destitute frontier society into an image of late-nineteenth-
century "goodness" acceptable to national political and religious leaders.[3]

My assessment of the westward movement of Presbyterianism in the
1870s makes no attempt to grapple with the complex doctrinal concepts
debated then by Presbyterian theologians. Rather, the intent is to place the
story of the trials and tribulations of well-meaning missionaries and their
families in the context of their times. Rather than try to relate every incident concerning every missionary and each congregation, I have instead
developed the stories of those individuals who, in my judgment, had the
most revealing experiences. In many cases, I have incorporated the words
of the participants themselves in order to present, as much as possible, a
realistic appraisal of their most intimate concerns. In that quest I have
relied extensively on the Sheldon Jackson collection of correspondence
and on his scrapbooks, currently at the Presbyterian Historical Society in
Philadelphia, Pennsylvania. Jackson's colorful accounts of his travels
throughout his superintendency in the 1870s have been particularly revealing. That material, added to other published and unpublished recollections of pioneering missionaries in numerous repositories in the West,
has, I hope, helped me to achieve my goal presenting a study that is not
"dry as dust" church history.

   I want the reader to have a sense of the kind of Presbyterianism that
evolved in the Rocky Mountain West as a result of the efforts of Sheldon
Jackson and his colleagues. Subjected to the supposed radical and democ-
ratizing influences of western society, did western Presbyterianism become

noticeably different from its counterpart in the East? Or did old traditions and doctrines emerge relatively unscathed from association with the frontier? Although it is always difficult to provide a definitive label for any historical event, the reader should still be able to find a place for Presbyterianism on the Rocky Mountain frontier, a place shaped by the views of the people who lived through that challenging adventure.

I am indebted to many people for their kind and generous assistance in making this work possible. Fred Heuser and his staff at the Department of History of the Presbyterian Church were very helpful, as always, in providing pertinent documents from the department's collections. Naomi Bender at the office of the Presbyterian Synod of Colorado made available for my use the annual reports of the General Assembly of the Presbyterian Church. At the regional office of the National Archives in Denver, Colorado, Joel Barker guided me to the microfilm records of the Office of Indian Affairs. Librarians at the University of Colorado, Boulder, Colorado; at Westminster College, Salt Lake City, Utah; at Wasatch Academy, Mt. Pleasant, Utah; at Menaul School, Albuquerque, New Mexico; and at the Princeton Theological Seminary, Princeton, New Jersey, devoted much time to locating items for this study. Many people supplied church histories of great value to my project, and those publications have been gratefully acknowledged in appropriate footnotes. Portions of the material used in this book have appeared previously in *Montana*, the journal of the Montana Historical Society; *Colorado Magazine*, formerly the journal of the Colorado Historical Society; and the *Midwest Review*. I wish to thank the editors of those publications for permission to include that material in my book. Finally, my deepest thanks are extended to Debbie Scott, who provided indispensable typing services in the production of the manuscript.

Winning the West for Christ

1 | The Evolution of a "Border Missionary"

*It was to be [for] the mission service that I was dedicated
in infant baptism....*
—SHELDON JACKSON, DECEMBER 7, 1857

On Prospect Hill in Sioux City, Iowa, stands an impressive monument overlooking the Missouri River and the great expanse of prairie to the west. The monument is inscribed

ERECTED BY IOWA PRESBYTERIANS
IN MEMORY OF
REV. SHELDON JACKSON
REV. T.H. CLELAND
REV. J.C. ELLIOTT
PIONEER MISSIONARIES WHO ON
APRIL 29, 1869 FROM THIS HILLTOP
VIEWED THE GREAT UNCHURCHED
AREAS AND AFTER PRAYER WENT OUT
TO WIN THE WEST FOR CHRIST

Speaking before a meeting of Iowa Presbyterians in 1905, Sheldon Jackson recalled that memorable event. He wondered if his audience appreciated the full significance of the great work started so many years ago. He remembered being overwhelmed by emotion in April of 1869, when he and his companions knelt in prayer as the Holy Spirit opened their eyes to see the vast extent of spiritual desolation stretching to the western horizon. Concluding his remarks, he paid tribute to the courageous Iowans who had been selected by God to inaugurate a movement that would establish the Presbyterian Church within one-half of the United States.[1]

Iowa Presbyterians may have been selected by God to organize the great forward movement, but they were also selected by Sheldon Jackson to serve as a vehicle for his own aspirations to initiate and oversee the westward

3

expansion of the Presbyterian Church after the Civil War. In 1869 the young missionary was determined to make a name for himself in the ranks of those who were advancing the standard of Presbyterianism into the "great unchurched areas." Convinced that decision-makers on the Board of Domestic Missions of his church were reluctant to allocate scarce funds to any new missionary enterprises in the West, Jackson had decided to force the issue by securing an endorsement from the Iowa brethren to push ahead on his own. Although some of his superiors on the mission board were appalled by Jackson's audacity, others of his colleagues who recalled his background and record of church service may not have been particularly surprised by the news from Sioux City.

Jackson's early life had never been far removed from the influence of a conservative Christian family. At the time of Sheldon's birth, on May 18, 1834, his parents, Samuel and Delia Jackson, lived in Minaville, New York, a small town in the lower Mohawk Valley where Samuel operated a mercantile establishment. Hoping to find a more prosperous location for the family business, the Jacksons soon moved to Esperance, a community about ten miles south of Minaville. Sheldon's sister, Louise, was born there shortly after they arrived. While residing in Esperance, Samuel and Delia Jackson decided to make a public confession of their Christian faith by seeking admission to the local Presbyterian church. Delia received the rites of membership on December 23, 1837, and a few months later the congregation accepted Samuel as a member. The final step, of course, in the decision by any family with small children to make a total Christian commitment was the baptism of the children. That joyous event took place on December 11, 1838. Although Sheldon probably could not recall in later years the specific details of the ceremony, he firmly believed that by that action his pious parents had dedicated his life to eventual service as a Presbyterian missionary.[2]

While Samuel and Delia Jackson would always recall the year 1838 with fond memories of the baptism of their children, many other Presbyterians in the United States would associate the date with a tragic event. In 1838, at the annual meeting of the General Assembly, the national governing body of the denomination, the church divided into Old School and New School branches. Besides differences of opinion on complex theological matters, one of the principal issues in this division was a controversy over home mission activity. Old School adherents called for control of the administration of missionary funds by their own denomination. The New School branch was willing to pool available resources with interdenominational missionary enterprises such as the American Home Missionary Society and its principal sponsor, the Congregational Church. Remaining steadfastly loyal to the Old School faction, the Jacksons continued to raise their children in an environment where—according to a later friend of Jackson's—"the word of the Lord was the law of the household. . . ."[3]

A few years after settling in Esperance, the Jacksons moved again, this time to a nearby farm. Determined to secure an education for their son that would prepare him for the rigorous challenges of later seminary studies, Jackson's parents carefully selected only schools conducted by reputable Christian teachers for his early training. After passing successfully through the lower grades, Jackson enrolled in 1849 in a Presbyterian academy in Haysville, Ohio. The academy was conducted by a former pastor of the Esperance church, in Haysville, Ohio. A fellow student later remembered Jackson as "diligent, painstaking and conscientious as a student, giving close attention both to his classroom and religious duties. . . ."[4] In 1852 the young scholar entered Union College in Schenectady, New York. A classmate at that institution recalled Jackson as a plodder who, nevertheless, "stood well up in his class, being accorded a place as a speaker on commencement day."[5]

Following his graduation from Union College in 1855, Jackson entered Princeton Theological Seminary, the next step along the path prescribed for talented candidates for the ministry in the Presbyterian Church. During his three years there, he followed a carefully prescribed study program. In the field of classical languages he now moved beyond Latin and Greek, which he had learned at Union College, to concentrate on Hebrew. In addition, he had to master such erudite subjects as "Biblical Criticism and Interpretation," "Didactic and Polemic Theology," and "Ecclesiology." Other courses in his curriculum included "Church History," "Geography and Antiquities," and "Homiletics," the art of preaching. Also required of all students throughout the course of study were exercises in composition and delivery. Clearly, a graduate of Princeton Seminary in the 1850s would have been well prepared to cope with the spiritual element of his pastoral responsibilities.[6]

During his summer vacation in 1856, Jackson received his first official assignment. He was to spread the Word literally about his faith by distributing religious publications for the Presbyterian Board of Publications in the counties near his home in New York. In the following summer, he accepted an appointment as an agent of the American Systematic Beneficence Society of Philadelphia. In that capacity he encouraged pastors and their congregations to give regularly to the various worthy programs of their church. By the end of the summer, Jackson, always a meticulous record keeper, had surely impressed his employers with his report. During his three-month tour of duty in an area extending as far west as Kansas, he had conversed with seventy-five ministers and preached thirty-two sermons before fifty-three congregations comprising a total audience estimated at twenty-four thousand listeners. Anyone with a knowledge of his record of achievement could only have regarded Jackson at the time as a young man whose career as a laborer in the Lord's vineyard would bear watching.[7]

As he neared the end of his course of study at Princeton, Jackson made a decision regarding his future. In December of 1857 he wrote to the Board of Foreign Missions, offering himself as a candidate for a foreign mission field. Although his preference was for work in Asia or South America, he dutifully yielded to the wishes of the board and accepted an offer for assignment to a duty station at an Indian reservation in the United States after graduation.[8] The following months were busy ones for the diligent student. In January of 1858 he passed, without missing a question, an examination designed to test his qualifications for the ministry. After his graduation from Princeton on April 27, he was ordained to the ministry in a service at Schenectady, New York, on May 5. Pleased, no doubt, by his scholarly achievements, he also participated in another ceremony destined to have a lasting effect on his personal life. On May 18 he married Mary Voorhees, a friend from his boyhood whose parents lived near the Jackson home.[9]

Jackson soon learned of the specific challenge awaiting him with the Indians. In the summer of 1858, the Board of Foreign Missions advised him of his selection for a teaching assignment at Spencer Academy, a school for Choctaw boys in the Indian Territory. Sheldon and Mary quickly prepared for their trip to the remote duty station, knowing that their presence was expected for the opening of the fall term. Their long journey was arduous but relatively uneventful. They traveled by train to Quincy, Illinois, where they took passage on a river steamer that carried them down the Mississippi to Napoleon, Arkansas, near the mouth of the Arkansas River. There they transferred to a smaller riverboat that took them to Little Rock, where they boarded a stage for the continuation of their trip to Washington, Arkansas. At Washington they hired a private carriage to take them the rest of the way to Spencer Academy, which they finally reached on October 6.[10]

Spencer Academy, named for Secretary of War John C. Spencer, was located in the southeast corner of the Indian Territory, about fifty miles west of the Arkansas border. It was one of several schools established in the Choctaw Nation after passage of "An Act Respecting Public Schools" by the General Council of the tribe in 1842. The Tribal Board of Trustees appointed to supervise the operation of these schools soon called upon the Board of Foreign Missions of the Presbyterian Church to provide a superintendent and teachers for the Spencer Academy. Attendance at the school gradually increased, until the records show more than a hundred boys enrolled by 1850. When the Jacksons arrived, their impressions of the school facilities and their living quarters were very favorable. The classroom buildings and student dormitories were in good condition, and the house they occupied was quite adequate for their needs.[11]

Less favorable were Jackson's impressions of his students. Short of stature himself, he found that some of his boys who exceeded his height defied his efforts to maintain strict discipline in the classroom. His only recourse on those occasions was to administer whippings with a strap that he always carried with him for that purpose. He professed to dislike the method of punishment, but other teachers assured him it was the only way to keep order. When he could exercise his pedagogical talents undisturbed, he endeavored to teach the elements of what he regarded as a proper education. These included geography, arithmetic, grammar, reading, spelling, and writing. On Sundays, teachers and students devoted most of the day, of course, to Sabbath-school classes, in which the boys memorized portions of the Bible, and to morning and evening church services.[12]

In addition to meeting his teaching requirements, Jackson often traveled to small communities in the vicinity of the academy, preaching and conducting occasional wedding ceremonies for those among the Choctaws who had accepted conversion to Christianity. He frankly admitted that he enjoyed these experiences much more than his association with the Choctaw boys in his school. While her husband occupied his time with these responsibilities, Mary kept busy fulfilling the duties expected of a missionary's wife. She mended the students' school uniforms, visited students and faculty members who were ill, supervised the work of the janitorial staff, and tended to the multitude of housekeeping tasks in her own home. After describing one of her busy days to her sister-in-law, she asked, "What do you think of our work? No time you perceive for calling or receiving calls, taking walks or attending concerts, but I doubt not we are as happy as you."[13]

Regrettably, whatever happiness the young couple shared in their lives at Spencer Academy was soon overshadowed by factors that convinced Jackson to submit his resignation early in 1859. In his letter to the foreign mission board he spoke of the confining aspects of his teaching obligations, which had produced an adverse effect on his health. Also, in his opinion, the climate of the Indian Territory had contributed in a large degree to protracted spells of dizziness and what he described as bilious fever. Although the symptoms mentioned by Jackson might at a later date have been partly attributed to psychosomatic causes, the distraught missionary saw a change of residence as the only cure. There is no indication in existing records of the precise date on which the Jacksons left Spencer Academy, but by the spring of 1859 they were at Galesburg, Illinois. Jackson's parents had moved there from their home in New York, and Sheldon and Mary enjoyed a brief visit with their relatives while they awaited a new mission assignment.[14]

That call was not long in coming. On June 6, 1859, the Board of Domestic Missions appropriated three hundred dollars to support Jackson as a missionary for one year in a vaguely defined area in the southeastern corner of Minnnesota. With his wife's concurrence he finally decided on La Crescent, a little settlement on the Mississippi River twenty miles north of the Iowa border, for his headquarters. After moving with Mary into a small rented house in La Crescent, Jackson conveyed his impression of his new challenge to his family back in Galesburg. "On many accounts," he wrote, "it will be a hard field to cultivate, but doubtless it is the same throughout this whole western country."[15] At La Crescent, Jackson exhibited the zeal destined to make him a cultivator of hard fields *par excellence*. In addition to preparing the way for establishment of a church at La Crescent, he visited the nearby town of Hokah, where he accepted an offer to use the Masonic Hall for church services. In September he received a commission from the Board of Domestic Missions to serve as pastor to congregations at La Crescent, Hokah, "and vicinity." Armed with this document, he officially organized his first church in the area at Hokah on September 20, 1859. The church had four members.[16]

When organizing a church, Jackson would have followed the procedure established by his denomination: Persons desiring organization as a church would first prepare and sign a petition expressing their intent. After examining letters of dismission from former church members and approving professions of faith from new members, Jackson would proceed to the election of one or more ruling elders. These men, who were expected to exercise control over the spiritual conduct of the congregation, would then be ordained by Jackson in a ceremony that included answering questions such as "Do you believe the Scriptures to be the word of God?" and "Do you approve of the government and discipline of the Presbyterian Church?" After satisfactory completion of these preliminary steps, Jackson would forward a notice of his action to appropriate officials in the hierarchy of the church; they would acknowledge the organization in their records.[17]

Interpreting the designation "and vicinity" in his commission in the broadest possible context, Jackson traveled far and wide throughout southeastern Minnesota and western Wisconsin in his quest for locations where there was support for a church organization. Without a horse and buggy of his own, he was at first obliged to walk more often than not. After a typical journey of 110 miles early in 1860, he found that he had walked eighty miles and caught rides for the other thirty. Although his strenuous journeys were surely tiring for a person not blessed with a powerful physique, Jackson was rewarded by expressions of genuine joy and gratitude from those he encountered who were eager to hear his message. "When I meet such people," he wrote after one of his more lengthy trips, "I forget all my weariness and trials and bless God for permitting me to be a border missionary."[18]

For the Jacksons, their experiences between 1859 and 1864 at La Crescent were often rewarding, sometimes discouraging, but never monotonous. In the spring of 1860, they found time to visit friends and relatives in the East. Mary enjoyed spending several weeks with her parents while her husband attended the annual meeting of the General Assembly of his church in Rochester, New York. Jackson seized the opportunity to obtain funds from old acquaintances for the construction of a house of worship in La Crescent, where he had organized a church on December 28, 1859. Aided by these contributions and other donations received from solicitations by mail, he announced completion of a modest sanctuary for his congregation in the spring of 1862. For the building process, he personally transported, with a borrowed ox team and wagon, the needed timbers and stone from the banks of the Mississippi about a mile and a half from the construction site.

In addition to financial support for his church, Jackson derived another benefit from his Eastern journey in 1860. He visited Princeton Seminary and recruited three young graduates for assignments in his mission field. But although initially successful in his attempts to supply leaders for his scattered flocks, he soon found himself handicapped in his efforts by events beyond his control.[19]

Noticeably lacking in Jackson's correspondence at this time is any comment about the issues drawing the nation closer to civil war. Still, he and his church were not immune from these disruptive forces. Sectional division in the Presbyterian Church had actually preceded the secession of the South from the Union. Reacting to differing viewpoints on the slavery issue, the New School faction in 1858 and the Old School adherents in 1861 divided into northern and southern branches. When the war began in April of 1861, shock waves from the great conflict reached Jackson's faraway mission field in the form of drastically reduced financial support from the Board of Domestic Missions. Any reduction in the already meager level of support for home missionary work on the western frontier could only have diminished the desire of young missionaries to accept these demanding positions.[20]

While the struggle between North and South intensified on battlefields in the East, Jackson continued to minister to the needs of Presbyterians in his domain. He did not comment upon the bloody uprising of the Santee Sioux at their reservation in southwestern Minnesota in the summer of 1862. Military units from Fort Snelling and other garrisons in the vicinity quelled the rebellion after several weeks of hard fighting, but Jackson, along with all white settlers in the area, must have been concerned about the consequences if the soldiers were not successful in subduing the Indians. In the summer of 1863, Jackson decided to make a more personal contribution toward alleviating the suffering caused by the war. Responding to a call from the United States Christian Commission for volunteers "to promote the spiritual and temporal welfare and improvement of the men of the Army and Navy," he accepted a commission from that organization on July 28, 1863, to provide his services to the Army of the Cumberland in Tennessee. His responsibilities included distributing Christian reading material, visiting the sick and wounded to comfort them and help them write letters home, aiding surgeons in the care of the wounded, and addressing soldiers "for their personal instruction and benefit, temporal and eternal."[21]

During his brief period of service with the Christian Commission, Jackson faithfully carried out his prescribed duties. Stationed behind the lines near Winchester, Tennessee, he distributed religious tracts at a field hospital and at a camp for Confederate prisoners. For his supply of these tracts, Jackson could have selected, from material available at the time, volumes bearing titles such as *Sinners Welcome—Come to Jesus Christ*; *Something for the Hospital*; *Little Lizzie's Letter to a Soldier*; and, of course, the *Soldier's Pocket Bible*. He held daily prayer meetings and was pleasantly surprised when he discovered much religious interest among soldiers of both the North and South. Although he felt that he was doing much good in his job, he reluctantly terminated his commitment to the worthy cause at the end of August, when he received news from Minnesota that Mary was ill. Jackson did not specifically identify the cause of her indisposition in his correspondence. The birth of their daughter Delia, whom they nicknamed Daisy, occurred soon after his return to La Crescent, however, and Mary may have experienced difficulties in her pregnancy. In any event, by the end of 1863 Jackson's professional interests began to focus on a new challenge. It was in Rochester, Minnesota, a rapidly growing community located about fifty miles west of La Crescent.[22]

Jackson had organized a church with four members at Rochester on February 17, 1861. From then until the end of the year, he made a biweekly round trip to preach to the small but growing congregation. The church members finally secured as their regular pastor a missionary who had taught with Jackson at the Spencer Academy. On March 12, 1864, the Rochester Presbyterians, adopting a plan for reorganizing ministerial responsibilities in their church, asked Jackson to accept a position as their co-pastor. According to the terms of this rather unusual proposal, Jackson would tend to the spiritual needs of the congregation while his partner would conduct visits to outlying preaching stations. As to Jackson's financial remuneration, the brethren in Rochester, intending for their new pastor to be "free from worldly cares and avocations," pledged an annual salary "according to the ability God giveth us."[23]

Soon after the Jacksons moved to Rochester in the summer of 1864, he was successful in obtaining enough funds from local subscriptions and donors in the East to erect a church building. At one point while the building was under construction, the members of the congregation participated in a ceremony anticipated by the traditions of their church. On November 16, 1864, they conducted an installation service for their new leader. Jackson's father and mother, who were visiting their son and daughter-in-law at the time, were pleased to witness the memorable event, although the surroundings were considerably less than appropriate for so solemn an occasion. Gathered together in an abandoned storeroom, the participants in the ritual had to sit on board benches surrounded by empty shelves, boxes, barrels, and refuse. Happily, the completion of the new church in 1865 brought an end to dependency on such crude accommodations. The finished building, which cost about five thousand dollars, had a spire, stained-glass windows, and a bell—all traditional accoutrements of a proper church.[24]

Another event in 1865 was also a source of gratification for Jackson. The General Assembly, at its annual meeting, authorized creation of the Presbytery of Southern Minnesota as part of the Synod of St. Paul. To understand the terminology used in this organizational structure, it is necessary to be aware of the Presbyterian Church's long association with a chain-of-command concept of governance: At the lowest level, the individual member of a local church was expected to abide by the decisions of his ruling elders, who were elected from the congregation and who reached decisions on local church issues acting together as a session. The pastor of the church was technically a preaching elder who moderated session meetings without a vote. Several churches in the same general locale composed a presbytery. The pastor and one elder from each church in the presbytery attended meetings of the presbytery to review the actions of each member church and to determine presbyterial policy. The synod exercised supervisory responsibilities over a number of presbyteries in a still larger geographical area. The General Assembly met annually to consider issues that required policy decisions by the highest judicatory of the denomination. For Jackson in 1865, the creation of the Presbytery of Southern Minnesota acknowledged the success of his efforts to establish churches in that area.

The members of these congregations could now derive the satisfaction of knowing that, from that time on, their leaders could act together at the presbyterial level on matters pertaining to their concerns.[25]

On a more personal note, the Jacksons welcomed a new addition to the family when another daughter, whom they named Elizabeth, arrived in the spring of 1866. While Mary doubtlessly found much of her time occupied with the care of the new baby and her elder daughter, Delia, during the post–Civil War years, Jackson busied himself with the requirements of his congregation in Rochester and with his continuing concern for the needs of other missionaries in southern Minnesota. Although he had no authority from his superiors on the Board of Domestic Missions to assume a supervisory role, he acted on his own initiative to provide the coordinated support function that he felt was sorely needed in his mission field. The two avenues of approach he selected were calls for missionary boxes and solicitations for monetary donations. Members of eastern congregations had traditionally prepared boxes of clothing for missionaries in remote outposts throughout the world. Jackson's voluminous correspondence to his acquaintances in churches in the East brought many timely contributions to needy missionary families.[26]

Jackson's approaches to individuals, churches, and Sabbath schools calling for cash contributions were equally productive. In his overtures to children, he skillfully worded his letters to appeal to juvenile readers. In a communication sent to sixteen Sabbath schools in the fall of 1865, for example, he stated, "It was very sad to see so many children growing up without religious privileges. Through all that beautiful country [southern Minnesota] there is scarcely a Sabbath school and very seldom any preaching." Of course more Sabbath schools should be started at once, so that children could hear about Jesus, and that goal could be achieved quite simply. "This you can do," Jackson concluded, "with your missionary by sending money. . . ."[27] Jackson collected the money received from all of these sources in an account he called his Raven Fund, using a designation apparently derived from the biblical story of Elijah, who was fed in the wilderness by ravens. Although this form of private solicitation was not endorsed by the Board of Domestic Missions, Jackson used these unorthodox measures to respond to what he regarded as the do-or-die conditions faced by frontier missionaries at the time.[28]

Jackson revealed the desperate nature of the situation in a letter to the pastor of a church in New York City. "A great emergency has arisen threatening to stop all forward movement," he wrote, "if not to break up and scatter our little congregations already established." The great emergency was twofold in nature. First, and of immmediate concern, was the failure of the wheat crop in southern Minnesota in 1867. Jackson blamed the economic depression resulting from that natural calamity for a drastic decline in the level of local support from the members of struggling little churches. To alleviate the sad state of affairs, he hoped that Presbyterians in the East would give even more generously to ensure continuation of the good work by the Western missionaries. Although the problem called for heroic relief measures, Jackson identified an even more dangerous threat to "forward movement." The Board of Domestic Missions, citing a lack of funds in the treasury, intended to reduce all allotments to missionaries in the field and to disallow the commissioning of recruits for new assignments. If the mission board adopted this ill-advised policy, then, according to Jackson, "we must abandon several of our most important missionary fields, and thus throw the work back an indefinite number of years. This we cannot bear to do."[29]

Jackson's opposition to the mission board's regressive policy led to an unpleasant period of rivalry with his superiors at the home mission headquarters in Philadelphia. Particularly offensive to the board in this time of financial crisis was his campaigning to raise funds for his own needs by directly soliciting prospective donors. In the eyes of the offended board members, this unilateral action undermined their authority to act as distribution agency for all contributions to the home mission program. Matters came to a head with selection by the board of a new corresponding secretary in 1868. George Musgrave had worked for the national church in various administrative positions and had served with distinction as corresponding secretary of the Board of Domestic Missions. He had also earned commendation for his work as pastor to prominent churches in Baltimore and Philadelphia. His peers, who described him as devoted to pure Calvinism, considered Musgrave a foremost advocate of orthodox Presbyterianism.[30]

Musgrave and other members of the mission board soon decided to take the offensive in the struggle for control of the solicitation and disbursement of donations. Readers of the October 24, 1868, issue of the *North-Western Presbyterian*, published in Chicago, learned of a serious problem confronting the Board of Domestic Missions. A resolution by the executive committee of the board appeared in that issue in an article entitled "A Caution." George Musgrave, author of the article, deplored the actions of missionaries who raised and distributed funds on their own responsibility. Musgrave condemned the actions of these nonconformists, writing that they "[are] unjust towards other missionaries in other parts of the field, and are adapted to diminish the receipts of the Board; therefore, Resolved, That this committee disapproves of such operations."[31] In the annual report of the mission board, Musgrave, who compiled the report, later de-

clared that much, if not all, of the unauthorized fund-raising occurred in
Minnesota. The board secretary concluded his comments with a warning:
"The disbursement of funds so collected might be perverted to selfish and
ambitious purposes."[32]

Jackson would have vigorously denied any selfish or ambitious intent
on his part. With the purest of motives, he could argue, he had bypassed
customary channels of collection and disbursement of home mission funds,
out of genuine concern for the pressing needs of the missionaries in his
field. Aware of the board's opposition to his policies, Jackson made a critical decision near the end of 1868. Deciding to burn his bridges behind him
and place his future in the hands of Divine Providence, he told the leaders
of his congregation in Rochester of his intention to submit his resignation
effective on or about January 1, 1869. As his reason for this drastic decision, he simply noted his wish to move into more general mission work in
the West. On January 28, 1869, the members of the Rochester church
officially accepted their pastor's resignation.[33]

Freed of his responsibility, Jackson attempted, at first, to abide by the
procedures governing his relationship with his superiors. Writing to George
Musgrave early in the spring, he requested a rather general commission to
organize new churches on the western frontier. The board secretary, unwilling to provide carte blanche authority for Jackson to plunge ahead with
his undefined schemes, sought to buy time by calling for him to be more
specific in his request. Did he have a preference for work in a particular
state or territory, and, if so, which? Exactly what kind of work was intended? Did Jackson propose to act simply as an explorer, or did he con-
template traveling as an itinerant missionary within a limited field? Probably
anticipating this evasive response by the mission board, Jackson had already made up his mind to act on his own. He was determined to marshal
his local support for decisive action at a meeting—destined to become famous in the pages of Presbyterian history—of the Presbytery of Missouri
River. The meeting was scheduled for the end of April in Sioux City, Iowa.[34]

Meanwhile, however, in the nation's capital on March 4, 1869, Ulysses
S. Grant delivered a brief inaugural address following the solemn oath-
taking ceremony proclaiming him president of the United States. Predicting early retirement of the large national debt incurred during the Civil
War, he exulted, "Why, it looks as though Providence had bestowed upon
us a strong box in the precious metals locked up in the sterile mountains of
the far West, and which we are now forging the key to unlock."[35] The key
to unlocking the great treasure box envisioned by the new president was
the transcontinental railroad. In April of 1869, as Jackson journeyed to
Sioux City, Iowa, for his fateful meeting with the Presbytery of Missouri

River, a thousand miles to the west, in northern Utah, the Central Pacific was laying track east from Sacramento, California. The Union Pacific was constructing its line west out of Omaha, Nebraska. The two had finally accepted a location near Promontory, Utah, as the spot where officials of the railroads would drive a golden spike on May 10 to commemorate the completion of their heroic task. Discerning the trials ahead, one of Jackson's friends asked, "What is God opening up to us through His Pacific R.Road? This is the nation He is blessing, and will bless unto the end, but the work must be done by us poor, weak erring mortals."[36]

Should Presbyterian missionaries be assigned to new settlements along the great railroads? Of course, and with no delay, replied travelers along completed portions of the Union Pacific. Typical of such comments was the statement of a passenger riding to end-of-track on the Union Pacific in October of 1868. This worried correspondent noticed little observation of the Sabbath in towns along the way, save perhaps for an influx of miners from the mountains. He found "dance houses and dens of prostitution and gambling halls more frequented on this than other days. Otherwise, Sunday would pass without recognition."[37] Another witness to this shameless conduct called for Presbyterian mission board members to come and see the extent of the depravity for themselves. Immediate action was required because:

> 1. The railroad companies are prepared to grant church and mission sites all along the line to such *churches as will promptly occupy them.* The Baptist Mission Committee have already taken the field in this good work.
> 2. Satan has already taken possession of all points along the line. . . . The Church must do the whole work of Christian civilization, as in the case of the army, only here we have not the powerful restraint of military discipline in aid of law and order.[38]

To judge from these remarks, competition for missionary work could be expected not only from Satan but also from other denominations. Sheldon Jackson certainly regarded seizure of strategic outposts along the soon-to-be-completed railroad as a top priority. When he arrived in Sioux City at the end of April to attend the meeting of the Presbytery of Missouri River, he hoped to obtain recognition of his status as a roving missionary from Iowa presbyteries with known interests in western expansion. He may have succeeded even beyond his expectations. At the conclusion of the convocation in Sioux City, the delegates unanimously designated Jackson "Superintendent of Missions for Western Iowa, Nebraska, Dakota, Idaho, Montana, Wyoming, and Utah, or as far as our jurisdiction extends."[39] At the same time, the presbyteries of Fort Dodge and Des Moines approved similar resolutions that, in effect, gave Jackson presbyterial authority to do whatever he deemed necessary to win the West for Christ.[40]

As Jackson later recalled, the adoption of this semi-independent position by the presbyteries was the result of a simple misunderstanding between the Iowans and the Board of Domestic Missions. This rather bland explanation may have served Jackson's purpose of minimizing the growing tensions between the brethren in the West and the home mission board. Nevertheless, his strategy in encouraging these decisive actions was again designed to bring pressure on the board to follow his lead in responding to what he visualized as clear and present opportunities to sow the seeds of Presbyterianism in unbroken but fertile soil. Whatever the motives behind these events, Jackson was prepared to let the board members catch on to his flying coattails if they so desired. When he announced to George Musgrave the results of the meeting in Sioux City, Jackson said that he would continue to represent the board's interests, just as if he had been appointed by the board members. He also wished Musgrave to know that the three presbyteries would rejoice when the board could find the funds to commission him formally for work in the vast field designated by the Iowa brethren.[41]

The mission board members were now challenged to make the next move. Regrettably, the confrontation was beginning to appear more a bitter power-struggle than a congenial joint effort to advance the Lord's work. The board members decided to postpone the matter, at least for the time being, politely acknowledging Jackson's new association with the Iowa Presbyterians as a fait accompli. Inasmuch as Jackson had accepted the appointment from the presbyteries and had already entered upon the work, apparently in Musgrave's opinion any action by the board was unnecessary. Since the matter was obviously one of great importance, the executive committee of the board preferred to take all the time needed to reach an appropriate decision on the matter. Jackson may have been annoyed by this evasive action, because he could have certainly used to good advantage the money accompanying a regular board commission. His appointment from the presbyteries carried with it no provision for financial support, and so he could rely only on continuing contributions to his private Raven Fund to cover his initial expenses. He followed with great interest events in the East that could result in increased funding for crucial home mission programs.[42]

When the angry guns of northern and southern armies ceased their thundering at Appomattox, Virginia, on April 9, 1865, many influential leaders of the Presbyterian Church in the North perceived a divine purpose behind the tragic Civil War. If a sinful nation had required punishment in blood for its transgressions, then peace would surely bring redemption and a renewed challenge to advance the interests of God's kingdom. Additional encouragement for such an endeavor came from evidence of reconciliation between the Old School and New School factions of the church in the North. During the war years there had been friendly interchanges of conciliatory resolutions between the two groups. And, by ending their affiliation with the interdenominational American Home Missionary Society in 1861, New School members had apparently accepted the Old School position of noninvolvement with other churches or agencies in home mission work. After a complicated sequence of committee meetings, the Old School and New School General Assemblies convened simultaneously in New York in May of 1869, and achieved agreement on the terms of reconciliation. One observer of these proceedings was inspired by the great expectations for advancing the banner of Presbyterianism following the reunion. Reflecting on prospects for future conquests by the united church, he saw two great sections of the Lord's host falling into line, "not for the satisfaction of exulting in the sense of greatness or indulging in mutual gratulations, but for the purpose of pushing Christian efforts with more vigor."[43]

Brave words, indeed, but in what direction should the great push be applied? The same writer who called for more vigorous efforts to Christianize the nation had some strong views on this subject. He wanted the reunited church to strengthen its position in the urban centers of the East, because the church that held those cities would certainly shape the religious character of the country.[44] Not so, replied the many others, who were drawn to events taking place west of the Mississippi River. Good brethren in the West, they said, were not receiving the ministrations of their church. The Sabbath was violated there and sin was flourishing in many forms. Strategic points were in danger of occupation by rival denominations, and donations of property for church structures were available to the first arrivals. Surely the united treasury of two former home mission boards could support the planting of missionaries and churches in this critical area.

Sheldon Jackson was certainly counting on the latter assumption as he prepared to initiate his campaign for conquest in the West, beginning along the line of the new Union Pacific Railroad.[45] Confident that his worthy cause would eventually be blessed with adequate financial support, he had daringly started to recruit missionaries to assist him even before he attended the Sioux City meeting at the end of April. In the preceding month he had visited students at several Presbyterian seminaries in the East. From those contacts he had selected four young men. As soon as he received his commission from the Iowa presbyteries, he called them to spend their summer vacation preaching at various points in the eastern portion of his vast

and vaguely defined mission field. He also summoned three other missionaries—who had agreed to help him during the summer if his plans
materialized—to reconnoiter along the Union Pacific. He asked J. N.
Hutchinson, a young man recently licensed to preach, to take that part of
the railroad from its origin at Omaha to Julesburg in the northeastern
corner of Colorado. John L. Gage, who had worked as a missionary with
Jackson in Minnesota, received responsibility for the section from Julesburg
to Rawlins, Wyoming. Melancthon Hughes, who had resigned his pastorate at Bellevue, Nebraska, accepted the area from south-central Wyoming
to Corinne, in northern Utah, as his field of endeavor.[46]

While Jackson's recruits traveled to their new duty stations, their superintendent returned briefly to Minnesota to close out his affairs with his
former congregation in Rochester. After amicably concluding this task,
near the end of May Jackson moved with his family to Council Bluffs,
Iowa, just across the river from the Omaha terminus of the Union Pacific.
On May 28 he started on his first tour of inspection along the railroad,
intent on visiting John Gage in Cheyenne, Wyoming. Cheyenne, at that
time, undoubtedly conveyed the impression of a typical, wide-open, any-
thing-goes railroad center to visitors from the East. Founded in the summer of 1867 as a service center for the rapidly approaching Union Pacific,
the town's population was estimated at four thousand when the tracks arrived on November 13. Reflecting on the life expectancy of the bustling
community, one visitor warned that it could become just another here-
today, gone-tomorrow enterprise. According to that pessimistic reporter,
"The infant metropolis out here is born at dawn, teeths [sic] before breakfast, attains robust majority by noon, riots until sunset, and disappears at
midnight only to reappear an hundred miles further west, faster and freer
handed."[47] The construction crews had moved on in the spring of 1869,
but Cheyenne was still a going concern; in Jackson's eyes, it still harbored
much of its original wickedness. Undaunted by the evidence of ungodli-
ness on all sides, Jackson was more determined than ever to organize a
church among the iniquitous inhabitants because, as he firmly believed,
"There are a few who love Jesus."[48]

Jackson found several of those "who love Jesus" when he decided to
preach on one of the street corners in Cheyenne. A man of lesser fortitude
might well have hesitated before placing himself in a position where he
could be ridiculed by the more rowdy elements among the passersby. Jackson, however, bravely went ahead with his plans, and his story of the results provides a rather humorous picture of a religious service staged in
distinctly irregular surroundings. To achieve the desired elevation, Jackson recalled how he had had to use an empty dry-goods box for a pulpit.

He had also hoped to embellish his oratorical efforts with hymn-singing from some of the equally courageous among the Cheyenne Presbyterians, recruited for the purpose. Unfortunately, when the time arrived for the choristers to perform, their efforts were suddenly disrupted. According to Jackson, as he ruefully described the incident, "The choir were seated in a buggy, when the horse became frightened, and away went the choir, singing as they went."[49]

Discouraged, perhaps, by these experiences, John Gage was not really sure that the time had arrived to go ahead with a Presbyterian organization. The number "who love Jesus" was quite small, and he wondered if the Presbyterians, for the time being, could worship together with the Congregationalists, who had already invited a missionary from their denomination to come out and start a church. Jackson would have none of that. Good Presbyterians, no matter how few, should receive the Presbyterian message unblemished by association with the beliefs of any other faith. Acting on that conviction, the two missionaries met with several residents of Cheyenne who had identified themselves as Presbyterians, and they discussed plans for organizing a church. At the meeting, Jackson demonstrated his own support for the project by impulsively pledging five thousand dollars for the erection of a church building for the fledgling congregation. Encouraged by the gesture, those attending the meeting obtained the names of twenty-seven residents in their community who promised "hearty cooperation and support in the effort to plant and maintain a Presbyterian Church in this city."[50]

After assuring the Cheyenne Presbyterians of his intention to return soon and finalize the organization of their church, Jackson decided to conduct a hurried fund-raising expedition to the East to obtain the five thousand dollars he had promised for the church in Cheyenne. For a week he visited prospective donors in Pittsburgh and New York who, touched by his description of the depravity in the West, made generous pledges for the support of his work along the Union Pacific. While Jackson was trying to raise money in the East, the members of the Board of Domestic Missions, at their meeting on June 15, decided to offer him an appointment as district missionary for Nebraska, Colorado, and Wyoming at an annual salary of fifteen hundred dollars, without traveling expenses. When George Musgrave conveyed that news to Jackson on July 7, he included a clear statement of the board's wishes concerning the future conduct of the new district missionary. If Jackson elected to accept the offer, he must abandon his unorthodox policy of raising and disbursing missionary funds on his own.[51]

One can only speculate on Jackson's reaction to this peremptory edict. Certainly he did not want to give up the title of superintendent, which the

Iowa presbyteries had selected for him, to comply with the board's preference for district missionary. He may have discerned in the position taken
by his superiors a rather petty reluctance to acknowledge the loftier designation, a designation that might have suggested usurpation of the board's
authority. Although Jackson would deny any intention of defying the mission board just to inflate his own position, it is reasonable to assume that
he did relish this token of the importance of his position. As to the order to
refrain from openly soliciting money for his own missionary projects, Jackson, who had just returned from a journey in the East devoted precisely to
that purpose, had no intention of abandoning a policy he perceived as essential to the continuation of the great westward movement. Finally, he
may have decided simply to ignore the delineation of his mission field by
the board, as it did not include areas in the West that he had already resolved to secure for Presbyterianism.[52]

Whatever his thoughts on these matters, Jackson decided to accept the
board's offer and then proceed with the plans he had already formulated.
At this time, the tangible results of Jackson's ministry were already substantial. While he was in Minnesota, he had organized, or assisted in organizing, twenty-three churches; he had secured twenty-eight ministers to
labor in his mission fields; and he had collected approximately $13,500
and more than 150 missionary boxes for the support of these recruits.
Sheldon Jackson was prepared to accept the role of iconoclast if, by so
doing, he could advance the standard of Presbyterianism into the great
unchurched areas described on the monument to the Sioux City meeting.
He was zealous, energetic, personally ambitious, an acknowledged leader
among his peers, and a skilled propagandist. He would not hesitate to ignore the directives of his superiors by soliciting direct financial support
from his many contacts in the East. He motivated these people to contribute with his vivid descriptions of the hardships encountered by his missionaries as they tried to plant the seeds of the Gospel in a harsh frontier
environment. While all of these attributes may have been useful for any
missionary endeavoring to win the West for Christ, it remained to be seen
how Sheldon Jackson would deal with the new and more difficult challenges he would encounter in a field described later by a colleague as a
region "where godlessness and anarchy reigned."[53]

2 | Seizing Prominent Points

*It was going out to the churchless, Sabbathless, growing
communities of the frontier—to the wild, lawless, gambling,
saloon-cursed mining camps where gravitate the most abandoned,
hardened, and desperate characters of the country.*
—SHELDON JACKSON, "A STORY OF EARLY HOME MISSION
   WORK," 1904

"Usually a church organization on the frontier commences
with from five to twenty members, occasionally with two or three. It is a
question not of present membership, but of future growth. If the place has
a 'promising future,' the earlier the organization is made the better."[1] These
comments by Sheldon Jackson, delivered near the end of his long and distinguished career, illustrate his approach to organizing churches in the
Rocky Mountain West. Sometimes his assessment of a promising future
for a new community proved faulty, and the seeds he planted fell on barren
ground. Prospects for future growth might be shattered by unforeseen economic tribulations or other factors he could not anticipate. Since such things
were beyond his control his criterion for creation of a church organization
in any location was usually based on a single principle: if those who initially pledged their support to the endeavor proved worthy, the church
would surely flourish. On the other hand, if the members of a new congregation did not have a firm commitment to the cause, efforts by Jackson and
others to nurture and expand the enterprise would be of little or no avail.
Although Jackson would hardly have embraced propositions advanced at
the time by Charles Darwin and others, propositions that seemed to be at
odds with portions of the Bible, he might have been inclined to agree with
the notion of the "survival of the fittest" when he sought for an explanation for the successes or failures of frontier churches. Whatever his thoughts
on these matters, early in the summer of 1869 Jackson embarked on the
first of his many organizing expeditions. On Sunday, July 18, he was back
in Cheyenne, where he met with the nine residents of the town who had
consented to be enrolled as the first members of the new Presbyterian
church. After conducting an organizational service in the schoolhouse in

the morning, Jackson preached in the evening to members of other churches, who met in the Episcopal church. He also secured a contribution of two city lots from the Union Pacific Railroad to accommodate the church building that he had proposed on his previous visit. Jackson closed his report of these proceedings, which was published in a Presbyterian journal under the title "Cheyenne, the Magic City of the Plains," with the statement, "But the train whistles, and I must be off westward."[2]

Jackson's objectives, as he continued his travels, had been outlined for him by Melancthon Hughes, the minister recruited previously by Jackson to reconnoiter the region along the Union Pacific from southcentral Wyoming into northern Utah. In addition to his own place of residence at Corinne in Utah, Hughes had mentioned the railroad towns of Rawlins, Laramie, and Bryan in Wyoming as communities deserving closer attention. The mining camps of South Pass City and Atlantic City in the Sweetwater Mining District of Wyoming also looked promising. Finally, an acquaintance from Montana had told Hughes of the rapid development of that territory, making special notice of Helena, a boom town that was said to have a population of eight or ten thousand inhabitants. Planning an itinerary based on these suggestions, Jackson set out on an extraordinary journey.[3]

His first stop was Bryan, a small town in southwestern Wyoming where the Union Pacific had built machine shops and a roundhouse in 1868. Forced to stay overnight in Bryan until he could secure passage by stage to the Sweetwater Mines about one hundred miles to the north, Jackson was appalled when, in the morning, he noticed three intoxicated men in the office of his hotel. Soon after this encounter he found one of the men lying on the ground, stabbed to death by one of his comrades. When a resident of this depraved community stated his belief that there was not a single Christian in the place, Jackson decided that a more prolonged visit to Bryan would wisely be deferred until a later date. He set out on the next available stage for the Sweetwater Mines. The trip, which regularly took fourteen hours, followed an arid and desolate route along which the stage company had erected fortified relay stations every ten or twelve miles to guard employees and livestock from hostile Indians. Passengers received loaded rifles for their own defense in case the coaches should be attacked between relay stations. Jackson was understandably relieved when, at the end of a long day, he reached South Pass City safely.[4]

Melancthon Hughes had provided Jackson with a brief description of conditions at South Pass City after a visit a month before. He regarded the mining camp, which had been established near a rich gold strike in the fall of 1867, as a rapidly growing and very promising community. He estimated the population, in the spring of 1869, at about eight or nine hundred souls. According to Hughes, the attentive listeners to his preaching in the courthouse had expressed great pleasure with his visit.

The morning following Jackson's arrival, he posted notices in the town announcing his presence and his intent to preach that evening. As the time for his scheduled service drew near, he sent out a boy with a bell to proclaim the location of the gathering. Jackson preached as advertised before a small congregation in a warehouse that had been cleaned up for the purpose. Before leaving the mining district, he received a request to visit a dying man in the nearby camp of Atlantic City. He found the young man, whom he described as a graduate of a well-known eastern college, at death's door. He offered Christian solace to ease the last moments of the unfortunate lad. And always ready to publicize the depravity he encountered, Jackson described in his report of this touching scene how a companion, who sat watching the expiring man "and wiping from him the damps of death, was reading a low novel."[5]

When Jackson heard reports of what he described as "Indian difficulties" in the area, he was convinced that the time had not yet arrived for establishment of Presbyterian churches in the camps of the Sweetwater Mining District.[6] He continued on to Corinne, Utah, where he visited briefly with Melancthon Hughes on July 23. When he resumed his journey, he turned northward once again to Helena, Montana, a mining camp established in 1864 in a remote location colorfully designated Last Chance Gulch. After four days of continuous staging, Jackson finally reached that isolated community in the rugged mountains of western Montana. Although his arrival there in the summer of 1869 is deservedly acknowledged as a great pioneering achievement in the annals of Montana Presbyterianism, Jackson was not the first missionary of his church to preach the Gospel there. Five years earlier, the Reverend George G. Smith had reached Bannack, site of the first great gold discovery in Montana, with an exploratory commission from the Committee of Home Missions of the New School branch of the church. Smith's recollection of his arrival at one of his preaching stations provides a delightful commentary on the reception that might be anticipated by a Presbyterian missionary in a new mining camp in the West.[7]

After placing a preaching notice in the local post office, Smith stepped to a corner of the room to observe the results:

> One fellow read it and shouted. The crowd gathered and he read it again, aloud, and they all shouted. They wanted to know what a preacher was, what was his business, and what was a Presbyterian preacher. Some fellow, evidently an oracle among them, explained,

and said they were a religious sect and very high toned. . . . Some one exclaimed, if he had been a Methodist exhauster he would not have been surprised, but a regular starched Presbyterian in that country was an anomaly and Barnum ought to have him, and concluded by saying, "Let's all go around and hear the animal."

At that day Sunday was the big day. Everybody was in town. Bedlam was let loose. Business and sin were at their very worst. Next door to my preaching compartment was a large gambling hall with full band of brass, and my preaching that day was certainly attended with much sounding brass and tinkling cymbals. In the midst of my sermon the band struck up a lively dance tune and the hob-nailed miners began to beat time with their feet upon the bare floor. I was completely thrown out, and stopped and folded my arms. Just then the ringleader, a long, lank, lean fellow in buckskins called out, "Boys never mind the music. The elder has the floor. You listen to him. Elder, go on. You shall not be disturbed again." And I was not.[8]

Smith's colorful description of the dynamic society encountered in a promising mining camp would not have provided an accurate portrayal of conditions in Helena when Jackson arrived. Although Melancthon Hughes had estimated the population in Helena at ten thousand, the boom period, according to one of Jackson's correspondents in the area, was now over. In fact, times were extremely dull and a general feeling of despondency prevailed throughout the region. Jackson chose to ignore this discouraging report when, the day after his arrival, he made a house-to-house survey in Helena and obtained expressions of interest in a church organization from eighty-one professed Christians. Encouraged by these results, on August 1, 1869, with thirteen residents of Helena ready to sign the membership roll, he organized the First Presbyterian Church of Helena. Recalling that solemn and courageous event, an early historian of this church boasted, "There was not another church (except Indian missions) of the same denomination in a region stretching westward to Portland, Oregon, southward to Cheyenne, eastward to the churches of Minnesota, and northward to the pole."[9]

This claim to fame by the proud Helena congregation was soon undermined by Jackson's subsequent organizing efforts. Leaving Helena, he returned to Corinne, where he preached to a small gathering recruited by Melancthon Hughes. He regarded plans for a church organization in Corinne as still premature, however, so he set out once again to find audiences more receptive to his message. As he retraced his route eastward in Wyoming along the Union Pacific, he stopped at Rawlins, a division point established on the railroad in 1868. While there, Jackson received a written request signed by six residents who called for him to organize a church in their little town and send a pastor to minister to their needs as soon as possible. Touched by this expression of faith, Jackson conducted an organizational service on August 8, 1869, in the dining room of the railroad hotel.[10]

From Rawlins, Jackson continued on to Laramie, a town created by the railroad in the spring of 1868 where its tracks crossed the Laramie River. During this break in his return journey Jackson met John Gage, the missionary he had stationed in Cheyenne, Wyoming, who gave him a petition signed by six citizens of Laramie requesting that Jackson organize them into a Presbyterian church. Assured by Gage that the small nucleus of faithful petitioners would soon grow into a flourishing congregation, he organized the First Presbyterian Church of Laramie in the local schoolhouse on August 10, 1869. Eager now to get back to his home in Council Bluffs, which he had left almost a month before, Jackson tried to hurry through Nebraska. But he could not resist other invitations to establish churches at four more towns along the railroad. He left in his wake church organizations at Grand Island, Columbus, Blair, and Fremont, communities where his recruit J.N. Hutchinson had found receptive audiences when he had scouted the area. Exhausted but triumphant, Jackson finally reached his home on August 17. There he found a letter from George Musgrave informing him of his formal appointment, effective July 1, 1869, as district missionary for Nebraska, Colorado, and Wyoming, with an annual salary of $1,500.[11]

Jackson's next journey took him to Pittsburgh in November of 1869 to attend a meeting of the Old School General Assembly. At the same time, New School delegates had gathered in that same city at a nearby location for their own General Assembly meeting. Following the preliminary negotiations on the subject of reunion the past May, the presbyteries of both groups had overwhelmingly voted during the intervening six months to approve that long awaited action. The great day had now arrived when the rival bodies would announce their intention of joining hands to form one great denomination in the North. After two days devoted to procedural matters, on November 12 the commissioners to both meetings adjourned into the streets where they formed parallel ranks and tearfully clasped hands symbolizing a pledge of support to the reunited church.[12]

Besides relishing the opportunity to participate in the joyous reunion, Jackson also came away from these meetings with some tangible recognition of his own work. One of his colleagues recalled how he had managed somehow to secure approval for addition of the territories of Utah and Montana to his mission field. Perhaps of greater significance, Jackson also had received authorization for creation of a new Presbytery of Colorado, to include churches in Utah, Montana, Wyoming, and Colorado. Jackson had not visited Colorado in his exploratory work, but he knew of several Presbyterian congregations already established in Denver and some of the nearby mining camps. He was now eager to accept the challenge presented to him by a Colorado missionary, who had asserted, "There are Presbyterians in this country who love the gospel, and thousands of sinners who need it."[13]

Although Jackson would not have been completely aware of the origins of Presbyterian missionary work in Colorado, he did know how it had begun shortly after the discovery of gold in 1858, at a place later called Denver City. The following year, the rush of prospectors brought with it Lewis Hamilton from his church in Lima, Indiana. Concerned about his poor health, Hamilton's congregation had given him a six-month vacation with full pay to restore his vitality in the mountains. On June 11, 1859, he had arrived in Denver, where he preached in an unfinished building on the following Sabbath. When many of the gold-seekers moved to a new site in the mountains west of Denver, Hamilton followed them to the diggings, where he continued his preaching to receptive audiences. On one occasion, when requested to start a hymn during one of his services he obliged with "Come Thou Fount of Every Blessing" and, according to a colleague who later recalled the incident, "The miners and saloon keepers joined in the singing while they kept right on with their work."[14]

When Hamilton returned to his church in Indiana his health again deteriorated, and he decided to take up permanent residence in Colorado. Unsure of what the future held in store for the fledgling mining camps, he had made no effort in 1859 to establish churches there. By 1866, however, he and other Presbyterian missionaries who followed in his footsteps had organized churches in Denver and other nearby communities that exhibited evidence of continued growth. In that year, leaders from three of these churches had daringly tried to secure formal approval from the Old School General Assembly for creation of a Presbytery of Colorado. Meeting in Denver on January 15, pastors and elders from the three congregations had resolved "that the accomplished union of such churches with such others as may be formed, in a Presbytery would subserve greatly the interests of the cause of the Redeemer and strengthen each particular church."[15] The Coloradans were understandably disappointed when their proposal died in committee at the assembly meeting. While acknowledging the desirability of organizing a Presbytery of Colorado "as soon as practicable," members of the committee decided that a longer time for testing the waters was needed before a new presbytery could be justified.[16]

The moment arrived when Sheldon Jackson succeeded in obtaining approval for establishing a Presbytery of Colorado at the General Assembly meeting in the fall of 1869. In February of 1870 he set out for Colorado to attend the first meeting of the new presbytery. He traveled by train to Cheyenne, where he transferred to a stagecoach that carried him the remaining one hundred miles. When he reached Denver, which now boasted a population of almost five thousand, he was surely impressed by the majestic prospect of snow-covered mountains that defined the horizon to the west. He had read reports describing Denver as a wicked place indeed. When he arrived in the community, however, he perceived that the growing influence of society's better elements had contributed to a noticeable improvement in morals. Writing for a Presbyterian periodical about his visit, he said that he was sure that the "tidal wave of wickedness, the cesspools of iniquity, and the desperadoes that came in with the surging mass of gold-seekers have passed on, and a more permanent population taken their place."[17]

How was he to satisfy the religious needs of this permanent population, not only in Denver but in other Colorado communities as well? That basic question received prayerful consideration at the presbytery meeting. Joining Jackson at the gathering were pastors and elders from churches in Denver and vicinity. On Friday evening, February 18, he led religious exercises for his small but dedicated band in the basement of the Baptist church. The next day the delegates disposed of various business matters, but in his subsequent account of these proceedings Jackson noted that the mission work of the church in the territory of Colorado was the greatest concern on the agenda. Although members of Presbyterian churches in the East were scattered across the region, according to Jackson, "Some have made shipwrecks of their hopes . . . in some instances becoming Sabbath-breakers, blasphemers, and drunkards. Others have become careless and indifferent."[18]

Recognizing the urgent need to redirect the steps of these fallen individuals to the straight and narrow path, Jackson decided to visit other communities in Colorado to determine which would be most receptive to the establishment of Presbyterian churches. He traveled first to southern Colorado where he organized churches at Pueblo, the largest town serving a ranching and agricultural region along the Arkansas River, and at Colorado City, a small settlement nestled at the base of the great mountain known as Pikes Peak. He then returned to Denver, where he prepared a travel itinerary designed to carry him to several of the mining camps in the mountains to the west. He hurriedly visited the neighboring communities of Black Hawk, Central City, Georgetown, Idaho Springs, and Golden City, organizing churches in all of those places except Central City, where a small group of Presbyterians still belonged to a church established by Lewis Hamilton in 1862.

Returning to Denver, Jackson rested for a few days and then departed
to check on the progress of one of the churches organized in 1869 in Wyoming along the Union Pacific Railroad. In Rawlins, Wyoming, the date of
March 13, 1870, was a memorable one indeed in the history of the local
Presbyterian church. On that date, Jackson joined with the congregation
in a service dedicating the recently completed church building. Of the five
hundred dollars promised to Jackson for this project by members the previous year, only two hundred dollars had been collected; Jackson graciously
offered to make up the difference from his own funds.[19]

After completing his part in the Rawlins dedication, Jackson returned
to his home and family in Council Bluffs. He resumed his travels in May of
1870 when, as the pastoral delegate from the Presbytery of Colorado, he
attended the first General Assembly of the reunited church on May 19 in
Philadelphia. He was, on the whole, pleased with the agreements reached
on matters of particular concern to himself. For example, a drive would be
initiated at once to try to raise five million dollars as a memorial fund with
which to create and strengthen church institutions at home and abroad.
Jackson surely visualized part of that vast sum directed toward sustaining
his enterprises in the Rocky Mountain West.

He also learned how home mission work for the reunited church would
continue under the supervision of a board designated simply as the Board
of Home Missions. The headquarters of the board would move from Philadelphia to New York. The important function of board secretary would
now be shared by representatives of the New School and Old School groups.
Henry Kendall, secretary since 1861 of the former New School Committee on Home Missions, would represent his faction. In 1864 Kendall had
journeyed to Colorado, Utah, Nevada, California, and Oregon, but his
function had been to observe and not to organize. From his observations,
however, he viewed the West as a prime target for Presbyterian missionary
enterprises. To Jackson's surprise, Cyrus Dickson, a prominent Old School
churchman, now replaced George Musgrave to serve as co-secretary with
Kendall. Musgrave had chosen to relinquish the responsibility because
advancing years had brought infirmities.[20]

There is no record of Jackson's reaction to the news of Musgrave's resignation. One could surely surmise, however, that he was relieved by the
departure of his old adversary. Cyrus Dickson's history of service to his
church included a record of distinguished leadership in several influential
congregations in the East. At the meeting in 1870 the delegates also named
him clerk of the assembly, a position that would require a considerable
amount of his attention. For that reason, Jackson assumed that Henry
Kendall would determine, in large part, the supervision of his role as dis-

trict missionary. Considering his previously cordial relationship with Kendall, Jackson no doubt felt that he would soon receive the support he needed for his mission field, which he now regarded as encompassing the territories of Montana, Wyoming, Utah, Colorado, and New Mexico.[21]

After the General Assembly meeting ended, another concern arose requiring Jackson's attention. At the end of the summer of 1869, Melancthon Hughes had left Corinne, Utah, after completing his reconnoitering assignment in western Wyoming, Montana, and northern Utah. Hughes had left some vivid impressions of Corinne for Jackson to consider. He had selected the town as his headquarters, in the first place, because he had recognized it as the largest gentile town in Utah. That description, at the time, referred to the distinction between Mormon and non-Mormon settlements in a territory that had been occupied in 1847 by members of the Church of Jesus Christ of Latter-day Saints and their leader, Brigham Young. Fleeing from persecution in the East by gentiles (as they called non-Mormons), these nonconformists had erected the bustling metropolis of Salt Lake City as the focal point of their extension into the Rocky Mountain West. Without mentioning the obvious opposition he would have received in the strongholds of Mormonism, Hughes defended his selection of Corinne as his residence by simply saying that, in his opinion, its location on the main line of the Union Pacific ensured its future as the most important community in Utah.[22]

Hughes's prediction of future greatness for Corinne was enhanced, to say the least, by a reporter who may have overstepped the bounds of reality in his grandiose description of the little community's future: "It is about equi-distant from the great centers of European, Asiatic and Australian trade and industry," the enthusiastic observer wrote, "and may one day become the world's exchange, where the pigtails of Peking and the well-nurtured side-whiskers of London will meet to compare notes and drive bargains."[23] For Melancthon Hughes, however, these flamboyant comments had no relationship to the immediate challenges facing his ministry. In his first religious service, conducted in a crude structure designated the city hall, his preaching was well received by a capacity audience. But the benches, borrowed from a gambling hall to accommodate his listeners, had had to be returned in time for the evening game of keno, a popular card game on the frontier. Disheartened by this open disregard for the Sabbath, Hughes admitted to Jackson, "I am much discouraged some times. These western towns are terribly wicked places."[24]

When Jackson had visited Corinne in the summer of 1869, during his trip to the Sweetwater Mining District in Wyoming, he had decided that Cheyenne, which he had previously considered the Sodom of the West, was a paradise compared with Corinne. He found four-fifths of the inhabitants there living in tents on an arid, alkali, sagebrush plain. Temperatures reached 110 degrees in the shade during his visit, and he believed that Melancthon Hughes or any other minister who could stay there should be greatly admired. Dismayed by Jackson's description of this hell on earth, a writer in a Presbyterian periodical lamented, "In many places the name of Christ is never spoken, except with blasphemous lips. It is sad to see guileless youths come from the home of a praying mother and the family altar, to find no minister to speak of heaven—no church bell to remind of the Sabbath morning. So vice is honored and walks abroad at noonday unrebuked. The enemy triumphs."[25]

Certainly Sheldon Jackson was not prepared to acknowledge the triumph of the enemy; his forces, after all, had just entered the field. In the spring of 1870 he secured the services of Edward E. Bayliss, pastor of a small church in DeSoto, Iowa, to minister to the needs of a small band of Presbyterians in Corinne. Bayliss reached Corinne on April 5, 1870. The only accommodations he could secure were in a hotel where the proprietor charged him a staggering eighteen dollars per week for room and board. He received relief from this intolerable burden at the end of the month, when several generous donors contributed three hundred dollars for construction of a small parsonage.

Bayliss obtained temporary permission to conduct his Sabbath services in a building that had been erected as an Episcopal church. From his first impressions of the quality of life in his new surroundings, he concluded, "There is not a better regulated community even in Pennsylvania. It is simply the high civilization of the East carried across the Rocky Mountains, and here planted to take root against surrounding ignorance and semi-barbarism." Encouraged by this report, which seemed to contradict previous impressions, Jackson returned to Corinne, where he and Bayliss organized a church with ten members on July 14.[26]

In September, Jackson moved with his family, which had been grown by the birth of a daughter on January 1, to Denver, a location better suited than Council Bluffs to serve as headquarters for Jackson's mission field. A local newspaper reporter warmly welcomed Jackson. "He has erected a fine dwelling house," the writer noted, "and we bespeak for him the kindly attention of our people and predict for him a career of great usefulness in the West."[27] Sadly, soon after their arrival, the Jackson's infant daughter, named Louise after Jackson's sister, was stricken by scarlet fever. In a few days she died, despite the best efforts by doctors. The bereaved parents took the body of the deceased child to Galesburg, Illinois, where they interred her by the side of their first daughter, Mary Helen, who had died there in 1861. When they returned to Denver, the despondent Jackson prepared for one more trip to Corinne, where he had consented to participate in the dedicatory service of a new church building.[28]

It appeared, for a moment, that this eagerly awaited occasion would take place without the presence of Edward Bayliss. The pastor of the Corinne church had told Jackson early in October that he was seriously considering submitting his resignation. He had become discouraged by what he perceived as a "lack of hearty cooperation" from his congregation. There was little interest in the spiritual prosperity of the church, according to Bayliss, and the only objective of his members "appears to be a church which will for its architectural beauty be an ornament to our town."[29] Fortunately, Bayliss's usual optimism soon returned. With renewed vigor, he supervised the final plastering of the interior of the building so that the dedication could proceed as scheduled on November 20. On that Sabbath morning, Sheldon Jackson preached the dedicatory sermon to an audience seated on chairs borrowed from the opera house. Pleased with his comments regarding their spiritual expectations, the Corinne Presbyterians were also grateful to Jackson for a more tangible contribution toward the success of their venture. Members of the church gratefully acknowledged "the promised presentation of a triple plated communion set from the Superintendent of Missions, Reverend Sheldon Jackson and his estimable lady."[30]

Jackson must have regarded the dedication as a step in the right direction, but he knew that the good work in Utah would have to be expanded beyond Corinne. His next objective was Salt Lake City, and he arrived there on July 1, 1871, hoping to find support for a Presbyterian church. After meeting with Presbyterians who had been recommended as preliminary contacts by Bayliss, Jackson came away ready to proceed with his organizational plans. He found a minister for the proposed church in the person of young Josiah Welch, a recent graduate of Princeton. Welch met Jackson in Denver, and on October 5 they traveled together to Salt Lake City. Three days later, on the Sabbath, Jackson preached to an audience of twelve prospective church members in a room over a livery stable. Encouraged by this small but apparently dedicated nucleus of support, Jackson returned to his home satisfied that Welch would make a determined effort to spread the word about his intentions. The happy culmination of this audacious experiment among the Mormons occurred on November 12. On that Sabbath day, Jackson returned to participate in the organizational exercises for the First Presbyterian Church of Salt Lake City. According to Jackson, "Thus the dark spiritual outlook of a few months before had given place to bright hopes and devout thanksgiving."[31]

Jackson was involved directly in only one other attempt to brighten the "dark spiritual outlook" in Utah, but the story vividly illustrates the difficulties of organizing a frontier church. Prominent among the mining camps in Utah in 1873 was the town of Alta, located in the mountains about twenty miles southeast of Salt Lake City. Discoveries of rich silver deposits in 1869 had attracted prospectors to the area until, in 1872, the population of Alta and vicinity was said to have reached five thousand. To prepare the way for a Presbyterian church in Alta, Jackson had recruited James Schell from the graduating class of Union Theological Seminary in New York City. Although Schell, who arrived in Alta in the spring of 1873, was the first Presbyterian missionary stationed at this location, the work of bringing the gospel to the area had begun in the summer of 1872. At that time, a representative of the American Bible Society had, according to his meticulous records, distributed 400 Bibles and 230 New Testaments during his visits to 2,650 families from August 26, 1872, to February 15, 1873. This industrious gentleman did admit that his figure for families might be inaccurate: "I am not satisfied that I know how to count families in Utah, as there are some peculiar arrangements there not found elsewhere."[32]

Jackson would have regarded these efforts as commendable, but his goal, as always, was to establish a permanent bastion of Presbyterianism, complete with resident pastor, dedicated congregation, and proper house of worship. Intending to observe at first hand the conditions faced by Schell, Jackson traveled to Alta at the end of May. He found Schell living above a grocery and liquor store. In an attempt to insulate his room against the cold, he had lined the ceiling and walls with cotton cloth, and he had obtained pieces of carpeting to wrap around his feet and legs. Despite these hardships, the young missionary seemed determined to carry on with his ministry. Encouraged by Schell's fortitude, Jackson left the community convinced that in a short time the results of Schell's efforts would warrant organization of a church in Alta. When Schell announced early in July that the snow was about gone, that strangers were flocking into the area, and that the situation looked promising, Jackson quickly returned to Alta. He and Schell organized a church on July 20. That date marked the end of Jackson's organizational work in Utah. [33]

After having organized a church in Helena, Montana, on August 1, 1869, Jackson had paid little attention to that remote part of his mission field. But in the eyes of many "boomers" of the Rocky Mountain West, Montana was destined for greatness among the galaxy of new stars soon to be affixed to the flag of the reunited Union. In the 1860s a great treasure vault of mineral deposits had been opened in the mountainous western portion of the Montana Territory. Communities, such as Helena, Virginia City, Bozeman, Deer Lodge, and Missoula, had been established as mining camps or as supply points for mining districts. By 1872 it appeared that the isolation of these towns would soon be ended by the construction of the Northern Pacific Railroad, which had been chartered to run from Lake Superior to Portland, Oregon. Construction crews were preparing to extend their track westward, and, with the banking house of the celebrated financier Jay Cooke engaged to secure funds for the construction, prospects early in 1872 for Montana's continuing growth and prosperity appeared very favorable indeed.[34]

Convinced by these reports that the time had arrived to plant the standard of Presbyterianism at all promising points in the area, Jackson planned an expedition early in 1872. To serve the churches contemplated in his plans he had recruited William Frackelton from the Presbyterian seminary in Chicago and James Russel, a recent graduate of Princeton Seminary. On May 16 the two young men and Jackson left Denver for Corinne, where they left the railroad to begin the arduous trip by stage to Montana. Jackson's account of this incredible journey left little to the imagination. With nine passengers packed into the coach, and nearly as many on the outside, the party traveled on the first day through camps of Shoshone Indians and scattered Mormon settlements. The journey continued unbroken through the night, which prompted Jackson to lament, "The miseries, torture and living death of a night ride in a crowded stage must be experienced to be known."[35]

At the first station encountered, the passengers received the unfortunate news that they must continue their journey in a crude lumber wagon. Their driver threw all of their boxes and trunks, as well as the mail sacks, onto the bed of the wagon, and the members of the party found perches on top as best they could. On they went through the darkness and a drizzling rain until midnight, when they reached a creek where the bridge had been washed out by heavy rains and runoff from the spring thaw. Calling upon their ingenuity, the driver and his passengers constructed a raft of logs to ferry three or four trunks and as many passengers at a time across the swollen stream. After the horses had managed to pull the lightened wagon across, the travelers resumed their journey in what could only be described as the most miserable of conditions.[36]

Thankfully, the weather and terrain improved on the third day of this ordeal. Passing through a region of low hills and small streams, the wayfarers reached a junction of the stage line at nightfall. There, much to their disgust, they learned that their connecting stage had not yet arrived. They tried to make themselves as comfortable as possible until, at about 11 P.M., an official of the stage company appeared with an extra coach he had commandeered to enable the weary party to proceed. On the fourth day, the exhausted travelers reached the mining camp of Bannack, where gold had been discovered in 1862. After only a brief stop at this town, the first encountered since leaving Corinne, they pressed on. That night the passengers were awakened by the driver, who requested they alight and walk across a bridge threatened by destruction from another torrent. Finally, on the fifth day of their trip, the stage and its cargo reached Helena, where, Jackson later remembered, "the arrival of three Presbyterian ministers brought great joy to many loyal hearts."[37]

Jackson and his two recruits lingered in Helena for three days recuperating from their exhausting journey. They then decided on a plan of action to fulfill their commitment to organize new churches in Montana. James Russel would remain in Helena to prepare the way for reorganization of the church started and then abandoned by Jackson in 1869. Meanwhile Jackson and Will Frackelton would try to organize churches in other communities where the residents seemed receptive. At the end of a veritable whirlwind of organizing activity, the two missionaries could look back at churches established at Gallatin City with five members, at Bozeman with eight members, and at Hamilton with only two members! On June 4, the intrepid wayfarers reached Virginia City, and the next day they posted placards throughout the bustling territorial capital announcing preaching that evening in the senate chambers. At the conclusion of that well-attended service, Jackson organized a church with five members, including the territorial auditor and the wives of the governor and secretary of state.[38] Impressed by Jackson's story of his adventures, one admiring resident of Virginia City commented:

> In the Rev. Sheldon Jackson the Presbyterians have a man who worthily magnifies his office. One would think this field big enough for half a dozen bishops, and quite too big for one man to keep pace with its growth. But if the record of the past twenty days is a fair specimen of his powers, he will provide all these states and territories with churches as fast as they are needed. At that rate, the Methodists will have to look out for their prestige.[39]

Continuing to provide Montana with churches "as fast as they are needed" was precisely Jackson's objective. "The establishment of the Presbyterian Church in Montana permits no loitering by the way," he wrote at one point during this whirlwind journey.[40] Leaving Will Frackelton in Virginia City, he hurried on to establish a church with seven members at Deer Lodge on June 9. One observer of the organizing service noted, "The house was filled with attentive listeners who were well pleased with the sermon. . . . The reverend gentleman [Jackson] will be certain to meet a hearty welcome whenever he may find it convenient to visit us."[41] The "reverend gentleman" felt compelled to visit one more town before rejoining Frackelton and Russel in Helena. On June 12 he organized a church at Missoula, although he could find only two persons who consented to be members. Finally, on June 16, Jackson reached Helena, where he proceeded to effect a reorganization of the church. Six of the members from the initial organization in 1869 who still resided in Helena joined with fourteen others to form the nucleus of a revived Presbyterian congregation in their city.[42]

With the organizing process in Montana completed for the time being, Jackson and his two companions decided that Frackelton would care for the needs of the churches at Bozeman, Virginia City, Gallatin City, and Hamilton. James Russel's area of concern would be the congregations at Helena, Deer Lodge, and Missoula. It remained to be seen, of course, if Jackson had correctly assessed the strength of Presbyterianism in the communities he had visited in Montana. Counting on Frackelton and Russel to nourish the seeds he had planted, Jackson set out on June 21 for his home in Denver by a roundabout route indeed. He traveled by stage north from Helena for about 140 miles until he reached Fort Benton, the head of steamboat navigation on the Missouri River. At that outpost in the wilderness he noted with pleasure the presence of two earnest Christian women who organized Sabbath services for a handful of listeners, with their husbands taking turns reading printed sermons. He boarded the steamboat *Mary McDonald* on June 22 along with an assorted group of companions, including a few tourists, army officers and their wives, employees of fur companies, and, according to Jackson, "criminals and desperadoes who have fled from the face of society and buried themselves among the various Indian tribes."[43]

Jackson's account of this journey included revealing comments about the Indians he observed along the way. When the boat passed Indian encampments, the occupants of the tipis would flock to the riverbank to watch the steamboat pass. Occasionally, as Jackson recalled, they fired their guns at the boat just for the fun of seeing the startled passengers scatter. Jackson also remembered seeing Indian funeral biers in trees or on platforms. Although these sites were sorrowful enough to behold, he found it sadder "to see the frequent graves of wood-choppers and trappers who had fallen victims of the scalping knife." Finally, after ten days aboard the *Mary McDonald*, Jackson reached Sioux City, Iowa, where he boarded a train for Denver. He arrived at his home on July 4 at the conclusion of an extraordinary five thousand mile journey. Reflecting upon the results of his efforts to organize churches in Montana, he believed the hardships and dangers "were more than compensated by the spiritual joy of founding Gospel institutions which shall assist in moulding the rising public sentiment in that beautiful Territory, so soon to be the home of tens and hundreds of thousands."[44]

Perhaps feeling a bit guilty about devoting his organizing efforts for such a long time exclusively to the challenge in Montana, Jackson spent the months of July and August in a tempestuous round of church organizing in Colorado. Among the stories of Jackson's participation in the establishment of six churches at that time, one event related to his work at a mining camp near the headwaters of the South Platte River, in the mountains about seventy miles southwest of Denver, is particularly noteworthy. Named Fairplay in 1859 by miners who had left the neighboring camp of Tarryall complaining of unfair treatment, the camp had prospered over the years from rich gold deposits discovered nearby. Jackson organized a church of eight members there on August 11. A friend of Jackson's recalled hearing the following story while on a vacation trip to the area shortly after Jackson's visit:

> At a mining camp on Mount Bross [near Fairplay], where as yet only two of the workmen had brought their families and were living in homes, the question was asked, "Do you ever have preaching up here?" "Oh, yes," was the reply, "Sheldon Jackson was here last Sunday and we all met in this building—a house for crushing ore—the largest in the place; and he stood upon the engine and gave us a rousing sermon."

Impressed by this remarkable story, the narrator of the tale concluded, "My friend Jackson, I know, would not hesitate, if he thought he could reach an old hardened sinner, to mount a locomotive and let fly a Gospel message at a group by the wayside while going at a speed of forty miles an hour."[45]

Certainly Jackson would have appreciated the services of a locomotive pulling a train at forty miles an hour on the last of his lengthy organizing expeditions in 1876, but that means of conveyance was not available to him. His goal on that occasion was Tucson, Arizona, where he proposed to organize a church in a territory that had been added to his superintendency by an action of the General Assembly in 1875. His interest in moving quickly to occupy the area for Presbyterianism was kindled late in 1875 when he learned from a friend of the intention of the Congregational Church to send a missionary to Tucson. Another informant confirmed this news with the exhortation to Jackson, "As things now are, if Arizona is saved at all to our church you must do it, and there is no time to lose—not a day."[46]

While Jackson might have wished to respond to this urgent appeal at once in the fall of 1875, other commitments had forced him to delay his plans until the spring of the following year. In any event, in March of 1876 he traveled from his home in Denver to Santa Fe, New Mexico, where he secured a seat on a stagecoach that carried him to Silver City in the southwest corner of that territory. From there he had to continue his travels under conditions that were uncomfortable, to say the least:

> Late in the afternoon we left Silver City on a one-seated "Buck Board." There were 400 pounds of mail heaped on in front and back, so that there was no alternative but to sit bolt upright. Once I tried to crouch down between the seat and the dash-board, but small as I am, it could not be done with comfort, so strapping myself to the seat lest I should get asleep and fall I got through the night as best I could.[47]

Finally, six days after leaving Santa Fe, the weary traveler arrived in Tucson, a town with a population estimated by Jackson at about four thousand, located in southern Arizona about seventy miles from the Mexican border.[48] An announcement publicizing his arrival and a preaching service he would conduct in the courthouse on April 9 appeared in a Tucson newspaper:

> The Rev. Mr. Jackson comes highly recommended. The ladies will certainly be there. They are always forward in every good word and work. Let them suggest to their husbands and male friends for once to neglect the everlasting contemplation of profit and loss, or to forego the last sensation, the problems of politics, the comic weekly, the agile billiard ball, the seductive seven-up [game of chance], or the Sunday morning nap, and wend their way to the house of worship.[49]

Jackson was pleased when about one hundred of Tucson's citizens did find their way to his improvised house of worship. One of those attending the gathering noted that their guest speaker, who "displayed no unctuous or gushing piety in his style," had proved to be "a plain, earnest, sensible man, and an able preacher." A choir of three, "extemporized" for the occasion, was accompanied by a member of the congregation playing a small cabinet organ.[50] Responding to a request signed by five petitioners, Jackson then conducted an organizational service in the evening to create the First Presbyterian Church of Tucson. Reporting on the successful culmination of all of these activities, one witness to the events believed that the new enterprise would doubtlessly have the "hearty co-operation" of good Christians of all denominations in the community.[51]

When he left Tucson, Jackson decided to forgo a return journey that would retrace his tiring route through Arizona and New Mexico. Instead he followed an itinerary that took him eventually to San Francisco, where he could return to Colorado by train via the Central Pacific and Union Pacific railroads. When he finally reached his home in Denver early in May, he could look back with satisfaction on an extraordinary record of church organization.[52] In some places, of course, church organization had occurred before his appearance on the scene. For example, in addition to the churches already established in Colorado before his arrival in 1870, churches had also been organized in New Mexico at Santa Fe on January 13, 1867, and at Las Vegas on March 21, 1870.[53] Other churches were established throughout his superintendency during the 1870s, his missionaries in the field often carrying out these responsibilities.[54] At the end of the decade, as he regarded these achievements, Jackson must have been pleased with the results, at least in one respect. He had apparently shown that there was a desire for Presbyterian churches in the Rocky Mountain West; his hope was that decision-makers in the East would provide the funds and personnel to sustain the new congregations.

Unfortunately, some of the organizations attempted by Jackson and his missionaries did not survive. There were those who regarded some of Jackson's organizing as foolhardy, to say the least. For example, reflecting on his organization with only two members at Missoula, Montana, delegates at the meeting of the Presbytery of Montana in February of 1880 noted, as a case in point, that one of the members, a freighter who was in Missoula for only one night, "was induced to act the part of ruling elder for the occasion.... The other member ... was a Methodist woman who had a quarrel with her pastor."[55] On the other hand, there were those who applauded Jackson's organizational strategy. "He was constantly searching out the land," wrote one of his supporters, "sowing beside all waters, organizing beside all railroads. Too much of it, do you say? Organized too much? The hunter does not begrudge a lost shot now and then, if he yet bags abundance of game. O, for more Jacksons to follow up Jackson, to build up what he began."[56]

As for Jackson's own views on his approach to organizing churches, he sought to justify his actions in a historical sermon prepared in 1876. "It was a grappling with unseen difficulties," he wrote, "a laying of the foundations of the church ... amid exigencies for which our Form of Government makes no provision."[57] In other words, he might bend the rules a bit in the organizing process if the means employed were directed to acceptable ends. For example, organizational guidelines prescribed by the national church called for presbyteries to appoint a committee of ministers and elders to visit prospective members of a new church to conduct the organizational exercises. While Jackson may have wished to comply with that requirement in all cases, in his vast mission field it was certainly more practical, in view of travel expenses, for him to serve as a committee of one for the purpose. Commenting on this fact, he noted, at the end of these expeditions, the following: "I reported to presbytery my action, which was then ratified, and the churches I had organized were received and enrolled, by action of presbytery, in due form."[58] In the final analysis, the result of Jackson's organizing efforts, whatever the *modus operandi*, would be evaluated, in part, by the growth of the new churches. Knowing this, Jackson might have wondered, as he organized his western churches, if frontier conditions might not significantly alter the kind of Presbyterianism that he and others of his background considered essential in their plan to win the West for Christ.

3 | Creating a Proper Appearance

But let a pleasant house of worship be reared, and the people will not only know that there is a Presbyterian church in the town, but they will desire a place within its walls.
—"HUNTING FOR A CHURCH," *Rocky Mountain Presbyterian*, JULY 1876

When one considers the Presbyterian churches established in the Rocky Mountain West in the 1870s, it is evident that the members of the new congregations were determined to erect, as soon as possible, a church building resembling those back in the States. One traveler in the West in 1876 related his experiences in trying to find a Presbyterian church in a western town. He knew that there was a church of this denomination, because he had seen it listed in the minutes of the General Assembly. He could not obtain information on its whereabouts until someone finally recalled "a Presbyterian *meeting* held once in four weeks over Smith's grocery." He went on to deplore this sad state of affairs, holding out little hope that the congregation would ever become stronger without a genuine house of worship.[1]

The first Presbyterian missionary arriving in a new western town might find it necessary to accept, at first, the crudest kind of structure in which to hold his preaching services. Perhaps the most extraordinary of these early improvisations occurred in Phoenix, Arizona, in 1879. With no other building in town available for their worship exercises, the new pastor and his small congregation erected an enclosure described by one witness as "a booth covered with bushes. . . . It is named the 'Tabernacle.'"[2] Writing to Jackson, the pastor noted how this strange arbor suited them very well during the hot months when the wind did not blow, but he said that it would not be acceptable in the cooler winter months. Besides, they could hardly place an organ or other proper church furnishings in such a preposterous edifice.[3]

The Phoenix Presbyterians, and others of their faith throughout the West, understood, of course, that the use of unconventional facilities for

Sunday worship services was only a temporary expedient. The next step was usually the securing of a hall that could be rented for a small fee or, if a public building, could be obtained free of charge. When Melancthon Hughes, for example, started the church in Corinne, Utah, in 1869, he preached in the city hall, a room measuring about sixteen by eighteen feet and made of rough, unplaned boards. Light came not only from the windows but also from the large cracks between the boards. In the spring of 1871, Jackson experienced a rather unpleasant disruption to the preaching service he conducted on his first reconnoitering expedition to Evanston, Wyoming, a ranching community along the Union Pacific Railroad in the southwestern corner of the territory. He had arranged for the use of a hall on the second floor of a rough frame building that also housed a saloon in the room below. He recalled how the service had proceeded smoothly before a capacity audience, although, at one point, he deemed it necessary to call upon the sheriff to stop a fight among the patrons on the lower floor.[4]

A classic recollection of the hardships endured in such makeshift surroundings was a tale about Alex Darley and his early church work at the small town of Del Norte in the San Luis Valley of southern Colorado. Darley, a graduate of a Presbyterian seminary in Chicago, had been recruited by Jackson to establish a church there early in 1875. The local Methodist pastor recalled how, in 1877, he and Darley had shared the use of the courthouse above the jail in 1877 for their church services. Sometimes the prisoners below would deliberately disturb the congregation above by stamping their feet, talking loudly, singing, or shouting. One Sunday morning Darley found the chimney on the upstairs stove stopped with soot. Being an enterprising individual, he tried to blow it out with a charge of black powder, not knowing that the chimney also connected with the room below. The resulting explosion blew the cover off the downstairs stove and set the jail on fire. Awed perhaps by this manifestation from on high, the prisoners were quiet from then on.[5]

A few years later, Alex's brother George arrived in Del Norte to minister to the congregation. George had had no formal seminary training, but he had become convinced that he would like to become a missionary like his brother. He was commissioned by the Board of Home Missions as a "Missionary Preacher" early in 1877, and at a meeting of the Presbytery of Colorado on May 9, 1878, the delegates formally ordained him to the ministry. When he arrived in Del Norte, George found that he would have to preach in the same facility, above the jail, that his brother Alex had used. It seems that the prisoners in the jail had resumed their disruptive antics. "The only room I could get to hold services at that time," he recalled, "was a small room over the calaboose, and because the audience downstairs did not consider listening to preaching part of the penalty inflicted by law, they would occasionally object in a way that made it very unpleasant for the audience upstairs."[6]

Quaint recollections like these have become an accepted part of the folklore of the West. It was not the way, however, that the Presbyterian Church intended to fulfill its mission to win the West for Christ indefi- nitely. Providing a suitable building in which to worship always had a high priority in planning sessions among the new congregations. The first build- ing did not have to be a cathedral, yet it was expected to conform with the design of modest frame church buildings common to most small commu- nities in the East. When Bayard Taylor, the celebrated world traveler, passed through Black Hawk, Colorado, in 1866, he had observed a crude settle- ment "where the sole pleasant object is the Presbyterian church, white, tasteful, and charmingly placed . . . above the chimneys and mills in the uniting ravines."[7] Many of the Rocky Mountain congregations had to remain content with simple church structures, but, if a town continued to grow and prosper, the Presbyterians would strive to erect a more stately edifice as befit- ted their role as second to none among Protestant denominations.

The determination with which this goal was pursued was well illus- trated on March 10, 1872, when Jackson joined with other Presbyterians in Denver in the dedication services for an imposing new house of wor- ship. Presbyterian tourists visiting the city the previous year had called for contributions from donors in the East toward the erection of this building, because Denver was important "as a religious center for radiating truth into the vast mineral regions of the mountains as well as over the sur- rounding plains."[8] Obviously proud of the successful completion of this project, Jackson provided a detailed description of the structure for the readers of the *Rocky Mountain Presbyterian*, a newspaper Jackson published and edited from his home in Denver beginning in March of 1872:

> The building is semi-Gothic architecture, 32 X 60 feet, with a tower and entrance through the tower. It has two basement rooms, is heated by a furnace, lighted with gas, the seats handsomely cushioned and the entire floor is covered with a beautiful carpet of the pattern known as the small scarlet cross. The windows are stained and enameled glass. They are all memorial and bear the names of the different Sab- bath schools and individuals who contributed them. It is altogether the neatest and handsomest church in the Territory, and cost with the ground belonging to it $12,075.[9]

The sense of pride in a job well done is evident in this commentary. Jack- son would have regarded this achievement as indisputable evidence that brush arbors or rooms above saloons and jails might serve initially as meeting rooms for Presbyterians in frontier communities, but proper church edifices could soon be constructed if congregations and eastern benefactors united wholeheartedly in raising the funds.

No matter the form of sanctuary for worship, a visitor to these churches on a Sunday morning could count on hearing hymn singing by the congregation and a choir. When Alex Darley organized a church at Lake City in western Colorado in 1876, he recalled how "our first choir music at a church service gives us pleasure and the promise of things such as characterize the homes of our youth."[10] This poignant reference to cherished moments from church services in the good old days back East expresses the need Presbyterians felt to re-create a traditional musical accompaniment to their Sabbath services in the West. A friend of Jackson's at the Presbyterian Board of Publications in Philadelphia supplied hymn books for the churches Jackson had organized along the Union Pacific in 1869. On one occasion he apologized because "they are cheaply bound, and are of an earlier edition, slightly different from that in use, but I think it will answer the purpose of your new churches very well."[11] James Russel, who began his preaching assignment in Butte, Montana, in a dimly lit room set up for a minstrel show, clearly identified the place of congregational singing in the new churches. He remembered that when singing time came the congregation took out candles to throw light on the songbooks, and, "It is good yet to remember how they enjoyed the singing, for we sang only the good old hymns upon which we had all been raised."[12]

While all of Jackson's missionaries advocated singing the "good old hymns" in their services, Delos Finks at the Fairplay Colorado church seemed to attach more importance than anyone to this form of worship. Finks was a young missionary who had graduated from Auburn Theological Seminary in New York in the spring of 1873. Writing to Jackson in 1874, Finks chose to reflect upon the success he was enjoying by emphasizing congregational singing in his church and Sabbath school. When he went to preach at Alma, a nearby mining camp, he found his listeners eager for him to organize a singing class, a responsibility that he gladly accepted, "feeling that to improve their wretched singing would be a good and necessary step to religious interest and profitable worship." Unfortunately, on at least one occasion the interest attracted by the singing at his church resulted in a rather startling result. "One day a drunken man straggled in," Finks recalled, "and forcibly illustrated the evil effects of drink. He undertook to join in the songs and could not stop at the right time and finally his whiskey tumbled him over and he had to be carried out." Despite an occasional embarrassing incident, Finks concluded that singing was the life of his prayer meetings, and "what I should have done here without music, I do not know."[13]

Although a cappella singing in the frontier congregations was acceptable when there was no musical instrument available for accompaniment, small cabinet organs could usually be obtained for the churches. Delos Finks, for example, felt much more at home in Fairplay when his own cabinet organ finally reached him undamaged in the summer of 1873. There was also an element of satisfaction in claiming a "first" with acquisition of an organ. At Alex Darley's organizational service in Lake City, Colorado, in 1876, he justified an expenditure of four dollars: "$2.00 being for use of Mrs. Wade's organ—the first organ and church choir used in the city—and $2.00 for hauling it half a mile and back again."[14] Since an organ required an organist, when one was not available, the pastor might feel a responsibility to try and play the instrument. William Rommel, a recent graduate of Princeton Seminary, had joined Will Frackelton and James Russel in the Montana mission field in 1872. At his church in Helena, Rommel took organ lessons from a piano player at a local saloon and, with a note of dejection mixed with relief, he explained, "After ten lessons . . . I only succeeded in learning how to play 'John Brown's Body,' when an organist was found."[15]

So the hills, valleys and plains of the Rocky Mountain West literally echoed with sacred music from the earliest days of settlement. An ambitious composer at the time, bent on creation of a great choral masterpiece of music of the West, would, of course, want to include the cowboy's lament and the Indian's tribal chant. His work would certainly have been incomplete, however, without the familiar hymns sung by many of the western pioneers. One other ingredient was still needed to complete the picture of a proper church—a church bell. Presbyterians, and other church goers in the West, found themselves somehow spiritually naked without this traditional introduction to their worship exercises. Reflecting an interdenominational rivalry on this matter in Denver in 1869, the pastor of the Presbyterian church noted remorsefully, "The Presbyterians are far behind the Methodists and Episcopalians in this Territory. . . . We need a bell for our church more than anything else except a blessing from heaven."[16] Duncan McMillan, a young minister whom Jackson had persuaded to leave his small church in southern Illinois to establish a church and school at Mt. Pleasant, Utah, in 1875, believed that a bell for his little church could be an effective missionary instrument. He expressed this thought to an elderly member of his congregation. The old man replied wistfully "that if a bell should ring out some Sabbath morning in this valley many a heart would melt down with precious memories of the long ago in other homes."[17]

Precious memories of churches back in the States would usually include fond recollections of a preacher who could inspire his congregation by his physical appearance, personal conduct, and pulpit oratory. The expectations were no lower in the western churches. When accepting a pastorate in a rough and tumble frontier settlement, a Presbyterian missionary could not assume for example, that he could dress in a manner incommensurate with his position. An instance occurred in Silver City, New Mexico, in 1874. Typical of the many complaints received by Jackson from churchgoers in the town was a report from one woman who described the missionary, who had arrived at the end of 1873 to try to organize a Presbyterian church, as "filthy beyond anything I ever dreamed of. . . . [He] goes around town without a shirt and no strings in his shoes. . . . I have made up my mind that he is either a bad man or partially insane." This distressed lady concluded her condemnation of this misfit by emphasizing the need for a really good minister in Silver City. "I never realized what it was to be without one until we came here three years ago," she explained, "and I feel we are all drifting on the road to ruin without a hand to save or encourage us to better things."[18]

Some of the pastors of the western churches were surprised to find, when they did strive to dress in attire suitable for a Presbyterian minister, that they raised questions among their brethren in the East about the hardships they were presumably enduring in frontier churches. When the pastor of the Laramie, Wyoming, church traveled in the East in 1876 to try to raise money for his mission field, he told Jackson how his plans had gone awry. He and his wife had scrimped and saved for months to outfit him with a new wardrobe for the journey. When he tried to portray himself, however, as a starving missionary before eastern congregations, he received little sympathy because "their idea of a Western missionary is that he must have an old coat, weather beaten hat, and other things to correspond. I did not fill the bill."[19] A representative from the Presbytery of Colorado who attended the General Assembly meeting in Brooklyn, New York, in 1876 noted how the other delegates were surprised to find him not clothed in buckskin, "giving an exaggerated expression to a very prevalent feeling in the East that far western people must necessarily be very rough and uncouth." He had tried to assure the skeptics that many westerners came from refined and cultured backgrounds back in the States, and that "they are as necessarily like the East as it is possible to be."[20]

Sometimes this better class of citizen who attended a frontier church took exception when their spiritual leader tried to carry his message of salvation to the lower classes. The pastor of the Presbyterian church in West Las Animas, a railroad town in southeastern Colorado, bravely decided in 1875 that he was duty bound to bring the Gospel message to railroad workers and others not religiously inclined in his community. His courageous efforts, as he told Jackson, were not well received by the upper echelons of society in West Las Animas:

> A week ago last Sabbath I obtained permission and preached in the largest dance hall and gambling saloon in town, to a respectful and attentive congregation of upwards of 100 of these men who never go to church. Wife and two other ladies went with me to sing. The church-going community regarded the procedure of doubtful propriety and expressed surprise that we were not grossly insulted. I believe that this is the only possible way of reaching the people who have given themselves up to wickedness. I expect to continue this kind of work as opportunity affords though it is not countenanced by many who ought to lend their moral support.[21]

Perhaps the most scandalous case of "doubtful propriety" associated with a Presbyterian missionary in the Rocky Mountain West took place at the church in Evanston, Wyoming. When a pulpit vacancy occurred there in 1873, Jackson found a replacement who, at first, appeared to receive widespread acceptance from the community and the congregation. Subsequent accounts of misconduct, however, soon claimed Jackson's attention. The young man seemed to exhibit worldly interests completely antithetical to Presbyterian doctrines. One resident of Evanston charged, "The other night it was announced and there was held at the Presbyterian Church a low traveling show."[22] When accusations of this nature continued, the Presbytery of Wyoming acted in the spring of 1874 to dismiss the nonconformist. His successor, who visited the congregation periodically from his home church in Corinne, Utah, found a sorry state of affairs on his first visit to the Wyoming church. He could locate only two women who still regarded themselves as faithful members. One of these ladies told him how the departed and disgraced minister had "preached all of the Christians out of the church and all of the gamblers and infidels into it."[23] Although the pastor from Corinne continued to visit the Evanston congregation, he admitted to Jackson at the end of the year, "If you can get that church out of the disgrace . . . brought upon it and get out of it those who are so shamefully disgracing it and themselves by drunkenness and worldliness you will do more than I have yet been able to do."[24]

Good Presbyterians could also avoid bringing disgrace upon themselves and their church by refraining from frivolous behavior at Sunday-morning worship services. When Jackson published an article entitled "Manners in Church" in his newspaper in 1874, he surely hoped that the admonitions included therein would be taken to heart by his readers. The writer deplored idle chatter in the sanctuary. Pointing his finger at the ladies in the audience, he declaimed, "What a spectacle for angels, who ever convene with God's people in their worship, to be witnesses of the animated tattle of two women, who should be subdued into awe at the thought of being in the presence of God!" This critic also advised against any manifestation of fine clothing by those attending church services. "To make the house of prayer," the judge of good taste continued, "a scene for exhibition of the latest fashions, the gayest colors, and the brightest jewels and thus bedizened, to appear before God, is out of all character. . . . Thoroughly refined people are always averse to making a display of themselves." The writer was sure that beneficial results would be derived by adhering to this policy, because "by an appearance of equality, the lowly may be encouraged to attend public worship."[25]

The "lowly" might indeed be welcome at Sabbath services, but their conduct outside the church would have to be above reproach before they could be seriously considered for membership. This requirement was well upheld by the missionary sent by Jackson to organize a church in Prescott, Arizona, in 1876. He later boasted that he had carefully screened those applying for membership, preferring to have a small group of true Christians rather than a larger body with a portion "whose lives are doubtful."[26] An embarrassing situation, arising from an error made in permitting a person leading a doubtful life into church membership, occurred in Salt Lake City in 1872. At the beginning of the year, Josiah Welch told Jackson about a woman member of his church who appeared to be of doubtful character. With no direct testimony to confirm his suspicions at the time, he could only hope that the Lord would show her the error of her ways. Welch did not mention the case again during the year, but in December he told Jackson how the governing body of the church had finally suspended the woman because "Mrs. _____ has been arrested for keeping a house of ill-fame, and I grieve that the grounds for her arrest are too true."[27]

Such were the ingredients blended together to create a proper Presbyterian church in the West. Picture, then, a Sunday morning, with the congregation assembled for the weekly devotional exercise. The culmination of the service, of course, will be the sermon delivered by their spiritual leader. What topic should the pastor select for his address? And what message should he expect his audience to derive from his remarks? One of Jackson's missionaries chose to expound on these questions in the *Rocky Mountain Presbyterian* in 1875. Writing about "Home Missions and Orthodoxy," he exhorted:

If the men whom our Board sends out into the waste places of the
country are going to deal in platitudes, whittle down the truth, give a
milk-and-water theology to mankind, spend half their time making
little creeds for the adoption of young converts, and conform their
teaching, as far as their genius will permit, to anti-dogma men, the
sooner the Church knows it the better.

The fact is, Mr. Editor, the life of our Church, as well as of
Christianity, is its distinctive doctrines, and if there is a pitiable object in
the world it is the minister of our communion who cannot comprehend
them, or comprehending them, has not the boldness to avow them.[28]

Jackson's recruits, on the whole, were definitely not "anti-dogma men."
They followed carefully the party line, so to speak, when they urged their
listeners in the pews to follow the straight and narrow path, avoiding all
temptations that might be contrary to righteous codes of conduct. William Rommel in Helena, Montana, for example, found himself at odds with
some members of his church during the holidays at the end of 1872. New
Year's Day was approaching, when leading families of the congregation
customarily held open house and offered refreshments, including liquor.
On the Sunday before the festive occasion, Rommel deliberately selected
as his text "Look not upon the wine when it is red." Assuming he could not
reach the men in his audience, he directed an earnest appeal to the women
of Helena not to offer intoxicants to their guests on January 1. He was
discouraged when, on the next day, the men of his church whom he met on
the streets refused to speak to him. He felt that he had aroused only opposition with his temperance sermon, but when he made sixty calls to homes
and business establishments in the town on New Year's Day, he found only
two places where liquor was served.[29]

In a similar vein, when the pastor of the church in Evanston, Wyoming,
preached his farewell sermon in April of 1873, he admonished his audience
to shun certain "pernicious" activities. "In his remarks," one listener recalled, "he gave a faithful delineation of the evils of gambling, enumerat-
ing card playing, billiard playing, dice, chess and croquet, recommending
the entire abstinence from all games of chance as being pernicious to morals and inconsistent with the teachings of the Bible."[30] And at the church in
Black Hawk, Colorado, in 1875, the minister told Jackson how the largest
subscribers to his salary had resolved to give no more money unless he quit
preaching about hell. "Now I do not propose to surrender," the beleaguered correspondent assured Jackson, "but will fight it out on that line if
possible, if it takes all summer."[31]

George Darley was another missionary who was determined to fight the good fight against conduct that could be regarded as contrary to the high standards of Presbyterianism. Darley's carefully preserved sermons reveal his concerns on these matters, as he preached them to congregations at several churches in Colorado. Presenting guidelines for congenial relationships in a Christian family, for example, his recommendations extended from filial devotion, in "What We Owe the Old Folks," to comments on the husband-wife relationship, in "The Family." In the latter he describes a good woman as one who keeps her place. "The noisy, blustering, arrogant, self-asserting [women]," he argued, "make the air hot with their voices, and trouble the world with their superabundant activities." Times of financial distress, when the family provider is unemployed, Darley explained, should be recognized as the voice of God calling men to repentance. The best kind of man in Darley's eyes, and presumably in God's, was the manly man, and "nowhere has this noble trait of character more admirers than in this western land." Manly men frowned upon anything detrimental to the best interests of society, while they encouraged all that was noble and elevating. The manliest men were "large hearted." Men who were all intellect might attain momentary adoration "by a certain class," but then their brilliance dimmed, as they were pronounced unsuccessful because they lacked heart.[32]

Darley saw himself in a special role as mentor to the young men of his church and community. He cautioned the young men to beware the pitfalls that had snared the prodigal son. Too much money hastened a young man's ruin, encouraging him to waste his substance in riotous living. The wastrel could always be detected because:

His bleared eyes, his foul smelling breath, swaggering walk, and leering look into the faces of respectable women as they walk our streets, all prove the waste of physical strength, energy, respectability, manhood, common decency, and altogether a looseness of morals that is deplorable. His dress is flashy, his language often smacks of "smartness" that has more impudence in it than common sense.[33]

Other targets for Darley's sermons were the young men who came west solely for adventure. Unfortunately, they could be seen nightly, "either drinking that which poisons, intoxicates and ruins, or wending their way to her house whose feet the wisest man said, 'Take Hold on Hell.'" Darley urged young men to be energetic in business; the acquisition of money, if men neither loved nor wasted it, was honorable and its possession helpful. After the rather remarkable statement that "business is business, and the only way to succeed in business is to attend to business in a business like way," he continued with words of encouragement: "Remember that many

who were poor in their youth have risen to the highest heights, and that
the world stands ready to advance you whenever you prove yourself worthy of advancement."[34]

In his sermon for young men on the right kind of books to read, Darley
showed how "poisonous literature leads downward, while literature of a
high order has elevated and enriched the minds of men." Satan whispers to
the reader to read both sides of every question, but "it is dangerous for
most people to read books written by . . . infidel writers, because they
subject our principles and virtues to needless tests." It was common knowledge, according to Darley, that the inmates of jails had been accustomed to
reading stories of crime and adventure, and that the reading of a novel
based on sensationalism rather than moral principle "has sent more than
one young man away with a fever for life setting his blood on fire."[35]

Darley was particularly interested in reminding his listeners on Sunday
morning of the threats presented by the Catholic Church as it tried to
further its own interests among competing denominations in the United
States. He described its menacing presence as "a strong and flourishing
tree, the owners of which hope to see its outspreading branches cover this
entire country." Darley describes the Pope as a power-hungry potentate who
directs the campaign to capture the nation for Catholicism. "The Pope's sympathy with and admiration for the United States," Darley charged, "reminds
me of the sympathy and admiration of the hungry wolf for the fat lamb." He
continued this theme in a sermon intended as an exhortation to patriotism,
"America and Her Greatest Enemy." In it, he denies that the discovery of
America by Columbus, who was aided by a Catholic queen, gives to the Pope
any special rights in America. On the contrary, "as Americans we should not
spend all our time picking flowers and throwing them at Columbus, but rather
spend our time gathering facts . . . for the protection of our beloved land."[36]

George Darley was obviously not one of those men whom the writer in
Jackson's newspaper had warned against—one who "whittled down the
truth." Darley was sure he knew the truth; his theology, and the lessons to
be derived therefrom, certainly echoed the spirit of his time. Presbyterians
residing in the Rocky Mountain West were content to establish churches in
their communities that re-created, in all aspects, everything they perceived as
good emanating from past religious traditions. And once their churches were
under way, they tried to keep them free from the debilitating influence of
churchgoers not of the Presbyterian persuasion. The pastor of the church in
Golden, Colorado, for example, made a strong case for early erection of a
church building on the grounds that his members might otherwise be driven
to affiliation with other Protestant groups, whose leaders, he insisted, were
"gross errorists" in their misguided interpretations of the Scriptures.[37]

Prominent among the "gross errorists," in the minds of Presbyterian missionaries, were those who regarded themselves as Universalists. When a woman of that faith, which espouses the belief that all people will finally achieve salvation, approached Delos Finks wondering if she could join his church in Fairplay, Colorado, Finks's first reaction was to deny her the privilege. When she gave every indication, however, of adopting Presbyterian doctrines of prayer, faith, and good works—essential ingredients in the screening process for selecting those who would enter heaven—Finks was inclined to believe that her old views would soon wear away. Besides, he needed her help in teaching a Sabbath-school class, and, as he told Jackson, she "was brought up in the better class of Universalists."[38]

Sheldon Jackson and his missionaries in the West often held views contrary to the policy on comity, or fraternal cooperation between denominations, endorsed by the General Assembly and the Board of Home Missions. At the General Assembly meeting in 1873, the home mission board outlined what it considered a practical approach to this issue:

> One of the evils, particularly noticeable at the West, is the great number of church organizations and church edifices in nearly every village. It is a great grief to many, that there should be so often found a Presbyterian, Congregational, Methodist, Baptist, and perhaps other churches in a place, and each with a minister and a house of worship, when the whole number of church-going people could be easily accommodated in one church edifice, and served by a single minister of Christ.[39]

This pragmatic line of reasoning never set well with the western missionaries. In their communities, they preferred a position of—to use the facetious expression—first among equals. That attitude prevailed early in 1877 in Ouray, a small community in southwestern Colorado, where one Presbyterian resident worried about efforts to establish a Methodist church before a Presbyterian organization could be achieved. Convinced that a Methodist minister would arrive at any moment, he wrote Alex Darley, pastor of the Presbyterian church in Del Norte, Colorado, about his concerns. A few of his neighbors of the Methodist faith were already trying to raise money for a church building, using methods "hardly becoming to a Presbyterian." Would he attend a Methodist church in Ouray if it were the only one in town? Certainly not! "I am Presbyterian all over," he noted. "It runs in my blood. My grandfather was fed on the catechism in old Scotland, and was an elder in the Presbyterian Church as is my father today." He concluded with the firm assertion, "I do not want the Presbyterian to be else than the first to build its society permanently in this place."[40]

If the writer from Ouray hoped that his warning would serve as a call to action, his goal was soon realized. A month after his report, Alex Darley's brother George traveled to Ouray to announce his intention of organizing a Presbyterian church in the town, and soon thereafter Sheldon Jackson appeared on the scene to accomplish that purpose. On other occasions, threats of rivalry from other denominations brought similar results.

Early in 1874, a writer in the new town of Monument, located a few miles north of Colorado Springs, Colorado, told Jackson how Monument had earnestly embarked on the path of progress. Those interested in establishing a church in their town were prepared to affiliate with either Presbyterians or Baptists, depending on which denomination would furnish a good minister and assist in erecting a church building. Although Jackson might have resented being challenged to outbid a rival denomination for the privilege of placing a church, he obviously made satisfactory pledges to the people in Monument: on January 20 he organized a church there with six members. And in Idaho Springs, Colorado, in the fall of 1874, Jackson hastened to fill a pulpit vacancy when the angry clerk of session wrote, in a rather crudely constructed commentary, "What fiew [members] we have are thuraly Presbyterian and can be nothing els, but if we can't have a Presbyterian to preach for us we will take a Methodist or anyone els we can get for we dont intend to be cast of intierly."[41]

Jackson's greatest headache over comity, however, came from efforts of the Board of Home Missions to hold fraternal conferences, beginning in 1874, with representatives of the Congregational Church. The goal of these meetings was to develop some sort of policy for establishing one union church, at first, from members of each denomination in new and unstable western communities. The minister for the mixed congregation could be either Presbyterian or Congregational, depending on who was available. A similar initiative taken in 1801 known as the Plan of Union, for placing new churches in the frontier areas of the Ohio Valley, had resulted in dissatisfaction from the Congregationalists, who finally abrogated the agreement in 1852. At mid century, one spokesman for this disgruntled faction charged that the Presbyterians "have milked our Congregational cows, but have made nothing but Presbyterian butter and cheese."[42] Ready to try again, the delegates to the meeting in 1874 concluded their deliberations by issuing a joint statement deploring "the wicked waste of funds in the support of two feeble churches, both of which must be weak, and which might become involved in bitter, protracted and unholy strife."[43]

Regrettably, "unholy strife" occurred over these considerations at one of the churches in Jackson's superintendency in 1874. In the May 13, 1874, edition of the *Rocky Mountain Presbyterian* there appeared a notice of a proposition from the Congregational church in Longmont, Colorado, a small farming settlement about forty miles north of Denver, that it unite with the Presbyterian church in that community. The proposal called, however, for resignation of the pastor of the Presbyterian church and for the Congregational minister to serve both churches. The Presbyterians rejected this overture because it involved the expulsion of a man with whom they were well satisfied, and the acceptance of a man in whose call they had no choice. After a prolonged period of committee work, the session of the Presbyterian church decided at the end of the year to take no further action until the Congregationalists agreed to leave the consolidation matter to an impartial committee with a membership drawn from areas outside Longmont. Resumption of committee work on this subject in 1875 came to naught, and both parties finally agreed to abandon the proposal. When the Congregationalist element then completed and dedicated a church building in Longmont, the pastor of the Presbyterian church rejoiced at the failure of the union plan because the Congregationalists were "throwing open their doors to all the 'isms' in the world."[44]

The issues raised by the Longmont case received thorough analysis later by the pastor of the Presbyterian church. An appraisal of his views provides insight into the depth of feeling on this matter. In a history of the Longmont church prepared by this gentleman in 1876, he insisted that "these Congregational members have not spirituality enough nor sound faith enough to live and work in the Presbyterian church." Besides, they employed as their leader "a renegade Presbyterian minister of questionable character." This historian then closed his narrative by congratulating the stalwart Presbyterians who refused to abandon the faith of their fathers. "Seeing danger ahead," he exulted, "they rally their forces therefore, gather around their standard, fortify themselves, and prepare to fight the battles of the Lord in the blue ranks of the regular army, and upon the old battle fields of Presbyterianism."[45]

Henry Kendall, in New York, asked Jackson in the fall of 1874 to provide the Board of Home Missions with information on the number of communities in which both churches existed in the same community. Within his mission field Jackson made a very thorough study on the matter, and he published a copy of his findings in the *Rocky Mountain Presbyterian* in March of the following year. The results clearly revealed his views on the topic. He found forty-four Presbyterian and eleven Congregational churches in the region. Nine communities had churches of both denominations, but, with only one or two exceptions, in those places the Congregational church was noticeably weaker than the Presbyterian. And since the great bulk of continuing immigration to the area was Presbyterian, according to Jackson's analysis, it was obviously incumbent on the Presbyterian congregations to maintain their own distinctive identities. Relying on Jackson's opinions and those of other western missionaries, the home mission board reported to the General Assembly in 1877 that efforts at denominational comity in the West had proved, in large part, ineffectual. Complaints coming to the board blamed their Congregationalist brethren, but doubtlessly the same complaints to the Congregationalist mission board placed the blame on the Presbyterians. Assembly delegates reading these comments could only conclude that the translation of theories on comity into practice in frontier communities presented insurmountable barriers indeed.[46]

When all was said and done, the Presbyterian churches founded in the Rocky Mountain West during the 1870s were hammered, sawed, painted, mortared, and furnished into reasonable facsimiles of their progenitors in the East. Worshipers in these sanctuaries on the Sabbath would be adjured to adopt righteous lives and shun wicked pursuits. If the listeners followed these guidelines, everyone presumably would benefit from the results. An example of this line of reasoning appeared in a report on the dedication of the Presbyterian church building erected in Cheyenne, Wyoming, in 1870. Elated by the new evidence of civilizing influences in his community, the writer now regarded the town's earlier reputation as a godless and transitory railroad camp as no longer appropriate. "Never have we before witnessed such a change in society," the reporter concluded, "such a rapid and healthy growth of refinement and morality as has taken place in this city. . . . Crime and immorality have sought more congenial quarters, and churches, schools, and other evidence of a good civilization have taken their place."[47]

This observation from Cheyenne sums up the whole story of religious acceptance in the Rocky Mountain West. Crime and immorality in Cheyenne in 1870 probably did seek more congenial quarters, not because the arrival of the churches drove them out but because the heyday of railroad construction that nourished their existence had ended. But a rational understanding of cause and effect in this situation was immaterial to the conclusions drawn by the better class of citizen. They could now perceive "evidence of a good civilization," and the idea of "good" was tied, in no small part, to the presence of a church. Not a booth covered with bushes or a borrowed courtroom, but an authentic reproduction of something remembered from bygone days was the right ingredient for a community's permanence and prosperity. As for the Presbyterians, they generally preferred to keep their churches to themselves, resisting all overtures to form union churches blended of two or more congregations of similar denominations. Sheldon Jackson certainly sensed this feeling. He was lukewarm, to say the least, in his response to directives from his mission board on the matter of comity.

4 | The Role of the Field Commander

The Board do hereby appoint you to preach the Gospel to feeble Churches and Congregations, and to perform any other duties that may aid the work.

—J. F. Stearns, Chairman, Board of Home Missions, to Sheldon Jackson, October 1, 1872

"Is a District Secretary or Synodical Agent an unnecessary appendage to the Home Missionary Department of our Church?" Answering his own question, raised in the November 1876 edition of the *Rocky Mountain Presbyterian*, the unidentified writer replied bluntly: the supervisor is not necessary "if he only sits in his office, writes and receives letters, gets a good salary, and does no outside work. . . . But, if he is the right man in the right place he is essential in his position."[1] Writing in the same issue of the newspaper, Henry Kendall, secretary of the Board of Home Missions, defined the function of synodical missionary and the relationship with district supervision, as he saw it:

> To keep the feeble churches full of hope, and supplied with preaching; to explore wide sections of the new country; to organize new churches; to introduce new men into his field; to counsel and encourage, and, if need be, assist the young in their new and arduous labor; and to furnish exact and definite information of his whole field to the Board, taking long journeys by night and by day, in summer's heat and winter's cold, preaching nearly every Sabbath, and many times every day of the week—is what a Synodical missionary has to do.[2]

That description might well have been written expressly of the role assumed by Sheldon Jackson at the time. Certainly he did his best to supply his feeble churches with preaching by introducing new men into his field. He hoped to secure, if possible, men of exceptional talents to fill the western pulpits. In an article he prepared for publication on the subject, he concluded his appeal to men of ability with a resounding call to arms: "As the ablest military men are most needed where the danger is greatest," he wrote, "so the ablest ministers should be sent where the spiritual conflict is greatest. . . . For as it is universally conceded that the West will control the political destinies of the continent, so she must eventually, control the religious."[3] Jackson would have been pleased if he could have obtained an elite cadre of missionaries for assignment to the Rocky Mountain West. He soon realized, however, that it would be difficult to attract experienced men with good reputations to posts in his mission field. Eastern men serving prosperous churches were quite content to add their endorsements to home mission appeals, but they were not ready to sacrifice their secure positions for a nebulous assurance of spiritual reward in some western Sodom or Gomorrah. Thus Jackson had to rely heavily on recent seminary graduates to man his frontier outposts, and he knew, realistically, that he would experience many disappointments to go with the occasional successes.

On the whole, Jackson's superiors at the Board of Home Missions gave him a free hand in the recruiting process for western missionaries. The problems he did have with the board members were related, primarily, to his title. The board members consistently opposed Jackson's use of the word superintendent, and, at a special meeting called at the end of November 1870, they resolved to refer to all men holding positions similar to Jackson's as synodical missionaries. In faraway Colorado, the resident director of home mission work in the Rocky Mountain West chose to ignore their action. At the end of 1870, using placards and business cards, Jackson called for all Presbyterians desiring church organizations, a minister, or plans for a church building to contact him in Denver. Impervious to the mission board action, he described himself in bold letters in these announcements as Superintendent of Presbyterian Missions for Colorado, New Mexico, Montana, Wyoming, and Utah.[4]

The bickering over this issue continued until Jackson made a telling argument that finally brought the board around to his point of view. Regarding his use of the term superintendent, his purpose, he insisted, was only to save money for the board. Railroad officials would invariably give him a free pass if he represented himself with the more impressive designation, whereas he could get only half fare as a synodical missionary. There were no more reprimands for his use of the title. A member of the home mission board, speaking years later at a meeting of the Pueblo Presbytery in Colorado, was asked why the board now condoned the use of the term superintendent. Echoing the precedent established by Jackson, the visitor replied that the title was used "on account of its being better understood by railroad officials, and the only term recognized in securing reduced rates for these men, and not with any intention of giving them authority over the ministers or churches."[5]

Jackson never presumed that he could exercise authority over the ministers or churches in his area. His recommendations would usually carry great weight concerning decisions about church affairs in the congregations he represented, but the actual authority for making those decisions resided in the hierarchical structure of the church government. A session, composed of those selected to serve as elders, supplied the mechanism for local church governance. This group provided rules and regulations for the conduct of the church. At the Lake City, Colorado, church, for example, when the session met for the first time following Alex Darley's organization of the church in 1876, the elders adopted a constitution for the Bible school that prohibited the use of any books, papers, or other publications except those approved by the session. In addition, the school was instructed to use the publications of the Presbyterian Board of Publications in preference to all others. Later, after an unexplained problem arose pertaining to the composition of the choir, the session minutes noted, "It was unanimously decided to keep the choir under the control of the Session, and in the future no person can be admitted in the choir without the unanimous recommendation of said choir to the session who is then to decide upon his or her admition [sic]."[6]

The elders of the session were also expected to serve the bread and wine at Communion services. If they were remiss in their responsibilities, the service could not take place. At the little mining camp of Rosita in southern Colorado, the clerk of the session in 1879 ruefully recorded the following in the minutes: "Two weeks ago it was announced that the sacrament of the Lord's Supper would be administered today. The elders failing to provide the emblems [elements], there could be no celebration."[7] On the rare occasions when a church found itself without any elders available to offer Communion, the congregation might devise rather novel solutions. When Jackson wanted to conduct the first Communion service at the church that he had organized in 1870 at Golden, Colorado, about twenty miles west of Denver, five people were accepted as members of the congregation, but they were all ladies. An imaginative improvisation saved the day. "On this and other communion occasions," a historian of the church wrote, "for some time after when a ruling elder was required, one was borrowed from Denver and safely returned at the close of the service."[8]

The church session was also expected to provide guidelines for acceptable conduct by the members of the congregation. There was no question about condemning acts that were obviously sinful in nature, such as gambling and the imbibing of spirituous liquors, but were there other forms of recreational activity that good Presbyterians could enjoy that would not carry the stigma of blatant misbehavior? Could they, for instance, indulge in social dancing outside the home? Not if Alex Darley, in Del Norte, Colorado, had anything to say about it. He told Jackson early in 1876 that dancing was becoming an evil in his congregation. The session had gone on record as being opposed to dancing, but now there were hints of rebellion against the decree. In fact, some of the elders' wives had been observed dancing! Darley intended, however, to test the session on this matter very soon, and, knowing his uncompromising nature, one might assume that the official position of his church on the issue remained the same.[9]

If misconduct on the part of church members reached serious proportions, the session had the authority and responsibility to dismiss the wrongdoers from church membership. These actions, however, and all proceedings of the session were subjected to annual review by the presbytery, a body composed of the pastor and one elder from each church in the area. A sampling of comments from session records submitted for evaluation to the Presbytery of Colorado indicates that exceptions were usually of a technical nature, with occasional reprimands because it was not recorded that meetings were opened with prayer or because records were kept imperfectly. In the latter case, the clerk of session might be instructed to refer to the Specimen of Records in the front of his record book, which, presumably, had been acquired by each church from the Presbyterian Board of Publications.

Sometimes the presbytery was also obliged to rule on more important matters. Without a regular pastor at the Idaho Springs, Colorado, church, and with only one active elder in 1880, that gentleman, anticipating a sudden collapse of the church because of lack of interest, granted letters of dismissal to each member, to take effect if and when the church organization should be dissolved. The presbytery could not condone this unusual procedure, and it took exception to the action of the "one and only Elder" in issuing dismissals before the fact. Lest it appear that a condition of anarchy had descended upon the Idaho Springs church, the record keeper inscribed beneath the reprimand from presbytery, "No idea or intention of dissolving the church is expressed or implied. Justice is simply desired by the 'one and only Elder.'"[10]

Sometimes, when reports of questionable activities at one of the churches reached the members of the presbytery, they would arrange for a committee selected from their ranks to visit the session of the suspect church. The interrogators could then obtain information pertinent to the allegations for use in subsequent action by the presbytery. A crisis of that magnitude occurred at a meeting of the Presbytery of Colorado on March 19, 1874. The minutes of that gathering note that the presbytery had learned of certain "irregularities of practice" in the church at Black Hawk, Colorado.

Appointing a committee of three men to look into the matter, the members cited chapter 10, section 8, of the Presbyterian Form of Government, which stated that a presbytery was authorized "to visit particular churches for the purpose of inquiring into their state and redressing the evils that may have risen in them."[11]

At the conclusion of the investigating committee's visit to Black Hawk, one of the members announced the result to Jackson. The evils discerned at the Black Hawk church were, in essence, three in number. First, inasmuch as the church did not have a regular Presbyterian pastor at the time, its session had authorized, "in an irregular way," occasional preaching by a Congregational minister. Second, the session, acting in an informal manner without a regular meeting, had permitted an acknowledged Universalist to take Communion at the church. Finally, some children had been baptized despite their parents' noted indifference to religion. When censured by the visitors from the presbytery, the session members promised that the ministrations of the Congregational interloper would cease at once, and that the other infractions would not be repeated. With those assurances, the committee departed, with the sense that the brethren at Black Hawk would mend their ways in the future. "There seemed to be a disposition to work together amicably when we closed our session," the committee member reported to Jackson, "and I hope for good results."[12]

Presbyterial responsibility was not always associated with criticism of the improprieties of church sessions. The members of the presbyteries were also expected to provide an annual evaluation of their district superintendent. These reports were sent to the Board of Home Missions, which would decide if the record of its man in the field merited his reappointment for another year. The presbyteries in Jackson's mission field would customarily provide glowing endorsements of his achievements. Typical of these resolutions was the action taken by the Presbytery of Colorado in 1873. Proclaiming the fullest confidence in Jackson's "piety, zeal and faithfulness," the presbytery members announced their growing conviction of the need for a "faithful and judicious Superintendent of Missions to watch over the interests of Presbyterians in this great field, where there is much land to be possessed for Christ."[13]

One responsibility carried out by a presbytery in the quest to possess the land for Christ surely gave the members much pleasure. Recruits from theological seminaries in the East were often commissioned as licentiates, or trainees, while they were introduced to their first missionary assignments. When they felt qualified for ordination as full-fledged pastors in their church, they were tested in a number of areas by their presbytery. In 1880, when three of these young men appeared at a meeting of the

Presbytery of Colorado, they were examined all afternoon in the arts, sciences, Greek, Latin, Hebrew, theology, history, church government, and the sacraments. A committee of three then listened to their trial sermons. The candidates passed all of these ordeals satisfactorily, and in the evening their ordination service included an appropriate sermon by one of the members of the presbytery, responses to constitutional questions, an ordination prayer, and a consecration by the laying on of hands by all of those presbytery delegates in attendance. The ceremony then closed when a veteran presbytery member presented a charge to the candidates which, according to one observer of the ritual, "for completeness, practical common sense and piety, we have never heard excelled."[14]

Unfortunately, the experiences shared at presbytery meetings were not always joyous in nature. On rare occasions the members had to sit in judgment on cases involving serious charges against a pastor in one of the churches within the presbytery. That unpleasant situation occurred when the Presbytery of Wyoming in 1874 decided to dismiss the pastor of the Evanston church because he had sanctioned the use of his sanctuary for a "low traveling show."[15] That was not the only charge leveled against this misguided gentleman. He was also accused of renting the church building to the Mormon congregation in Evanston for their services. When the presbytery had considered his case at their meeting in November of 1873, a committee appointed to investigate the matter had concluded that disciplinary action might be premature: "We regard him as a young, but unwise and indiscreet man. Perhaps a bad man, but still we could see more of indiscretion and lack of judgment than real [evil intent]."[16]

This was not the end, however, of this sad affair. The presbytery soon learned of rumors circulating in Evanston that the credentials held by the beleaguered pastor would not meet the denomination's standards for leader of a Presbyterian congregation. The members of the presbytery decided, at that point, to seek guidance in their deliberations from the Board of Home Missions. Assembling all of the information available on the case, the presbytery sent it to the mission board headquarters in New York for an opinion. The response was not very helpful. The board, in effect, told the members of the presbytery that they alone could pass final judgment on the issues raised in the controversy.

Reporting to Jackson on this decision, one of the board members explained that the presbytery could not shirk its responsibility to act in an unpleasant situation brought on by its own carelessness. Certainly the presbytery had been remiss in accepting the man in the first place, as he was clearly "not sufficiently educated to pass a proper examination by our Book."[17] It then remained for the members of the presbytery to act, once and for all, on the matter. At their meeting in Cheyenne on May 19, 1874, they decided that the accused had deliberately withheld information on certain charges already made against him when he applied for the position at Evanston. Therefore, as he had not acted in good faith, his appointment was null and void and his name would no longer appear on the rolls of the presbytery.[18]

While the presbyteries in Jackson's mission field were often active participants in the chain-of-command structure of church governance, the same could not be said for the Synod of Colorado. Created by action of the General Assembly in 1871, this body, which had advisory and supervisory responsibilities over the presbyteries, at that time included the presbyteries of Colorado, Santa Fe, and Wyoming. At the end of the decade, the presbyteries of Montana and Utah had been added and the Presbytery of Wyoming dissolved, with its churches assigned to either the Presbytery of Colorado or the Presbytery of Utah. The new synod had been scheduled to meet at Pueblo, Colorado, in September of 1871, but because the quorum requirements under Presbyterian law—representation from at least three presbyteries—were not met, the inaugural meeting was rescheduled for the following year.[19]

On September 8, 1872, the first meeting of the Synod of Colorado was finally held, at Colorado Springs, Colorado. Delegates were present from the presbyteries of Colorado and Wyoming, and from the Presbytery of Montana, which had been approved by the General Assembly earlier in the year. After honoring Lewis Hamilton, the pioneer minister of Colorado, by appointing him moderator, and after disposing of several routine business matters, those in attendance unanimously adopted a resolution recommending the recommissioning by the Board of Home Missions of Sheldon Jackson as their district superintendent. They cited his "untiring zeal, faithfulness and efficiency." As they prepared to return to their home churches, the synod members concluded their formal session with a vote of thanks to the hospitable citizens of the host city, and to the various railroads that had provided reduced rates of fare for the churchmen who had journeyed from far and wide to reach Colorado Springs.[20]

Following the first convocation of the synod in 1872, meetings were sporadic for the remainder of the decade. The body did not meet in 1873, but on September 22, 1874, enough delegates to form a quorum gathered in Denver, where they voted to sustain the action of the Presbytery of Wyoming in dismissing the pastor of the Evanston church. In succeeding years, dates would be announced for synod meetings, but the meetings were usually canceled when the requirement for representation by three presbyteries was not met. At a meeting of the Presbytery of Colorado in

1877, some of the delegates voiced their concern on this matter: "As it is now three years since the Synod of Colorado has had a session," one member noted, "it will be hard to convince the brethren in these parts that Synodical representation is the proper thing."[21] But of course it was the "proper thing," and Jackson, perhaps in frustration, was not loath to bend the rules a bit at times to hold the semblance of a synod meeting. George Darley recalled, on one of those rare occasions, how Jackson, desperate to obtain a quorum, "suggested that enough of the brethren (for the present emergency) be given letters to other Presbyteries, that these Presbyteries might be represented. This suggestion being duly, orderly, and unanimously acted upon, we had a quorum and proceeded to business. Then at the close of the meeting gave these brethren their letters back to their respective presbyteries."[22]

Jackson struggled to maintain a pro forma synodical framework for his mission field, but he knew that the presbyteries were the most influential agencies in the structure of church government. And it was his own church in Denver, Colorado, that was involved in a dispute that called for all of the wisdom of the members of the Presbytery of Colorado in finding a solution. Jackson learned of the problem when he attended the first meeting of the presbytery in 1870. Bitter feelings among Old School and New School factions in the Denver church, which had been organized in 1861, had resulted in a division into two congregations. The larger, New School, group had retained possession of the church building, which had been constructed in 1863. Each of the rival groups now claimed ownership of the building, and each congregation wanted the coveted designation First Presbyterian Church of Denver. The questions faced at the meeting in 1870 were these: should both churches be admitted as members of the new presbytery, and, if so, with what names? In agreeing to explore the possibility of permitting the enrollment of both churches, the delegates to the presbytery meeting hoped that continuing negotiations would result in a decision acceptable to the contending factions.[23]

By 1871 the presbytery had agreed to accept representation from both groups, and the Old School church was listed in the General Assembly minutes for that year as the Stuart Memorial Church, while the New School church appeared as the First Presbyterian Church of Denver. After participating in the dedication services for a new church building for the Old School congregation on March 10, 1872, Jackson attended a meeting of the Presbytery of Colorado a few days later in Central City. From Denver, the Old School brethren had petitioned for permission to use the name First Church, instead of the Stuart Memorial designation. The delegates to the presbytery meeting granted their request.

When the presbytery convened again in Colorado Springs early in September, the members learned that the New School people were apparently ignoring the presbyterial directive to yield the First Church name to the Old School adherents. The delegates then firmly directed the New School party to accede, once and for all, to the wishes of the presbytery in this matter. In addition, the New School church should pay to the Old School congregation an amount equivalent to the contributions made by the Old School congregation to the construction of the church building which had been retained in the schism of the 1860s by the New School group. Clearly indicating their displeasure, the presbyterial delegates resolved "that both parties drop all controversy, treat each other as brethren, and agree to work together in harmony for the good of our common Master."[24]

Regrettably, getting the bickering parties to work together in harmony was easier said than done. Although the members of the presbytery thought they had resolved the matter once and for all, they at once learned from an article in a Denver newspaper, written by a New School spokesman, that the controversy had not been put to rest. Refusing to acknowledge any relinquishment of the First Church name, the angry writer insisted that the whole issue was still very much in doubt. These remarks brought a rejoinder a few days later in the same newspaper from the minister who had served as moderator at the presbytery meeting. After recalling how much time at the meeting had been taken up by long speeches espousing the points of view of each side, this gentleman noted, with regret, that the whole matter would probably be settled in the courts, as the New School group apparently intended to file a civil suit to obtain what they perceived to be their rights in the unfortunate dispute.[25]

In New York, repercussions from the turbulence in Denver had reached the offices of the Board of Home Missions. In June of 1873 the members had received copies of all of the papers relating to the controversy. After carefully examining these documents, the board noted with sorrow "that the brethren concerned have not been able to settle the differences without exposing them to the world, and thereby producing a scandal in that community which may prove detrimental to their growth and spiritual interest." The board's recommendation in the case was for the contending parties to compromise by referring the whole matter to disinterested and competent arbitrators.[26] At that point, Jackson stepped in as a mediator who was, of course, not disinterested but who could hope to be nonpartisan in his views on the subject. He suggested consolidation of the two churches under a new leader as a reasonable approach toward reconciling the feuding congregations. He prepared a lengthy defense of his proposition, arguing that consolidation would end all further litigation in the courts, that meetings of the Presbytery of Colorado could be conducted in a more harmonious fashion, and that the joining of both congregations in a combined church for Denver would certainly secure a minister of exceptional ability. In addition, a united church would have the financial capacity to erect a new church edifice that would make the Denver position as desirable as any in the larger cities of the East.[27]

Jackson was surely disappointed when the rival churches rejected his grand plan. He announced the results of the deliberations in his newspaper. Reconciliation but not consolidation was the order of the day. Each side was determined to retain its own identity. The New School group, however, had finally agreed to pay twenty-five hundred dollars to the Old School faction to settle the latter's claim stemming from contributions made to the construction of the church building presently occupied by the New School. Regarding the use of the name First Presbyterian Church of Denver, the contending parties consented to put the matter to rest once and for all by having each church adopt a new name that would not include the word First. With these issues now apparently resolved, both sides pledged to "work and pray for the largest measure of Christian harmony, love and true fellowship between the two churches."[28]

The compromises adopted on these issues were successful in restoring at least the semblance of a spirit of "true fellowship" between the rival congregations. The Old School group selected the name Seventeenth Street Presbyterian Church, and the New School faction chose to call themselves the Central Presbyterian Church. Those who favored a court action decided not to pursue that course any further.[29] Now, with these jurisdictional matters finally resolved, Jackson could return, with considerable anguish, to a corollary problem that had arisen at this same time in the Denver churches. While the incident was not directly involved with complex matters of church governance, it illustrates Jackson's role as the one who was expected to find ways to keep the peace when disputes arose between fractious missionaries serving under his supervision.

This disruptive situation, one that caused Jackson great anxiety, occurred in 1875. In the April issue of his newspaper, Jackson described at length an action taken in March by the members of the St. Paul's Congregational Church in Denver to shift their denominational affiliation from the Congregational Church to the Presbyterian Church. As their reason for taking this drastic step, the disgruntled Congregationalists noted, "We have not received, thus far, that encouragement and assistance to which we have felt that we were entitled."[30] Moving quickly to capitalize on this opportunity, on March 12 Jackson conducted an organizational service to enroll the church in the Presbytery of Colorado. Regrettably, within a short time this action, which should have diminished internecine strife among churchgoers in Denver, brought an outbreak of very bitter feelings indeed among the Denver Presbyterian churches.

The events that led up to this unpleasant situation began in a rather straightforward fashion. When the minister at the Central Church resigned to take a position in Chicago, the congregation secured the services of Willis Lord, who had been teaching in the theology department of Wooster University in Ohio. Described in Jackson's newspaper as "a gentleman of large experience, fine culture, warm heart and pleasing address," Lord received accolades as "the ecclesiastical sensation of the season in Denver."[31] Not so, said the pastor of the new St. Paul's Church. He took angry exception to a movement, allegedly instigated by Lord, to move the Central Church to a new location that would presumably intrude upon territory where St. Paul's drew much of its support. "His [Lord's] course upon this matter fills me with pain and astonishment," the irate minister complained to Jackson. "This looks far more Satanic than Christian. Brother, will this be allowed to go on? Is there no authority in the Presbyterian Church to check such cruel, wicked encroachment of the stronger upon the weaker?"[32]

Certainly Jackson did not have authority to order the Central Church to stay in its present location. He could only hope, once again, that a compromise of some sort could be found to resolve the rivalry between the contentious Denverites. Unfortunately, that did not happen. The pastor of the new St. Paul's Church continued his barrage of accusations. Ground had been broken, he acknowledged to Jackson, for construction of a sanctuary at the new location of the Central Church, but he had heard that money for the building project was coming in slowly because the members felt that Willis Lord had forced them into this foolish venture with a threat to leave unless they complied with his wishes. Then, enlarging the sphere of his calumny, he added the Seventeenth Street Church to the list of subjects for his invective. He had heard how the pastor's wife at that church was trying to manage not only him but everyone in the congregation, to the point where the members felt that their interests had been betrayed. The accuser then assured Jackson that everything at his own church was proceeding very favorably. In an extraordinary statement, he insisted that he was trying "to be very careful and not meddle in affairs which do not belong to [him]."[33] When both of the ministers who had been the targets of these attacks resigned their posts in 1876, the stream of vilification from the pastor of the St. Paul's Church ceased.[34] Jackson must have been relieved when he no longer had to deal with this feuding in the ranks, because he had encountered yet another divisive situation, in which he was accused of meddling in affairs that did not belong to him.

This problem had its origins in Greeley, Colorado, a farming community about fifty miles north of Denver, where Jackson had organized a church in 1870. Early in 1874, the pastor of the church announced his intention of resigning in June. Convinced that the small Greeley church was in danger of disintegrating, Jackson urged the union of the congregation in Greeley with that of the nearby town of Evans, under the leadership of the pastor at the church in the latter community. Apparently he also implied that the two churches could not expect any future financial assistance from the Board of Home Missions unless they acquiesced in the plan of union.[35]

To say that this suggestion met with an adverse reaction in Greeley would be an understatement. A minister who was serving at Greeley as the temporary replacement for the pastor who had resigned reported to Jackson that the Greeley Presbyterians would not accept consolidation with the Evans church on any terms. They even threatened to close their church if Jackson refused to abandon his ill-advised course of action, one that could result only in the ruin of Presbyterianism in Greeley. The man who had announced his resignation in Greeley told Jackson that the difficulties that had arisen "are those which you have created by your unwise, persistent and arbitrary course."[36] Realizing that he had stirred up a hornet's nest, Jackson quickly back-pedaled, insisting that he was never that serious about uniting the two churches. He did, however, admonish the rebellious Presbyterians in Greeley: "Perhaps I would be able to do more to your mind, if instead of finding fault, you would pray more for me in the many perplexities of the work."[37]

Jackson surely hoped that his stance would mollify the irate brethren in Greeley, but the specter of revolt arose again when the minister who had resigned changed his mind and resumed his pastorate with the approval of the members of his congregation. In the fall of 1875, with his animosity to Jackson still evident, he circulated a petition calling for Jackson's removal from the post of regional superintendent for Presbyterian home mission work. Early in 1876, in an exchange of letters between the two adversaries, the pastor in Greeley insisted that Presbyterians in Colorado could work together in harmony were it not for Jackson's unwise and unjustifiable policies. In his reply Jackson simply told his antagonist that his repeated and violent public attacks were unfortunately inspired by his own unfounded sense of mistreatment and were not supported by any of the other members of the Presbytery of Colorado. Jackson must have been gratified when his position was clearly sustained at a meeting of the Presbytery of Colorado on November 17. The members who attended adopted a resolution expressing "entire confidence in our Synodical Missionary, Rev. Sheldon Jackson . . . and we would especially request of the Board of Home Missions that he be continued in his present exceedingly important and useful position."[38]

This presbyterial endorsement represented, once again, a typical vote of confidence in Jackson's efforts to sustain and expand the cause of Presbyterianism in the Rocky Mountain West. There was only one occasion in the 1870s when he failed to secure this stamp of approval for his work. After a meeting of the Presbytery of Montana early in 1873, one of those attending recalled, "A Superintendent of Missions was asked for from the Board of Home Missions in order that he might prepare new fields and obtain ministers for them."[39] But there was already a superintendent of missions, whose field included Montana, in the person of Sheldon Jackson. An explanation of this apparent dichotomy can be found in an analysis of the events in that territory following the organization of seven churches there in 1872 by Jackson, Will Frackelton, and James Russel.

While Jackson was scurrying around Montana in 1872 organizing churches, the General Assembly of his church was meeting in Detroit, Michigan. On its agenda was a petition prepared by Jackson calling for creation of a new Presbytery of Montana, one that would include all churches in Montana and Utah. As part of his justification for this action, Jackson pointed out that churches in Montana were one thousand miles, and those in Utah at least five hundred miles, from the customary meeting places of the adjoining Presbytery of Wyoming. The creation of the new presbytery was, therefore, essential to establishing an opportunity for presbyterial supervision that could not be achieved by unwisely extending the boundaries of the Presbytery of Wyoming. Accepting this line of reasoning the assembly delegates approved Jackson's request, not knowing on the date of their adjournment, May 29, that Jackson had yet to organize the first of the new churches in Montana.[40]

Had Jackson learned of the General Assembly's approval of the Presbytery of Montana when he convened the first meeting in Helena? It would not have been out of character for him to go ahead regardless, confident that an affirmative action by the assembly would soon be forthcoming. In any event, on June 18, Jackson, James Russel, Will Frackelton, and an elder of the Helena congregation met in Russel's room at the International Hotel to approve plans for an orderly arrangement of presbyterial responsibilities. They accepted Jackson's report on the organization of seven churches in the territory. They also appointed committees on home missions, church erection, publication, and education. Anticipating Jackson's departure from the field in a day or two, they agreed that Frackelton would serve the churches at Bozeman, Virginia City, Gallatin City, and Hamilton, while James Russel would look after the congregations at Helena, Deer Lodge, and Missoula. At the conclusion of the business meetings, the delegates and others from the Helena church enjoyed a reception at the home of the Honorable R. E. Fiske, editor of the Helena *Herald*. "The large number in attendance," noted one observer of the gathering, "the rejoicing of Christian hearts at the possession of the church privileges from which they had long been separated, and the enthusiasm begotten by the unexpected strength of Presbyterianism in the community, made the evening one which will not soon be forgotten by those who were present."[41] Did Jackson overestimate the strength of Presbyterianism in Montana in 1872? Some of the delegates to a meeting of the Presbytery of Montana in Bozeman on February 21, 1873, obviously thought that this was the case when they petitioned the Board of Home Missions for a new superintendent to care for their needs. Will Frackelton, James Russel, and William Rommel attended the meeting along with Lyman Crittenden, who had joined the ranks of missionaries in Montana late in 1872. Crittenden, a man in his mid fifties who had a record of good work as a pastor at several churches in and around Pittsburgh, Pennsylvania, had settled with his family in Bozeman intending to open a Presbyterian school there. At first there must have been some doubt whether the meeting could be held at all. The temperature had dropped to forty degrees below zero and a deep snow had fallen. A coach finally got through, however, carrying James Russel from Deer Lodge and William Rommel from Helena, thereby providing a quorum with which to conduct presbyterial business. Hospitable members of the Bozeman church provided sleighs to transport the delegates from their lodgings to the local Methodist church where the meetings were held. In the division of responsibilities, Will Frackelton received the assignment to prepare the "Narrative of the State of Religion in Montana." In that document he admitted that the work to date could not be regarded as a complete success. He and James Russel convinced the other members of the presbytery to join them in sending the petition regarding Jackson's role and their dissatisfaction with conditions in Montana to the mission board.[42]

Feeling the need to explain this drastic action to Jackson, Will Frackelton wrote to him after the presbytery meeting about the grievances of the brethren in Montana:

> There have been some grievous mistakes made in the organization of Montana churches. Deer Lodge has no ruling elder nor can I see how it is possible for them to admit a single member to their communion. The Missoula elder has been in this valley a good part of the winter. Gallatin City was, as far as human sight can see, a very sad, sad mistake. . . . Russel feels terribly about Helena. . . . Ever since I have been here it has been work day and night.[43]

Jackson could no doubt understand the reasons for the displeasure of his comrades. First, several of his hurried organizations with only a handful of members may have been ill advised. And James Russel apparently now regretted his concurrence with Jackson's wishes that he relocate at the smaller and more remote churches at Deer Lodge and Missoula, leaving the Helena church to the new arrival, William Rommel. Finally, Frackelton was finding it difficult, if not impossible, to care for the needs of scattered congregations at Bozeman, Hamilton, Gallatin City, Virginia City, and the new church he had organized on his own initiative in December of 1872 at the nearby town of Willow Creek.[44]

Not all of the missionaries who attended the presbytery meeting shared the intensity of feeling exhibited by Will Frackelton and James Russel regarding Jackson's association with their endeavors. Soon after the meeting, Lyman Crittenden had second thoughts about the petition. "The resolution in regard to the Superintendent of Mission," he wrote apologetically to Jackson, "was not one which all of the members felt zeal for; indeed it was acquiesced in by the majority, I think, only to gratify the views of two of the members [Russel and Frackelton] who felt some change to be desirable."[45] William Rommel also assured Jackson that the presbyterial action had been taken without personal malice. Although Rommel felt that he could not agree with the wisdom of all of Jackson's efforts, he attributed any mistakes to an excess of zeal, and he offered his superintendent the following assurance: "I am willing to cooperate with you in the work here, and give you heartily all proper support."[46]

The number of Jackson's opponents in Montana was reduced by one when Will Frackelton left the territory in the spring of 1873. As for James Russel, he found time a year later to write Jackson a frank and often bitter delineation of his grievances. He charged Jackson, first, with dishonorable conduct in assigning William Rommel to the Helena church, a position that, according to Russel, Jackson had promised to him. Describing this action as "exceedingly shabby treatment," Russel viewed the entire matter as "an offense against righteousness and justice." Next, the angry missionary stated his belief that Jackson had never followed through on a promise to urge the mission board to increase his annual salary of one thousand dollars to a figure more commensurate with the high cost of living in Montana. He also accused Jackson of breaking a promise to secure compensation from the board for his traveling expenses when he journeyed to preach at other communities in the vicinity of Deer Lodge. Concluding his lamentations, Russel declared, "I do not wish to stir up an old quarrel. My object is to endeavor to settle once and finally an old dispute and if possible to live at peace with you and all men."[47]

Russel may not have intended to "stir up an old quarrel," but Jackson understandably felt that he must reply with a defense against Russel's charges. Regarding the assignments to Helena and Deer Lodge, he denied making any promises one way or the other. In fact the decision to place Rommel at Helena, according to Jackson, had come directly from mission board headquarters in New York. Regarding the monetary issues, Jackson insisted that he had tried to obtain the concessions mentioned, but the importunate letters to the board by Russel and the now departed Will Frackelton "had so dissatisfied the Secretaries that they felt a mistake had been made in sending you out; that you were not the men for the kind of work you were expected to do." Concluding his comments with a rather uncharacteristic display of anger, Jackson forcefully stated, *"Thus not considering myself guilty of your various charges I have no apology to offer.* . . . But I carried these grievances at once to the Cross and left them there, and have worked on with the same vigor for Montana as if they had not occurred."[48]

Jackson's association of the word "vigor" with his work on behalf of the Montana churches could certainly have been questioned, but he surely hoped that his rebuttal of Russel's accusations would serve to smooth the ruffled feathers of the troubled missionary. Russel was determined, however, to have the last word in this exchange. In a response to Jackson's letter, he insisted that it would be impossible for the two men to work well together in the future. Jackson had clearly indicated a lack of confidence in Russel, who certainly shared the same feelings about Jackson. If Jackson could find a suitable replacement, he would not hesitate to leave Montana and try to find employment elsewhere, where his work for the Master would be appreciated. "I came to Montana," Russel wrote, "to endeavor to glorify God and not you or the Board of Home Missions of the Presbyterian Church."[49]

The Board of Home Missions did not remove Jackson from his supervisory position with the Montana churches. As one of Jackson's friends recalled later, "A detailed statement correcting some misapprehensions and covering the entire ground of complaint was sent back to the Board [by Jackson] and apparently this ended the matter."[50] Although the petition of 1873 had not achieved its purpose, the mission board members were nevertheless not pleased with Jackson's work, or lack thereof, in Montana. After his quick trip to that territory in 1876, when he had failed in his efforts to bring along new missionary recruits for the field, Henry Kendall had spoken to him rather sternly about the unhappy situation. "We think you have never done any thorough work in Montana," Kendall wrote. "You have dashed in and dashed out again. The church has come to demand something better. We propose therefore that you go in there and spend three or four months at work. . . . No other part of your field seems to us so pressing in its demand at the present time."[51] That, of course, was more easily said than done. For Jackson, every part of his field had pressing demands, and he must have wondered how the mission board could possibly believe he could allot several months of his precious time to any one area at the expense of the others.

There had been only a few occasions in the 1870s when Kendall had felt it necessary to reprimand Jackson. One of those incidents occurred in 1877, when Jackson encountered defiance from a missionary in Colorado whose ignorance of "horse management" led him to oppose Jackson's selection of his mission station. John MacAllister, a seminary student, had accepted a summer vacation appointment to serve the church at Idaho Springs, Colorado, a mining camp in the mountains not far from Denver. When Jackson became convinced of the urgent need to establish a Presbyterian church at the town of Silverton in the booming mining fields of the San Juan Mountains of southwestern Colorado, he instructed MacAllister to move to that more remote community. The rather peremptory directive brought an unexpected response. The young man explained to Jackson how he had really come west to cure a respiratory problem, and that his physician could not recommend the climate of the San Juans for such a purpose. Besides, the journey to Silverton would be very difficult, involving considerable travel by horseback: "I have been only once in the saddle for six years, and have no idea of horse management."[52]

Refusing to accept these excuses, Jackson gave his views on the matter in a terse reply to the young rebel. When MacAllister came to Colorado, Jackson explained, he had placed himself under the direction of the Presbytery of Colorado. Acting for that body, Jackson felt that he could send summer men wherever the demands for their services were greatest. If MacAllister persisted in his defiant attitude, he could expect no additional financial support from the Presbytery of Colorado. Chastened, MacAllister did move to Silverton, where his work so pleased the residents that they sent a petition to the presbytery calling for his return during his vacation the next year. That should have ended the matter, but somehow Henry Kendall in New York learned about the dispute, which, it would appear, was a rather trivial one requiring attention only at the local level. Kendall saw it otherwise. He reproved Jackson for authorizing MacAllister's transfer without consulting the mission board. "The Presbytery of Colorado and the Synodical Missionary had better proceed with care," Kendall warned. "Both have enemies enough not to make others. We must not force things, and we must all be compelled to note where our authority and responsibility end. We cannot be too careful."[53]

There is no record of Jackson's reaction to this monition, but he must have wondered on many occasions in the 1870s just what the authority and responsibility of a Presbyterian synodical missionary, or "district superintendent," did encompass. Some answer came from the prescriptions, rules, and regulations of the church, but there was also a need to extemporize solutions to the many unusual problems arising in the remote areas of the West. At the General Assembly meeting in Chicago in 1877, a reporter who described the highlights of the gathering recalled how Henry Kendall had entertained in "a purely social affair" all of the synodical missionaries in attendance. "These pioneer workers," the observer noted, "without precedents to guide them, or the opportunities of mutual consultation, had been feeling their way toward the best methods of efficient work."[54]

Certainly Sheldon Jackson belonged in the category of those who were "feeling their way" toward development of policies that were admittedly inspired more by efficiency than conformity. But, if one subscribed to the notion that the end often justifies the means, the commendable results obtained from unorthodox practices were, in Jackson's view, surely warranted. Jackson knew that on many occasions he had gone beyond Kendall's description, in 1876, of the function of a synodical missionary. One responsibility, in particular, that Jackson assumed out of necessity was not mentioned by Kendall. Establishing new churches in frontier communities in the West was an expensive proposition. Faced with a constant need for funds to support his work, Jackson often turned to fund-raising devices that bypassed regular channels.

1. Sheldon Jackson as he appeared when serving as pastor of the Presbyterian church in Rochester, Minnesota, 1864-1869. (Courtesy, Presbyterian Historical Society, Philadelphia)

Above:
2. Sheldon Jackson as Superintendent of Presbyterian Missions for Colorado, New Mexico, Montana, Wyoming, and Utah. (Courtesy, Presbyterian Historical Society, Philadelphia)

Opposite:
3. Jackson suitably attired for his role as General Agent for Education in Alaska. (Courtesy, Presbyterian Historical Society, Philadelphia)

4. Mrs. Sheldon (Mary) Jackson in 1880. Acknowledging that not much has been written about Mary Jackson, a family friend still believed that "it may truly be recorded of her: 'She hath done what she could.'" (From Robert L. Stewart, Sheldon Jackson, *1908)*

5. Frances Haines, first Secretary of the Woman's Executive Committee of Home Missions, who thanked Jackson for giving her "facts as to the destitution in our own country that can never be forgotten." (Courtesy, Presbyterian Historical Society, Philadelphia)

6. *Lyman B. Crittenden and Mrs. Mary G. Crittenden-Davidson, founders of the Gallatin Valley Female Seminary in Montana "where parents may safely intrust their children, confident that they will be faithfully instructed...." (Courtesy, Montana Historical Society, Helena)*

7. *George Darley, a missionary in Colorado who spoke out from his pulpit against women "who make the air hot with their voices, and trouble the world with their superabundant activities." (Courtesy, Archives, University of Colorado at Boulder Libraries)*

8. *Duncan J. McMillan, Presbyterian missionary in Utah who Brigham Young allegedly denounced as "an imp of perdition, a minion of Satan, and a damned Presbyterian devil." (Courtesy, Montana Historical Society, Helena)*

9. *Benjamin M. Thomas, Jackson's ally as agent for the Pueblo Indians of Santa Fe, New Mexico. (Courtesy, First Presbyterian Church, Santa Fe)*

10. *José Ynes Perea, Presbyterian evangelist to the "Mexicans" in New Mexico in the 1870s. (Courtesy, Presbyterian Historical Society, Philadelphia)*

5 | Financing the Army in the Field

The new fields in Texas, Colorado, Montana, Idaho, Dakota, and on the Pacific Coast are far more expensive than the older and nearer fields. . . . The Board [of Home Missions] asks only for means to fulfill the promise of the Church to these missions.
—"HOME MISSION WORK," *Rocky Mountain Presbyterian,*
FEBRUARY 1873

Late in the nineteenth century, Josiah Strong, an eloquent Protestant clergyman, perceived a national emergency in the settlement of the western territories. Included in the issues he discussed in his book *Our Country: Its Possible Future and Its Present Crisis* were the perils of Catholicism, Mormonism, socialism, and intemperance as they applied to the westward movement. According to Strong, the nation could actually lose this vital region to the schemes of disloyal conspirators who were subservient to these evil influences. These bad men were not only un-American, they were also un-Christian, the first fault probably arising from the second. The emergency could be met, he concluded, only "by placing in the hands of every Christian agency there at work all the power that money can wield."[1] Money could, indeed, wield power. It was needed by Christian agencies to build churches and schools, pay the salaries of ministers, finance the travel of missionaries, and provide religious materials for the frontier congregations. Sheldon Jackson and the missionaries laboring under his supervision were never content with the level of financial support provided for their endeavors. Eager to win the West for Christ, they were, in their own thinking, retarded only by their perpetual lack of funds from attaining that great victory.

In the first place, they did not believe that they were getting their rightful share in the budgeting of denominational funds at the national level. After the reunion of the Old and New School branches in 1869, the General Assembly had authorized a drive in the following year for a five million dollar memorial fund to strengthen the reunited church. The goal was reached and passed in 1871, but from a western vantage point it did not appear that the frontier outposts were going to see much of this newfound wealth. On January 1, 1871, Jackson prepared an article for publication in the *New York Evangelist* soliciting funds for building a church in Laramie, Wyoming. In this appeal he noted that, in his view, an excessive amount of the great memorial fund was going to the eastern institutions of the church. Many devoted missionaries, discouraged by this lack of support, were beginning to question their commitments to frontier fields. Convinced that Christ's homeless churches in the West were in danger of being left out in the cold, Jackson concluded his appeal by raising this question: "When shall these extremities feel the Christian warmth of the great Presbyterian body and thus realize the oneness of the Church and the fellowship of the disciples?"[2]

While always ready to accept money from any source to nurture the "extremities" of his vast mission field, Jackson knew that he must rely on the Board of Home Missions for the funds with which to pay missionary salaries. As the campaign calling for contributions to the memorial fund progressed, the mission board members were not all pleased with the results. In the fall of 1870 the board had been embarrassed by a shortage of funds, which had necessitated a brief suspension of payments from the treasury. That painful condition was soon alleviated by new receipts, but some of the members saw donations to the widely publicized memorial fund reducing direct contributions to the cause of home missions. Apparently this concern was not misdirected. Although the custodians of the memorial fund proudly announced collections of $7,833,983.85 in a report dated August 1, 1871, Henry Kendall had to acknowledge woefully the sad status of the mission board's treasury near the end of the year: "Our debt still distresses us badly. We cannot do what we would, but we do what we can."[3]

The promise by the mission board members to do what they could in the 1870s was drawn from practical considerations of supply and demand. A budget prepared at the beginning of a fiscal year that contained salary commitments to missionaries in the field could be realized in its entirety only if expected revenue from contributions materialized. If the income anticipated by the board dwindled unexpectedly, missionaries were faced with a curtailment in their already scanty salaries. Unfortunately, such a disaster occurred in 1873.

That year, while Jackson contemplated the challenges lying ahead for his mission work in the West, he also considered the implications of the results of the recent hotly contested presidential election. Turning back the challenge of a coalition of Democrats and liberal Republicans, Ulysses Grant had won reelection for a second term. Pledging continuation of previous policies designed to promote recovery from the Civil War, the authors of the Republican party platform had noted that great financial crises had been avoided in the previous four years. With Grant returned to the

White House, "We start today upon a new march to victory."[4] Certainly Jackson would have welcomed any assurances that "great financial crises" would not occur, hoping that a robust national economy would be conducive to greater contributions from philanthropists for home mission work.

That was not to be. Near the end of September of 1873, newspapers in the East carried stories that shocked the nation. On September 18 the great banking firm of Jay Cooke and Company closed, thereby precipitating one of the most severe financial panics and depressions in American history to date. The impact of these events soon reached the headquarters of the Board of Home Missions in New York, in the form of a drastic decline in contributions to the board's treasury. In an appeal published in Jackson's newspaper in November, a spokesman for the troubled agency noted a debt outstanding on the board's accounts of more than forty thousand dollars. Anticipating trials and sufferings for missionaries in the field during the winter season, the board called for "the people of God" to look deep into their hearts, and purses, for funds that would enable the board to answer the many urgent calls for aid, "especially from the far away frontier."[5] Determined to obtain a firsthand impression of this calamity, Jackson journeyed to New York in November. Reporting back to the pastor of his church in Denver, he observed sadly how the devastating effects of the panic and depression had resulted in "everybody taking in all sail they possibly can under the circumstances."[6]

The sad state of affairs did not improve in 1874. When Jackson attended the meeting of the General Assembly in St. Louis in May, he learned from the annual report of the Board of Home Missions about the continuing monetary problems. Suddenly crippled by the great financial crisis, the board had been seriously hindered in its work by lack of funds. Of the $352,000 called for by the assembly in the previous year, less than $300,000 had been collected. When the board secretaries compiled their report, they noted that about $19,500 was past due to missionaries in the field.

The situation worsened following the assembly meeting. At mid year the board's treasury was more than sixty thousand dollars in debt, and in December readers of Jackson's newspaper learned that one-half of the pledges that had been made in response to the board's distress signals were still unfulfilled. One of the board secretaries ruefully told Jackson, "We are much discouraged for want of funds and the prospect of the future is still more forbidding. All the industries in the country are in a measure paralyzed."[7] In 1875 the annual report of the home mission board did acknowledge an increase in contributions, particularly from synods in the West. At the same time, however, because of increased demands on the board treasury, the appropriations for annual salaries to some missionaries in the field had been reduced to the point of "subjecting many brethren to trial."[8]

Inasmuch as 1876 was an election year, perhaps enlightened candidates would now appear who could offer solutions for the nation's fiscal problems. Jackson certainly understood the significance of the approaching contest for the depressed economy. "This is the year, among politicians, for president-making," he wrote in the *Rocky Mountain Presbyterian* early in 1876, "and those who claim to be wise in financial affairs say that business is not likely to improve much . . . until after the presidential election." Meanwhile, Jackson urged the readers of his newspaper to stop finding fault with the policies of the members of the Board of Home Missions who were straining every nerve to maintain existing mission stations.[9]

Rutherford B. Hayes, the candidate of the Republican party, finally emerged victorious in the controversial election of 1876. In his inaugural address on March 5, 1877, he acknowledged the continuance of the great depression, but he had observed indications all around of a return to prosperous times. Those indications were not apparent to leaders of the Presbyterian Church. The minutes of the General Assembly in 1877 referred to the previous year as one marked by a degree of financial distress unknown to the current generation. In 1878 the report of the Board of Home Missions at the General Assembly spoke of perplexing times that had actually forced the board to tighten its stringent fiscal policies. And in 1879, the board's report to the assembly included comments on the continuing financial distress of the country. Reacting with reluctance to the dismal situation, the board had to cut down expenditures by about 25 percent.[10]

Of course these reductions in financial support were hard on the missionaries laboring with Jackson in the Rocky Mountain West. Much of the correspondence he received from these men addressed financial concerns. In many cases, the writers simply lamented the inadequacy of their salaries. At Del Norte, Colorado, the always combative Alex Darley was the most vociferous of the complainers. A month after Darley arrived in Del Norte, in the spring of 1875, Jackson received a lengthy communication from him. The irate missionary had just received his commission from the Board of Home Missions, stipulating an annual salary of one thousand dollars. Darley noticed, however, a qualifying statement requiring him to deduct any amount contributed to him by his congregation from his base salary and return it to the board. This proviso shocked Darley, who had expected to keep any donations received, as he put it, from "working up my field." He informed Jackson that he would require a minimum annual income of fifteen hundred dollars, because things he regarded as necessities cost from 33 to 100 percent more in Del Norte than at his former home in Iowa. In fact, putting it bluntly, "extortion stares at a man over every counter in the San Luis Valley." Finally, Darley declared jealously, "Now our foreign missionaries get put down in foreign lands, house furnished, etc., and very light work in many cases compared to ours." A few days after penning this jeremiad, Darley wrote again to Jackson reiterating his concerns and concluding with the following assertion: "When I think of the absolute poverty to which I am and shall be reduced by the Board's absurd action . . . I can hardly forbear writing them an eye-opener such as never came from a missionary pen."[11]

If Darley wrote his "eye-opener" to the mission board, Henry Kendall did not mention it in subsequent correspondence with Jackson. But the sense of frustration felt by Darley and his colleagues with their niggardly compensation was quite evident in Darley's remarks. Relatedly, Josiah Welch in Salt Lake City, Utah, had replied in Jackson's newspaper in 1875 to a seminary student who was concerned about the financial uncertainties of employment on the frontier. "But as long as our board is under its present management," Welch wrote, "I never knew of a dollar that they promised to pay but was promptly paid."[12] His statement was manifestly incorrect. Quarterly payments by the mission board to missionaries in the field were too often delayed without explanation. A typical example occurred at the church in Las Vegas, New Mexico, in 1874. The distraught minister told Jackson, "The salary that was due me on the 1st of July reached me on the 1st of September. I was reduced to very great straits and perplexity. I wrote [to the mission board] two or three or four times and *telegraphed* once and received not a word of response until the salary came. . . . Are all the brethren treated so?"[13]

Jackson would have found it difficult to respond to the question. Not all of the missionaries serving churches in his superintendency encountered situations as extreme as the case just cited. Still, he did receive numerous complaints about the frustrating problem of unexplained delays in the payment of their quarterly salaries to his missionaries. In the summer of 1872, Jackson published an article in his newspaper entitled "Paying the Minister." The anonymous author emphasized the dilemma by concluding, "More ministers are made wretched and driven from their work by want of *prompt* payment than by short salaries."[14] While the failure by the mission board to at least notify those on the payroll of impending delays may seem inexcusable, at the same time the members of the board could point out that these situations would not occur if the churches in question were self-sustaining and able to pay their pastor from their own resources. A pay-as-you-go modus operandi in the operation of annual church budgets was always recognized as desirable in the frontier communities, but it was difficult to accomplish.

With the motto "God helps those who help themselves" to inspire them, many of the western congregations did try to pay at least part of their pastor's salary. This typically involved circulating a subscription paper once a year at the annual congregational meeting. Each member would then pledge an amount to be paid during the year. Unfortunately, translating promises into hard cash was often well nigh impossible. Of the many reports received by Jackson, an example from the church at Caribou, Colorado, a remote mining camp in the mountains about thirty miles northwest of Denver, can serve to illustrate the problem. "There is trouble in my field," the distraught missionary wrote in 1875. "It is financial. The ____ brothers pledged themselves for $400.00 toward my support, and now William writes me they never did. . . . [I] have during the nine months past only received from that whole field just $57.00."[15]

Distressed, of course, by these financial problems, the Presbyterian missionaries in the Rocky Mountain West hoped that their superintendent, Sheldon Jackson, could find ways, somehow, to obtain money over and above the support from the mission board. Jackson's reputation as an energetic and effective fund-raiser was well deserved. He still used his private Raven Fund, which he had created while serving as a missionary in Minnesota, to receive and disburse contributions received from donors in the East. Among his brief debit and credit entries in the little book that he used to record transactions there appears a set of three entries in 1870 that reveal, in part, an embarrassing situation he created that resulted in the issuance of a warrant for his arrest.

Jackson's dilemma began in 1869, when he had impetuously promised to raise five thousand dollars toward the erection of a church building for the new congregation in Cheyenne, Wyoming. He was also aware of a pledge of one thousand dollars from a donor in Rawlins, Wyoming, to build a sanctuary for the Presbyterians in that community. Determined to follow through on these projects, Jackson quickly made a fund-raising tour in the East, where he received numerous assurances of support for his building plans. Confident that he would soon receive the money, he went ahead and arranged for Lyman Bridges, a building contractor in Chicago, to supply small, prefabricated church structures for Cheyenne and Rawlins. Jackson had hoped to obtain partial funding for these enterprises from the Presbyterian Board of Church Erection, but he was disappointed in September when the board rejected his request for aid because of unusually heavy demands on its treasury. Undaunted by this setback, which he hoped would be only temporary, Jackson decided to proceed. His resolve to go ahead may have been prompted by a public declaration that he had made earlier regarding his expectations for support from the Board of Church Erection. Expressing his hope that the board would supply funds for these "cheap tabernacles," he had boldly stated, "I hope they will. But if they will not, I am determined to go on my own responsibility, buy the lumber on credit, and ask the friends of mission for the money."[16]

In November of 1869 Jackson received disquieting news. Bridges had shipped a building to the Presbyterians in Rawlins, but he had refused to release the package of building materials to Cheyenne until Jackson sent an installment payment. The worried Cheyenne Presbyterians, who had prepared a foundation for the anticipated structure, feared that the construction season would soon end with the arrival of severe winter weather. Although the members of the Cheyenne church were not aware of the reason for the delay, Jackson knew very well that Bridges was waiting for a payment on his contract before sending the building on to Cheyenne. Jackson simply did not have the money to comply with this demand. He had skated on thin ice before when making financial commitments, but this time his reputation was threatened, at the very least. His only recourse was to assure Bridges of his firm intention of paying everything that was due as soon as possible.[17]

In the spring of 1870, Bridges finally consented to go ahead and ship the construction materials for the Cheyenne church from his warehouse in Chicago. Reassured by Jackson's pledge of a payment of one thousand dollars on their contract when the building was raised, Bridges reported in June that the trustees of the church in Cheyenne had formally certified completion of the project. Fortunately for Jackson, in 1870 he received, as recorded in his Raven Fund account book, three contributions totaling forty-five hundred dollars that he could apply to the outstanding debt on the Cheyenne church. That still left a small balance due to Bridges, however, and in May of the following year, while Jackson was attending the meeting of the General Assembly in Chicago, the angry contractor confronted him with a demand for a final payment to settle the account. Jackson refused to concede the legitimacy of the claim, citing a continuing difference of opinion about a credit allegedly due for the plastering done on the building by the people in Cheyenne. The irate contractor had Jackson arrested and bound over for trial at some later date. Jackson countered by engaging a lawyer who secured his release pending his court appearance.[18]

Jackson's position in this matter suffered a damaging blow in October of 1871, when a great fire destroyed much of Chicago. Jackson had entrusted his records pertaining to the contract with Bridges to his lawyer in Chicago, and all of that material was destroyed in the great conflagration.

Jackson's lawyer thus advised him to pay Bridges's bill, which amounted to about five hundred dollars, as there was now little hope of gaining a favorable decision if the case ever came to trial. Unfortunately, Jackson didn't have the money. Finally, in 1872, Jackson's attorney persuaded Bridges to reduce his claim to $300; Jackson then borrowed the smaller amount from friends and sent the money to Bridges as payment in full. There is no indication that Jackson ever again made any personal contractual obligations to secure houses of worship for congregations within his mission field.[19]

Although the Bridges case was a setback for Jackson, his other exploits in raising funds were more gratifying. He accepted gladly the role of propagandist, the man who has the responsibility to impress those far from the field of battle with the pressing needs of the men at the front, with the great importance of the territory to be conquered, and with the awesome strength of the enemy. To achieve his objectives, Jackson skillfully used his newspaper, the *Rocky Mountain Presbyterian*, as an agency for directing appeals for funds to support home mission work to readers in the East. He tried to give his subscribers impressions of western society, usually balancing articles about the wild West with others that portrayed its residents as comparing favorably with the better classes of eastern society. His goal was to strike responsive chords from readers who would then feel inclined to contribute generously to the cause.

The image of the West as destitute and godless appeared many times in the *Rocky Mountain Presbyterian*. A classic example of this approach to loosening eastern pursestrings appeared in the edition of October 1876, in which a missionary described his visit to an isolated mining camp deep in the mountains of Colorado: it was bitterly cold, and "the Frost King was master of the ghostly world without, while Vice and Death held high carnival within." The town consisted of "frail tenements of cloth and rough boards," and the inhabitants included many bartenders, faro dealers, and "brazen-faced women."

> The motley crowds drawn from every rough locality in the four quarters of the globe were, respectively, poisoned, robbed, and stowed away in narrow bunks, to sleep as best they might amid all the din and confusion, in an atmosphere as hot as red-hot stoves, smoking lamps, and scores of lungs pumping out vaporized alcohol incessantly, could make it, and thick with the fumes of bad tobacco and blue with curses and obscenity.

This was the daily condition, the anonymous writer insisted, in hundreds of mining towns "where your sons are living and dying separated from the saving influence of the gospel." These poor lads were breathing "an atmosphere laden with moral pollution and death." The writer concluded with a challenge to provide the money that would give them the means of salvation through the Presbyterian home mission program.[20]

When he wrote "A Plea For Home Missions" for his newspaper in September of 1873, Jackson utilized this same kind of imagery, although his descriptions do not reach the level of vivid, Dantesque prose cited above. He writes of a young man from a pious home who falls into "gross sin" in a western mining camp. When a Presbyterian missionary finally reaches the depraved community, the poor lad shows him a letter just received from his sister, wherein she expresses her wish for him to "come and let me look once more on your manly face." It is too late, however, for such a reunion. "Poor girl! She'll *never* see me," the sinner vows. "How could I meet that dear, pure, loving sister? I never shall—never!" A few hours after this conversation (according to Jackson) the misguided youth commits suicide. "Oh, why did we not sooner send a missionary to that wicked village, and to that young man," Jackson concludes, "before sin had so enslaved him, and iniquity had sunk him so low."[21]

The wording employed in these commentaries was carefully calculated to encourage the eastern notion of western barbarism. Salvation for those who had strayed from the straight and narrow path could still be achieved if only the funds were available to establish mission stations in places "laden with moral pollution." On the other hand, when the motive of western propaganda was to convey an impression of permanence and growth potential, writers had to create a very different impression of the West. Eastern businessmen might have no more interest in sinking money into hopeless evangelizing than they might have in financing a mine with a poor assay report. For those targets, the publicists for western society adopted what might at a later date be described as a chamber-of-commerce approach in their remarks. Many of the towns in the West, they argued, could someday grow to rival the greatest cities in the East.

The sales pitch of these "boomers" for western society was evident in numerous articles in the *Rocky Mountain Presbyterian*. Espousing the cause of home missions in 1874, a writer who had recently visited Cheyenne, Wyoming, disputed the claim that mission funds could be better employed in areas other than the West. He regarded Cheyenne as a prime example of a western community whose growth had neither ceased nor regressed. He cited construction of brick houses and the presence of thriving businesses to justify his appraisal that the growing population was decidedly permanent. The reporter then insisted that Cheyenne was not an isolated case but, in fact, representative of most communities all over the West. Of course Cheyenne was blessed with a Presbyterian church that had surely contributed in a positive way to its commendable growth. Other cities with similar prospects for greatness would also attain their full potential, the writer concluded, if the Board of Home Missions could obtain the funds to enable missionaries "to go there and take possession of these territories."[22]

Expanding on the proposition that most western towns could compare favorably with communities of similar size in the East, several writers whose comments appeared in the *Rocky Mountain Presbyterian* were determined to challenge the idea that the occupants of mining camps were uncouth barbarians. One traveler in the West found that miners were, for the most part, "the very bravest and best men, generous, sagacious, enterprising, and competent to the noblest deeds."[23] Another tourist concluded that the miners, as a class, were intelligent. "There are graduates of Yale among them," he observed, "and in their cabins one sees scientific and philosophical books. There is a rough element, but it is no longer in the ascendant."[24] Finally, to dispel any lingering misconception about western missionaries' being misfits unable to obtain choice assignments in the East, a visitor to Colorado reported, "Our preachers out there are young men to be proud of; manly fellows with no whims; men with brains and no nonsense." Another traveler in the West heard a sermon that he declared "would do for Boston or Athens."[25]

While Jackson's newspaper served his purpose admirably in extolling the wonders of the West and in broadcasting the need to conquer the area for church and country, it was in the year before he began publication that he scored one of his greatest coups as a propagandist. Shortly before the meeting of the General Assembly in Chicago in May of 1871, a Presbyterian minister in Kansas City, Missouri, had advertised a special excursion for assembly delegates and their families. When their business was concluded in Chicago they would go by rail to Kansas City, where they could take advantage of reduced rates offered by the recently completed Kansas Pacific Railroad to continue their journey westward. They would travel across "the fertile prairies of Kansas and across the great 'American Desert' in its native wilderness to Denver where the lover of mountain views may find unending fascination."[26]

When Jackson learned of this impending excursion, he shrewdly offered his services as coordinator of sightseeing events for the excursionists while they were in Colorado. The results of his involvement may have exceeded his expectations. On Saturday morning, June 3, fifty-seven eager excursionists arrived in Denver after an uneventful journey across the plains of Kansas and eastern Colorado. Commenting on that part of the trip, one member of the party was amazed to observe the vast herds of cattle gathered at Abilene, Kansas, for shipment to eastern markets. On a less pleasing note, the sighting of only a few buffalo may have been accounted for by the many rotting carcasses and skeletons of the animals strewn all along the path of the railroad, where they had fallen, shot by passengers in the cars. Indicative of the high spirits prevailing in the group was a telegram sent to Jackson in Denver from a station along the way. The communication and response were as follows:

> To Jackson—Heap of preachers coming to Denver. Clear the track. Will attack the city Saturday morning. Better surrender at once.
> Reply—Good. We surrender. Send list of names immediately, so that we can prepare the lock-up to secure them.[27]

After partaking of a hearty breakfast following their arrival in Denver, the tourists drove around the city in carriages provided by their genial host, Sheldon Jackson. Impressed by such evidence of sustained growth as schools, academies, church privileges, and two first-class newspapers, one of the visitors decided that "the auspicious future of Denver is among the certainties of history." That observer was also pleased when some of the ministers in the party generously accepted invitations to preach for Sabbath services in Denver churches the next day. The large audiences attending those services were perceived to be intelligent and attentive. Sunday schools were "active and flourishing, and in literature, mode of teaching and general order, full abreast of our older schools in the 'States.'"[28] On Monday morning the excursionists began their expedition into the mountains west of Denver. Impressed by the magnificent scenery and the evidence of prosperous mining and milling operations, the tourists returned to Denver on June 8 and pronounced their trip of about 150 miles a complete success. When they boarded their train that evening to return to their homes in the East, they joined in an expression of thanks to their guide, Sheldon Jackson, who had been "unremitting in attentions" to the needs of their group.[29]

Jackson could recognize a good thing when he saw it. Three years passed before he could try to repeat the success of the great excursion, but in 1874 he guided another group of assembly excursionists as they visited Denver and other points of interest in Colorado. The travelers, nearly a hundred in number, left St. Louis on Wednesday, June 3. Jackson had secured round-trip train tickets for them from St. Louis to Denver and back for fifty-six dollars, a reduction of forty-nine dollars from the regular fare. Reaching Denver on the evening of June 5, the group then departed for a journey into the mountains that generally repeated the itinerary Jackson had planned for the excursion in 1871. When the tourists left Denver on their return journey, they proclaimed their thanks to him for his generous care and labor in planning and conducting the excursion.[30]

Published reports of these great excursions provided Jackson with precisely the results he had anticipated—favorable comments endorsing the cause of home mission work in his domain. One reporter decided that the whole region should be brought under the most powerful influence that Christianity could bear upon it. "The Territory is filling up," he proclaimed, "with young men of mental power who need all the moral restraint of the homes and the churches that they have left in the East." Another excursionist concluded, "We have been more than ever impressed with the importance of home mission work in the Rocky Mountains. Our church should occupy every field as it is opened." Still another member of the party praised the indomitable Sheldon Jackson, whose name "is clearly the synonym of energy and efficiency, and is known throughout the Church wherever Home Missions have a home in the hearts of the people."[31] As always there was the possibility of a great disparity between words and deeds, but Jackson surely hoped for some positive results from his efforts in the form of more money and men for the work in the Rocky Mountain West.

Did Jackson's various enterprises derive any direct benefit from the two great excursions? Although it would be impossible to know truly, Jackson at least was confident that his efforts had convinced the tourists of the importance of his mission field. Without exception, the published reports of the journeys spoke of the pressing need to sustain and expand the work of the Presbyterian missionaries committed to winning the West for Christ. The value of goodwill as an asset in any enterprise often defies precise measurement, but Jackson could surely hope that eastern decision-makers in his church who learned of these glowing reports would view his position as superintendent of the work in the West in a favorable light.

In his advertising for the second General Assembly excursion in 1874, Jackson offered a practical incentive for making the journey. He had secured a reduction of almost 50 percent in the round-trip train fare between St. Louis and Denver. For those of his party who then journeyed south of Denver to Colorado Springs and Pueblo, the Denver and Rio Grande Railroad provided a special free train for the tourists. Pleased by this generous expression of western hospitality, the excursionists sent the railroad officials a resolution of their thanks that included the declaration "that all that has been told us of the manifold attractions of this newly opened Territory has been verified by our own observation."[32] Always ready to take advantage of any piece of favorable publicity, Jackson printed a copy of this resolution in his newspaper for the eyes of readers in the East who might be contemplating a trip to the Rocky Mountain West. And for any of those prospective travelers who happened to be Presbyterian ministers, Jackson provided assurances of reduced railroad fares so that they and their families could visit "the great home mission field of the Church."[33]

Jackson's offer was only one of the many occasions on which he was instrumental in securing free or reduced fares for himself or anyone he endorsed as being qualified. Sometimes the railroads went even further. It was not uncommon for them to donate land to church enterprises. In return, they assumed that the added status attached to a western town by virtue of the presence of a church would be good for the community's growth, which should in turn contribute to continued expansion of profitable traffic on the line. An example of this coupling of mutual interests occurred with the construction of the Presbyterian church in Laramie, Wyoming, in 1871. To assist in that enterprise, the Union Pacific Railroad donated lots to accommodate the church and parsonage, and it permitted shipment of the lumber and furnishings from the East at no charge. This generous act elicited from a member of the congregation a statement that the Union Pacific "has not alone aided this church, but in the same proportion has helped all the schools, churches, public enterprises of our town and is worthy of all praise."[34]

Praise for the Union Pacific Railroad turned to harsh condemnation from many Americans in succeeding months, following the revelation late in 1872 of widespread graft and corruption in the construction of the line. Prominent individuals allegedly close to President Grant and some influential congressmen had accepted bribes to ensure the passage of legislation favorable to stockholders in the railroad construction company. Because the Union Pacific advertised in Jackson's newspaper and provided him with free or reduced-rate passes, Jackson was inclined to support the position of the railroad in this dispute. In the September 1873 edition of the *Rocky Mountain Presbyterian*, he printed an article from *Harper's Weekly* that denounced those who were bringing suit against the railroad. Referring to the article as "discriminating and just," Jackson argued that "the present development and evangelization of the Rocky Mountain territories would not have been accomplished without the building of this road."[35]

Jackson had pinned his hopes on the building of another railroad for the development and evangelization of a particularly crucial part of this mission field. When he had hurriedly organized seven churches in Montana in 1872, he and the people of the communities he visited were anticipating the momentary arrival of the Northern Pacific Railroad. "The favorable prospects for soon having railroad facilities," one resident of the territory had exulted, "are having a very beneficial effect upon the commercial interests of the territory and causing things to brighten very much."[36] These favorable prospects dissipated a year later with the collapse of the Jay Cooke investment firm, which had been engaged to market the railroad's securities. For the remainder of the 1870s the western terminus of the railroad remained in North Dakota, and it was not until 1880 that construction resumed to bring the line, finally, into Montana. While this calamity certainly added to Jackson's difficulties in trying to support Presbyterianism in the territory, his high regard for the western railways and their importance for missionary endeavors never diminished. Writing in 1876 in the *Rocky Mountain Presbyterian* about "Railways and Civilization," Jackson concluded his words of praise by declaiming, "Thus the mountains are being leveled down, and the valleys filled up, that railways may become a highway for the Lord."[37]

In addition to using the pages of his own newspaper to spread the word about the financial needs of home mission work in the West, Jackson also wrote articles for other publications. He welcomed every opportunity to speak to congregations in the East, and to address delegates to the annual meetings of the General Assembly about the need to strengthen and expand the western outposts. When he first began his work in the Rocky Mountain West, for example, he had secured publication of an article entitled "The Home Field" in a Presbyterian periodical. In it, he wondered how many parents who received notification of the death of a beloved son in some depraved western community "would give half they are worth if they could have had a minister visit him during his sickness, nurse him, [and] point him to Jesus." Alas, that could not have happened, in Jackson's hypothetical tale, because no minister had been available. "There might have been," Jackson declared, "had those parents, and all whom they could have influenced, done their whole duty towards Home Missions." Concluding this exhortation, Jackson called for those who occupied pews in eastern churches to respond to the monetary appeals of the secretaries of the Board of Home Missions "with an enthusiasm that shall not only fill the treasury to overflowing, but shall also arouse the whole Church to a missionary activity commensurate with the greatness of the work."[38]

Among his many fund-raising expeditions to eastern churches, Jackson's trip in 1872 was particularly noteworthy. During November and December he traveled throughout the East with Henry Kendall, beseeching Presbyterian congregations in the larger cities for funds with which to replenish the mission board's sadly depleted treasury. On one occasion, when Jackson spoke in Cincinnati in behalf of that worthy cause, he provided a revealing insight into his view, of the need to expand home mission work in the West. He told his audience how energetic and enterprising young men from the East were "planting the seeds of empire" in the western states and territories. Unfortunately, many of them, beyond the reach of any Protestant denomination, were becoming "rapidly demoralized by that state of things." These men would surely shape the destiny of the nation from their western vantage points. "It is our duty," Jackson reasoned, "not only as Christians, but as patriots, to carry to them the truths of the gospel, that they may be guided aright."[39]

While Jackson saw an obvious need for the right kind of guidance for young men who moved from the East to live in the western territories, he believed it was also necessary to make "the truths of the gospel" available to all others residing in the West. He shared the podium with Cyrus Dickson, one of the secretaries of the Board of Home Missions, at the General Assembly meeting in Cleveland, Ohio, in May of 1875, and the two men expounded on these concerns to a large and attentive audience. Standing before a large map of the United States, Dickson called attention to the great stream of emigration coming into western ports from China. He called for more funds for home mission work with which to influence this flood of migrants for good "ere it became a might torrent of heathenism which should sweep us and our inert Christianity before it." The listener in the audience who reported these events then described the impassioned oratory of the next speaker:

> Rev. Sheldon Jackson, whose clear voice and stirring words always secure a close hearing, chilled our blood by his vivid pictures of the horrors of heathenism existing on our own western and southwestern coasts. No far-off land in the Eastern Hemisphere surely can exhibit more scenes of fanaticism and hideous self-torture than disfigure the fair territories of New Mexico, Arizona and Colorado, through the frightful blindness of the Mexican population.[40]

Following the fervent speeches of Dickson and Jackson the reporter observed, "Those who were present, as Commissioners, could not fail to go back to their churches with new zeal for the evangelization of their own country."[41] All well and good, but translating zeal into cash was often a difficult or impossible task. It was a dilemma in eastern congregations and in mission churches in the West as well. The disparity between words and deeds in fund-raising endeavors was very evident to George Darley. Writing about the results of his missionary labors in Colorado, he provided a colorful recapitulation of his experiences. When organizing a church he had obtained an abundance of pledges from the members. "Oh, yes!" Darley noted, "Sounds well. Those who have subscribed are called upon. One says, 'I will pay,' but does not; another says, 'I thought so and so when I subscribed;' another leaves for parts unknown." Then, to compound the problem, comes a notice of reduced support from the mission board "because the church at large fails to furnish the money required to pay living salaries to her missionaries." Darley could not see how any mission church could survive under these circumstances. "The process looks to me a good deal like Paddy's experience with his horse," Darley lamented. "'One straw less each day,' but when the horse got down to one straw a day it died."[42]

While the western missionaries were understandably complaining about reductions in their salaries that gave them, in their opinion, considerably less than a living wage, their superintendent was enduring similar belt-tightening measures. Jackson began the decade of the 1870s with an annual salary of twenty-five hundred dollars, but that figure had declined by 1880 to eighteen hundred dollars. The yearly wages of the secretaries of the Board of Home Missions, however, remained constant at five thousand dollars during that same period. At this time of great financial distress, some of the missionaries might have questioned an appeal by their church that would divert precious funds from the great western crusade. The questionable campaign was associated with an observance of the one hundredth birthday of the Declaration of Independence at Fairmount Park in Philadelphia, where large buildings would be erected to accommodate agricultural, industrial, and cultural exhibits from all the states and many foreign countries. The Presbyterian Church was determined to do its bit for this gala by creating and displaying a large statue of Jonathan Witherspoon of New Jersey, a renowned Presbyterian who had been the only minister of the gospel to sit in the Continental Congress and to sign the Declaration of Independence. When these plans were announced, Jackson's newspaper carried an appeal to all pastors to call for contributions from their congregations to meet the anticipated cost of twenty thousand dollars for the bronze colossus: "a large sum has already been secured for the erection of a costly and elaborate structure . . . commemorative of Charles Carroll of Carrollton and three other Catholic worthies of the Revolutionary period."[43]

Jackson worked hard to raise funds for the home mission program of his church during his tenure as superintendent of mission work in the Rocky Mountain West. An eternal optimist, he never flagged in his belief that economic recovery for God's chosen people was just around the corner. "Though financial troubles have checked the growth of our Western towns," his newspaper proclaimed in 1875, "they have not destroyed them. In no long time these towns will be flourishing again."[44] As the nation rebounded slowly from the disastrous depression, Jackson took the initiative to try to convince one particular group within his church to coordinate their efforts in a great national program to benefit home missions. In 1873 he received a letter stating the following: "We shall always look to you to suggest objects of work and interest. If we can do them, of course we will." He knew that the writer was speaking for one portion of a vast reservoir of talented fund-raisers—the women of the Presbyterian Church.[45]

6 | Women's Auxiliaries for the Front Lines

*Do you not feel greatly encouraged when you know and realize
you have the* women *of this land awakening to their duty and
responsibility. I am. We have some glorious women near us who
are beginning to feel they are made for something better than
'ornaments.'*

—Mrs. E. W. Ten Eyck to Sheldon Jackson, March 11, 1875

Tucked away in the wording of the Republican party platform
prepared for the presidential election year of 1872 were these words: "The
Republican Party is mindful of its obligations to the loyal women of America
for their noble devotion to the cause of freedom. Their admission to wider
fields of usefulness is viewed with satisfaction."[1] Although Sheldon Jackson may have been completely unaware of this statement, he had resolved,
on his own part, to find ways in the days ahead to find "wider fields of
usefulness" for the multitude of Presbyterian women who had an interest
in home mission work in the West. Anticipating opposition from the male-
dominated heirarchy to any sudden or drastic change in the traditional
understanding of the limited role of women in church affairs, Jackson wisely
decided to move slowly on this issue. Church records did acknowledge a
few attempts in the early part of the nineteenth century to provide vehicles
for women's fund-raising efforts. Notable among them were the Cent Societies, formed by women in local churches to aid missionaries financially.
Following the Civil War, however, the extraordinary expense of winning
the West for Christ provided a plausible rationale, at least in Jackson's
view, for enlarging the sphere of women in the cause of home missions.[2]

When Jackson accepted the challenge to supervise the establishment of
Presbyterian missions in the Rocky Mountain West in the 1870s, the interest of Presbyterian women in the church's home mission work was being expressed in two ways: support from women's organizations in the
congregations of the mission churches themselves, and aid in the form of
boxes of used clothing from women's missionary societies in established
churches in the East. Jackson was quite content, at first, for the ladies in
the little churches in his mission field to fulfill their support function in

whatever manner they preferred. And the ingenuity of these stalwart fund-raisers in devising schemes to augment the treasuries of their churches was truly wondrous to behold. News items on these fund-raising projects appeared regularly in the pages of the *Rocky Mountain Presbyterian.* The issue of December 1872 carried reports of a fair and festival produced by the ladies of the church at Colorado Springs that had netted two hundred dollars for the church building fund. At the Golden, Colorado, church, the women members had organized a sewing circle that was planning an apron festival highlighted by an old-fashioned New England dinner. Proceeds from that gala would be used for the purchase of stoves for their church. And in Salt Lake City, the women's sewing society conducted a display and sale of their handiwork in the hall of a local hotel, intending to use the profits realized from the endeavor to furnish their new church building.[3]

Not to be outdone by the efforts of their sisters in Colorado and Utah, the ladies of the churches in Montana were exceptionally imaginative in planning their fund-raising ventures. A veteran of the Ladies Aid Society of the Bozeman church recalled how they had earned their first money at an ice cream festival where they prepared that delicacy in tin buckets. A later strawberry festival almost ended in disaster. The ladies imported the expensive berries from Helena, and the fruit arrived battered and covered with dust. Every woman went to work washing each berry, however, and a reporter noted, "The berries were a success, though they were a trifle gritty and made the cream on them a little cloudy."[4] Elsewhere in Montana, the ladies of the Helena church undertook a project during the summer to obtain money for a building fund. After obtaining a contract to operate a restaurant on the fairgrounds during fair week, they cooked enough food early each morning for three meals and then carried the various dishes to their booth on the fairgrounds. With every woman's kitchen in service during the week of the fair, they realized a profit after expenses of five hundred dollars.[5]

Perhaps the most ambitious money-making scheme occurred also at the Helena, Montana, church, where the women planned an elaborate fund-raising venture for the Christmas season in 1872. They conceived the project originally as a bazaar lasting several days and culminating in a Christmas dinner featuring plum pudding and fried oysters. When the ladies told their pastor, William Rommel, of their intention of including a dance and raffle on the program, they were surprised by his adamant opposition. The ladies explained how the Catholics in Helena had raised a large sum of money the previous year with similar events, but Rommel informed them that such sinful practices could not be condoned under the auspices of the Presbyterian Church. When Rommel threatened to resign his pastorate if the women refused to accept his ruling in the matter, the chastened ladies agreed to conduct the bazaar without any of the objectionable features. Although the ladies did not anticipate a very large monetary return without the dance or raffle, they were pleasantly surprised when the net profit totaled eight hundred dollars, which was set aside as the nucleus of a church building fund for the Helena congregation.[6]

While the ladies aid societies in the West were laboring diligently to provide financial support for their churches and their pastors, Jackson began to approach prominent Presbyterian women in the East to solicit their support for his mission field. In the summer of 1870 he began corresponding with Mrs. Cornelia Martin of Auburn, New York. That influential woman was an officer of a ladies missionary association in New York that had been organized as the Santa Fe Missionary Association in 1867 to support Presbyterian mission schools in New Mexico. In 1868 Mrs. Martin had also assisted in the formation in New York City of an organization entitled the New Mexico, Arizona, and Colorado Missionary Society. In September of 1872, Henry Kendall reminded Jackson of a recent letter from Mrs. Martin. In it, she had hoped that Jackson could find time in his busy schedule to visit Fort Garland in southern Colorado to preach and hold a Communion service for the small band of Christians there, who sorely missed those church privileges. Kendall urged Jackson to make the journey requested by Mrs. Martin: "she is quite a power in the land, and you will do well to cultivate her."[7]

Always ready to seize every opportunity to "cultivate" notable women in the East who appeared interested in his work, Jackson made the trip to Fort Garland carrying with him a silver-plated Communion service secured by Mrs. Martin for the garrison at the fort. In the summer of 1872, Jackson was pleased to hear from another important women in New York who had concerns for Presbyterian missions in the West. Julia Graham, leader of the Ladies Board of Missions of New York, had introduced herself to Jackson by complimenting him on the excellence of his newspaper, the *Rocky Mountain Presbyterian*. Expressing her interest in the mission churches at Santa Fe and Las Vegas in New Mexico, she wanted to send more help for that field, but "our Board is as yet a little thing." She concluded her introductory comments by rejoicing, "Thank God that the missionary is pushing his way out to the far West with the outgoing population, that the word of God may not be left behind."[8]

Mrs. Graham had modestly understated the significance of her Ladies Board of Missions. Founded in 1870 to enlist the ladies of the Presbyterian Church more actively in the work of home and foreign missions, it was definitely not "a little thing." A year after its organization, its membership roster had expanded to include forty-seven auxiliary societies. True, most of the money raised by these women was disbursed to foreign mission fields, but Jackson surely hoped, after opening a line of communication with Mrs. Graham, to use his persuasive talents to convince her to budget more of the funds collected by her board for his enterprises. Jackson's congenial relationship with Mrs. Graham apparently paid its first dividend early in 1873. In January a notice in his newspaper proclaimed, "The churches of Helena and Deer Lodge [Montana] have each been presented with a silver communion service from the Ladies Board of Home Missions, New York City."[9]

The attraction of female fund-raisers to foreign mission work rather than home mission projects was, of course, a matter of concern for Jackson. He tried to develop a line of reasoning to show how the latter cause deserved more support in a newspaper article early in 1873. In it, he cited a plea from the secretaries of the Board of Home Missions for increased contributions to aid the wives of home missionaries:

> Unable to have servants, [she] does her own work—looks after the direction and welfare of the children, undertakes too much of the necessary labor for outside matters in the church and congregations, and falls at her post. Many, many such wives have done their best, and will be remembered at the last, like one of whom it was said by our Lord, "She hath done what she could."

Emphasizing this woman-to-woman approach, Jackson concluded his commentary with his own appeal to all the godly women of the Presbyterian Church to remember their many sisters "who on our frontiers and in our feeble churches are doing as truly a missionary work as those who have gone to India or Japan."[10]

There is no way to pinpoint the precise moment in time when Jackson decided to try to develop a national women's home mission society in his church, but he must have been thinking along those lines early in his superintendency. At the end of 1873, evaluating the results of his efforts to interest the women of his church in home mission work, Jackson could point to some modest gains, at least in his own area of responsibility. Responding to his appeals, women at the churches in Denver, Pueblo, and Central City in Colorado had formed Ladies Home Missionary societies. To prevent these well-meaning groups from proceeding in a haphazard fashion, Jackson made available for their use copies of a formal constitution for a Ladies Home Missionary Society. Late in the year, at meetings of the presbyterys of Colorado and Wyoming, the delegates passed resolutions to the General Assembly calling for formation, as soon as practicable, of Ladies Home Missionary societies in all churches throughout the denomination. The first faltering steps had now been taken, and only time would tell if the end product would be on the scale envisioned by Jackson.[11]

At that point, Jackson knew that he had to address a dilemma basic to all of his plans: how could he convince potential donors that the home mission cause deserved as much financial support as the foreign mission work, if not more? For Jackson, one means to this end was his newspaper. In almost every issue of the *Rocky Mountain Presbyterian* in the 1870s there appeared an article extolling the virtues of women's work for home missions in general, and his own mission field more specifically. In January of 1874, for example, he wrote about "Woman's Work for Jesus." After quoting extracts from several heartrending letters from mothers seeking news of sons who had gone to seek their fortunes in the West, Jackson continued by explaining how these citations were only examples of hundreds of similar letters:

> But thousands of mothers and sisters do not thus write. They mourn and pray for the absent ones in silence. In tens of thousands of households there is great sorrow. Mothers are bowed down with grief for these wandering ones. Sisters are becoming more solicitous as the months pass by and no tidings from brother; and wives mourn in silence their enforced widowhood, while their husbands speculate and dissipate in the mines. And yet it is said there is nothing in Home Missions that appeals to the warm sympathies of our Christian women.

Concluding these touching observations, Jackson called for all Presbyterian women to form Ladies Home Missionary Societies in every congregation to manifest a much greater degree of interest in this good work.[12]

While Jackson hoped that his personal appeals would help to achieve the rather limited goals he had suggested, he waited to see if the General Assembly would provide some sort of official sanction for the bold concept of enlarging the scope of women's work for home missions. At the annual meeting of the assembly in St. Louis in the spring of 1874, the delegates seemed to avoid any indication of preferential treatment for either the home or foreign fields in soliciting support for mission work. This evasive action might have been derived from the continuing division in the ranks of church leaders on the issue of the role of women in church affairs. While some of the delegates to the assembly, for example, argued about women's work for missions, others discussed an age-old question.

Jackson published a report of the assembly debate on the controversial issue in his newspaper on June 17, 1874, in an article entitled "Shall Women Pray and Speak?" The topic had received attention at the assembly when the Presbytery of Rock River, Illinois, sent a petition to the gathering that called for a ruling on the question "Does the Assembly mean to enjoin that in the regular weekly prayer meetings of the church, no woman shall speak or lead in prayer?"[13] Associated with this matter was a report circulated at the assembly that a woman had been permitted to preach in the pulpit of a church in the Presbytery of Brooklyn, New York. Speaking against any deviation from church traditions, which had reserved these privileges for men only, one delegate to the assembly stated, "I believe when God created woman he threw over her the banner of his love by giving her a place he has never given angels, and it would be cruel to drag her down from it." Taking a more liberal stand, another speaker hoped that the brethren could "lift woman up to the level of speaking for the Lord Jesus and of working for him."[14]

While the first commentator in this exchange of views saw a woman's leadership role in praying and speaking as "dragging her down" from her familial position allotted by the Almighty, the other speaker felt it was time to "lift woman up" into a place where she could use her talents to speak and work alongside her brethren in the church for the great cause they all espoused. Perhaps recognizing the intensity of feeling on this subject, the assembly resolved to "express no opinion as to the scriptural view of woman's rights to speak and pray in the social prayer meeting, but commits the whole subject to the discretion of the Pastors and Elders of the churches."[15] Surely anyone reading the concerns expressed on all of these issues would have to agree that the Presbyterian Church was still not ready to adopt any broad policy that would lower women from their lofty and divinely ordained place of honor.

Meanwhile, Jackson continued throughout the year to try to secure the sympathetic support of Presbyterian women for home missions in the West. Continuing to use the pages of his newspaper as a forum for this campaign, he seized every opportunity to tell women in the East in no uncertain terms why their sisters on the frontier merited special consideration. Writing about "Woman's Work For Woman" in the summer of 1874, he explained:

> In the West they [missionary wives] scarcely ever find a parsonage ready for them to enter, as they often do in the East, lighted, warmed, carpeted and furnished with every comfort. Tumbledown shanties must be renovated and propped up to enable them to withstand the mountain gale. Often two or three removals must be submitted to within a single year, with severe toil and drudgery in every case; and yet they do it for the most part uncomplainingly. . . . All honor to these noble women.

Closing his commentary on these issues, Jackson pointedly asked this question: "And why should not these noble women receive the same substantial sympathy that is accorded their sisters in foreign fields?"[16]

Slowly but surely the moment was approaching when the policy-makers in the church would have either to approve or reject the concept of a national women's home mission society. The next step occurred at the General Assembly meeting in Cleveland, Ohio, in May of 1875. In the annual report submitted by the Board of Home Missions, the members noted favorable responses to the plan presented in the previous year for designating certain months during the year when the women of local churches would conduct special fund-raising drives for home missions. In a statement that Jackson must have contemplated with satisfaction, the board members attributed the initial success of the efforts by these women to "sympathy with their sisters who are building up healthy social and religious institutions in the West." Then, moving boldly beyond the position taken by the General Assembly in the previous year endorsing fund-raising programs that would benefit both home and foreign mission work, the members of the assembly's Standing Committee on Home Missions called for recommendation of a plan for a Woman's Home Missionary Society, with regional auxiliary societies under the advice and counsel of the Board of Home Missions.[17]

When the assembly accepted and approved the report of its Standing Committee on Home Missions, Jackson and Henry Kendall interpreted the wording employed in these statements as approval to start work on the initial planning stage for the new society. Kendall soon called on Jackson to make an extensive speaking tour in the East during the fall of 1875, to concentrate, as Kendall put it, "in working the matter up." In his instructions for this trip, Kendall told Jackson he was to "move among the masses, stirring up the women in the city and country in this great work." Jackson was to emphasize in his remarks the concept of women's and children's work in the East for the benefit of women and children in home mission fields. Underscoring the importance of this commission, Kendall referred to Jackson's assignment as the advance movement: "our only safe course is to push it with all our might." Finally, Kendall left no doubt about how he had selected the eleven churches and nine presbyteries for Jackson to visit: he stated, quite simply, "For here is the money."[18]

Jackson hardly needed these exhortations to press hard for a cause dear to his heart. Unfortunately, there is no existing account of the results of his long journey at the end of 1875. A friend of Jackson's did note, however, that the instructions from Kendall were carried out at the time designated. A committee of the home mission board had been appointed by Henry Kendall at the end of 1875 to consider ways of coordinating the fund-raising efforts of the existing women's home mission societies. That committee made its report to the board in January of 1876. Jackson must have been disappointed by the rather timid position adopted by his superiors. After discussing the committee report, the board members decided not to interfere in any way with the existing organizations. Instead, the board simply called for each presbytery to involve still more women in the good work by promoting the formation of local home mission societies in each church. The presbyteries should then "endeavor to secure systematic and harmonious action on the part of these organizations by any correspondence or combination or supervision that each Presbytery may deem most advisable."[19]

In the ensuing months, the mission board members did decide to try to move one step further in this process, by incorporating still another level of supervision in the growing presbyterial network of proposed women's auxiliaries. Why not direct each synod to appoint a committee of women each year called the Synodical Committee of Woman's Work for Home Missions? These women would then oversee the organization and operations for home mission work among their sisters within their respective synods. Jackson may have had mixed feelings when he read about this innovative proposal in the board's annual report in 1876. He would have appreciated any effort to provide new direction for women's work for home missions, but, at the same time, he would have hoped for some indication of progress in the planning for the national society recommended by the assembly the previous year. Jackson would have been pleased, however, when he noted in the board's report a special call for women to support churches and schools in the "solid unevangelized mass of 200,000 souls in New Mexico and Utah [where] the work must be carried on precisely as in foreign lands."[20] When the General Assembly met in Brooklyn, New York, in May of 1876, the delegates simply approved the report of the Standing Committee on Home Missions, which included a recommendation to implement the synodical proposal.[21]

At the end of 1876, any analyst of the official position of the Presbyterian Church on the role of women in home mission work could only conclude that there was still no clear focus. Numerous reports and resolutions on this subject had been adopted at every level of the church, but there remained a sense of bewilderment regarding the best course of action to follow. This dilemma was compounded, in some respects, by the action of the General Assembly meeting in Chicago in 1877. The report of the Board of Home Missions to that gathering called attention, once again, to the Utah, New Mexico, and Arizona mission fields, where there was much work to be done for "the degraded and deluded women and children." Because the magnitude of the challenge in that region from the Mormon and Catholic churches exceeded, by far, the demands placed upon home missionaries in other parts of the country, "a new agency, precisely such as is necessary to employ in foreign lands, must be employed [there]. Not that the preaching of the gospel is to be superseded or made subordinate to anything else, but that schools must be established as auxiliary and preparatory to the preaching of the gospel."[22]

Did Kendall and Jackson deliberately introduce the issue of mission board support for schools in certain sections of Jackson's mission field at this time to further reinforce the need for a strong national women's home mission organization that would raise funds for these new enterprises? Neither of these gentlemen ever openly acknowledged that motivation, but they did succeed admirably in convincing the delegates to the assembly of the merit of their proposal. The assembly authorized the Board of Home Missions to begin commissioning teachers to open schools in the areas identified as critical, and to enlarge this new endeavor as rapidly as women's societies could provide the funds. The board members, in accepting this responsibility, made it clear that they had no intention of undertaking a general educational work. On the contrary, their support would be directed only to "exceptional" people, and they would not try to give general help for schools elsewhere on the frontier. Concluding this appraisal of the new task before them, the board members appealed with confidence "to the Women of the Presbyterian Church, for aid to undertake and carry on this department of the great work laid upon it by the General Assembly."[23]

Henry Kendall and the Board of Home Missions lost no time in carrying out the mandate received from the General Assembly. In the March 1878 edition of his newspaper, Jackson announced the commissioning of ten lady teachers to Utah, two to Alaska, and six to New Mexico. "The work of sending out suitable Christian women to the heathen women of our own land," Jackson explained, "will be extended just as rapidly as the Ladies' Home Mission Societies will pledge the funds."[24] Meanwhile, Jackson traveled once again to speak before selected churches in the East on the subject of women's work for missions. Early in 1878 he addressed conventions of women at several locations in New Jersey. His success in stirring female emotions was evidenced when, at several of the conventions, the women resolved to raise the money required to send Christian women as missionary teachers to schools in Utah, New Mexico, and Alaska. An observer at one of these gatherings reported that the facts presented by Jackson were truly startling. She remembered vividly how the guest speaker "told us of the worship of wooden and clay images, of actual Baal-worship within the limits of these United States."[25]

The woman who prepared this report on Jackson's trip to New Jersey was Frances Haines of Elizabeth, New Jersey. Her interests in mission work, to that point, had centered primarily on support for those who labored in the foreign mission fields of the Presbyterian Church. She was impressed, however, by Jackson's description of the religious depravation prevalent in some areas of his mission field. "You have given us facts as to the destitution in our own country," she wrote to Jackson after his visit to New Jersey, "that can never be forgotten. The very interest that we as Christian women have been led to take in Foreign Missions, should now impell us to try to make our own land a more fitting and efficient light-bearer to the nation."[26]

Jackson was encouraged by the comments from Mrs. Haines and other ladies who had expressed their views in a similar vein. With the thought, perhaps, that it was now or never, Jackson decided to force the question of a single organization to coordinate the work of women for home missions at the General Assembly scheduled to convene on May 16, 1878, in Pittsburgh. Early in May, as part of his preparation for the meeting, he sent letters to several influential women in the East asking if they would consent to serve as officers in a new national women's board for home missions. Most of the replies he received were not encouraging. Some of those who answered, however, did share his views on the importance of women's work for missions. "Woman's power is only begun to be developed," one respondent stated. "Comparatively few of the Presbyterian women of this country have set themselves in battle array against the hosts of sin."[27] But another lady sent Jackson a copy of the letter she had written to a woman who advocated Jackson's great plan. The letter explained that she and her friends had already created one local society to help both home and foreign missions, and that they would regret any change in the arrangement. "I hope," she concluded, "he [Jackson] will not take any means to carry out such a plan."[28]

Jackson was not deterred from his purpose by these storm signals. He had a plan and he was determined to carry it out. While the delegates to the assembly conducted their regular business sessions, Jackson scheduled a women's meeting for May 24 at the First Presbyterian Church of Pittsburgh, to consider formation of a national organization of Presbyterian women to foster home missions. Without any direct endorsement from the Board of Home Missions to take such an initiative, Jackson apparently acted entirely on his own in making the arrangements for this gathering. The ladies who accepted his invitation to attend began their deliberations with the reading of various letters and reports expressing interest in the stated purpose of the meeting. Later, they listened to an essay prepared by Julia Wright, an authoress whose articles carrying inspirational messages for children appeared often in Jackson's newspaper. Realizing that the demands on women for home mission work were increasing dramatically, Mrs. Wright offered a proposal to meet the challenge. "My sisters, the answer is plain," she explained. "This work, which will be far greater next year than this, must be done, and can only be done by ORGANIZATION." The organization contemplated by Mrs. Wright should be achieved at once, in her opinion, to counter the insidious forces already at work. "The future of American liberties is enwrapt in this question of Home Missions," she pleaded. "This lovely land, these possibilities, these souls, are waited for by the destroyer. Romanism and infidelity are straining every nerve to possess all the West."[29]

Shall we organize now? That was the question put to the ladies after they concluded their discussion on the issue. Without revealing the actual numbers, the recording secretary simply noted the result of the vote: "Answered in the negative."[30] Although Jackson—who was in the audience of the meeting—may have been disappointed by the outcome of the vote, he knew that this action was not intended as a rejection of the plan, but was rather a postponement of the final decision. The delegates did resolve to appoint a committee of twelve women to confer with the Ladies Board of Missions in New York to determine if that powerful organization might agree to devoting its efforts henceforth exclusively to home missions. If that overture were unsuccessful, the committee was empowered to call a meeting of delegates from different churches, at a time and place to be selected, to go ahead with the organization of a new women's board for home missions. One of those who attended recalled that later, after the gathering at Pittsburgh had adjourned, "some felt sad at heart that the first general meeting in the interests of a cherished cause, should have been attended with such perplexities, and productive of such slight results."[31]

After the women completed their work, they must have wondered what action, if any, the delegates to the General Assembly would take on the issues they had raised. The report of the Standing Committee on Home Missions, which was approved by the assembly, called for efforts at all levels "to secure harmony of method, either by separate organizations for the different branches of the work, or by incorporating both [home and foreign] branches in one organization."[32] That seemed to say, Do what seems best to secure your goals, but we do hope that any results will be gained by harmonious negotiations rather than discordant ones. Certainly Frances Haines and the other women appointed to call on Julia Graham at the New York Ladies Board of Missions hoped that their discussions would proceed in a cordial atmosphere. If the meeting in New York did not produce satisfactory results, it was Jackson's recommendation that Mrs. Haines and her committee move quickly to create what Jackson called "A Provisional Board of Managers." That group should then make its presence known to all the synods with the announcement that it would now take charge of the interests of the new society. The provisional board could then prepare a constitution and bylaws to be presented for adoption at a women's gathering arranged in conjunction with the annual meeting of the General Assembly in the spring of 1879.[33]

So the stage was set for the pivotal confrontation that would decide the future of Jackson's plans for a national organization to coordinate the efforts of women's groups for the home mission cause. According to the wording of the resolution passed at the meeting in Pittsburgh, if the leaders of the Ladies Board of Missions in New York were to accept the proposal to change the emphasis of their efforts from both home and foreign missions to home mission work exclusively, there would be no need for the creation of any new board. One can only speculate on Jackson's thoughts as the date drew near for the meeting. He could not have openly expressed his own desire that the proposed course of action, which he could only have regarded as a halfway measure, come to naught, but he would surely have been disappointed if all of his efforts to make a bold new start on the issue had been in vain.

On July 11 the two delegations of women met at the Presbyterian Mission House at 23 Center Street. Henry Kendall had invited the ladies to use the vacant office of Cyrus Dickson, a colleague who shared the duties of secretary of the Board of Home Missions. Kendall wrote to Jackson while the women's meeting was in session. Although he could not predict the outcome, he viewed several things as "tolerably certain." He did not think that Mrs. Graham and her delegates would give up their association with foreign missions. If that were so, any subsequent effort to organize a new and separate board would produce a fight. Mrs. Graham had already interested most of the ministers in New York in her behalf, and they would not favor a new organization, nor would the Board of Home Missions because many of its members were pastors in New York.[34]

Kendall was correct in his assumption that the New York board would not divest itself of its commitment to foreign missions. Instead, Mrs. Graham offered a counterproposal. Her board would modify its position on home missions by having the presidents of synodical home mission groups become vice-presidents of the New York organization. Those women could then attend the meetings in New York and vote on all home mission issues on the agenda. Caught by surprise, the members of the Pittsburgh faction thought it best to defer action on the new proposal until the absent committee members could be consulted. Describing the outcome of this gathering, one of those present from the Pittsburgh group was bewildered. "Thus the second meeting for the purpose of securing systematic organization for Woman's Work for Home Missions met, deliberated and adjourned," she wrote, "leaving as a visible result only a few propositions in the hands of its chairman. What did it mean?"[35]

What it all meant, according to Julia Wright, who had made the impassioned plea for a new organization at the Pittsburgh meeting, was a lengthy delay. She told Jackson that most of the committee members would probably favor the Graham proposition to avoid a real showdown on the basic issue. Many of the ladies, in fact, considered the proposal as a divinely ordained response to their prayers for guidance on the matter. "Perhaps it is," Mrs. Wright suggested. "However, I think we have in this age got in the habit of talking a great deal of religious balderdash without knowing it." With a very pessimistic outlook for the future, Mrs. Wright concluded her observations with the prediction that it would be five years at least until the Graham plan could be proved a failure and creation of a new and efficient board could finally be achieved.[36]

Wright was wrong. A report of the meeting in New York went to all members of the Pittsburgh committee, along with a request for opinions on the Graham plan. A majority of those responding opposed any plan combining both home and foreign missions in one organization. Unsure of the next step, the committee decided to submit the whole matter to the Board of Home Missions for guidance and counsel before proceeding. The board members discussed the matter at their meeting on October 7. After expressing appreciation for everything the women had done to date for home missions, those in attendance stated, "We do not deem it competent for us to originate any new plans for the organization of woman's work in connection with this Board." After reviewing previous General Assembly actions related to the issue, however, the board decided to modify its position. The members urged the synods to authorize, if they had not already done so, committees of women interested in home mission work. Then, in a careful selection of wording, the board minutes noted, "It may be permitted to us to suggest that the several Committees of the Synods, as soon as possible after their appointment, may bring themselves into sympathy and cooperation by the appointment of a General Executive Committee who shall be their organ of communication with the Board, and that they report whatever may be done in this direction to the Synods and the General Assembly."[37]

Was this, finally, a go-ahead signal? Jackson and his female allies chose to interpret it so. Notices of the mission board action went at once to their synods. Then an organizational meeting composed of synodical delegations was scheduled for December 12, 1878, in New York. The meeting was well attended, mainly, however, by representatives from the synods of New York and New Jersey. The delegates decided to call the new coordinating body the Woman's Executive Committee of Home Missions. Election of officers followed, and Jackson was surely pleased when he learned that Frances Haines had accepted the position of corresponding secretary. "Plans of Work" and regulations were adopted, and after the gathering adjourned one of those who had been in the audience proclaimed, "Scattered up and down the land are companies of faithful women waiting to do what their hands and hearts shall find to do for Home Missions."[38]

So the die was cast. The officers of the executive committee went to work with a will in an office provided in the Board of Home Missions building in New York City. When they met again with delegations of women from the synods at the General Assembly meeting in Saratoga, New York, on May 23, 1879, they rejoiced that representatives from faraway Montana, Utah, and Colorado were now in attendance. A reading of the secretary's report indicated that ten thousand circulars promoting the home mission cause had been sent out, a simple form for organization of a women's home mission society in local churches had been prepared, and the Reverend Sheldon Jackson had promised to set aside a part of a page in each issue of the *Rocky Mountain Presbyterian* for news about the committee's work. The treasurer then reported that collections to date from twenty-nine synods amounted to $3,138.39. The report of the assembly's Standing Committee on Home Missions recognized these commendable achievements in the brief period of only five months. The assembly adopted the report, which included the following statement: "None too much space and none too much praise is given to the noble work accomplished, and the promise given for continued effort."[39]

Certainly all of the ladies who labored for the home mission cause deserved plaudits, but praise for the giant step forward should also have been directed to at least one man. Frances Haines told Jackson at the end of 1878, "You do not know how weak we all feel about this, but it does seem as if the Lord has guided us this far."[40] A realistic appraisal would have had to acknowledge that Sheldon Jackson, once again, had skillfully translated the Lord's guidance into programs designed to carry out His wishes. Another man who deserved congratulations for his efforts in behalf of women's work for home missions was Henry Kendall, secretary of the Board of Home Missions. Responding to a critic of the position taken by the Board of Home Missions, Kendall argued, "If they [Presbyterian women] may not assist in planting missions among the misguided Mormons, or the ignorant papists in New Mexico, or the 285,000 Indians in our own country, by what law are they bound to send the gospel across the seas? The work at hand is the first duty, and if our Christian women are let alone, we have no doubt they will divide their energies and contributions to the satisfaction of the Great Head of the church whom we are all trying to serve."[41]

In actuality, Kendall and Jackson were not content to leave Presbyterian women alone to decide how they would divide their energies and contributions. On the contrary, they exerted their influence on the ladies on many occasions in order to centralize a program for women's support for home missions. A rather extraordinary appraisal of the results of their efforts came, at a later time, from one of Jackson's colleagues: "Thus, at length, without friction or abatement of zeal for either cause, conflicting interests were harmonized and a great National Association of home evangelization grew up alongside of its sister organization for the evangelization of the world."[42]

The statement is clearly inconsistent with the facts. Of course there was rivalry between the home and foreign mission enterprises. Still, the end result of these proceedings was soon regarded as beneficial to the interests of the church at large. The same writer who spoke of lack of friction in the formative years of the women's home mission executive committee concluded, correctly, "None of the evil things which were prophesized concerning the division or transference of funds and the wrecking of the foreign work, in some sections of the land, ever happened in the practical working of these organizations."[43]

Few would question Sheldon Jackson's leadership role in the 1870s in pressing for a "practical working" organization to coordinate the work of women in support of home missions. His influence in the creation of the Woman's Executive Committee of Home Missions is usually regarded as one of the most significant of his many achievements.[44] Of course, Jackson had many concerns during the 1870s as he tried to shape national policy for his church, one of which was referred to in the annual report of the Woman's Executive Committee in 1880. In the preamble to that lengthy document, the writer raised the question "What is there for us to do to save our own land for Christ?" One of the answers, to provide "well qualified teachers, ready to be sent wherever most needed."[45] For Jackson, there was no question that the West was the place where the need for teachers was greatest. He and his missionaries believed strongly that a proper education was the appropriate response to the contributor in the *Rocky Mountain Presbyterian* who asked, "How, then, shall this scattered, wandering, homeless people grow up an intelligent, law-making, and law-abiding community?"[46]

7 | Education as a Weapon in the Presbyterian Arsenal

She [the Presbyterian Church] is in the world for aggression and conquest; and as we have seen she must widely pervade the atmosphere with intelligence, if she would find wide acceptance of her doctrine and polity.

—Report of the Special Committee on Education to the General Assembly, 1883

"The commingling of many nationalities, bringing with them all forms of irreligion, as well as corruptions of the true, will put to a severe test both our civil and religious systems." This was the concern voiced by a Presbyterian minister following an extensive trip throughout the Rocky Mountain West in 1874. "The moral, educational, and religious future of this backbone of the continent," the writer concluded, "is a theme of the deepest interest to the statesman and the Christian." The worried pastor offered a plan to ensure victory. "To assure the permanence of our civil freedom and our Protestant and Bible-loving religion," he argued, "the patriot and the Christian must be up and at work, to fill this Territory with schools, and academies, and churches, and the habitations of the incoming families with Bibles, books and all gospel influences."[1]

Amen to that, Sheldon Jackson would have replied. He and those who served in his mission field during the 1870s believed that education was the key to producing responsible citizens from the many nationalities who populated the area. The right kind of education would be derived, of course, from both secular textbooks and appropriate religious reading material. No one perceived this need more clearly than a Presbyterian minister addressing a meeting of the Synod of Colorado in 1878. He described education as a great power, and "it can be made a greater power for good or, if directed otherwise, a greater power for evil." He used the words "sold out and betrayed" to deplore the exclusion of the Bible from Colorado public schools, and he reminded his brethren that "a religious education is of vastly more healthful power than that of a purely intellectual order." The distressed pastor concluded his declamation by citing an alarming statistic. "Of the three thousand school children in Denver, how many," he asked, "are under moral teachings? Not one-half. They are growing up street Arabs, paupers and criminals."[2]

Such beliefs were not new in the Presbyterian Church. The church had a long and proud tradition of support for "moral teaching" in the classroom. From 1847 to 1870 the denomination tried to sustain a widespread system of parochial schools. The effort was not successful. The frontier communities, in particular, were not responsive to the program, being financially handicapped by meager support from a sparse and shifting population. A noticeable change occurred, however, after the reunion of the Old School and New School factions in 1870 and with the surge of population to mining camps and other growing communities in the West after the Civil War. Although the church refused officially to support a widespread program for general education, individual church members, especially women, became increasingly responsive to the pleas of Sheldon Jackson and others who manned the western outposts for support of a variety of educational endeavors.[3]

Jackson was no stranger to the challenges posed in a classroom situation. Early in his missionary career he had taught Indian students on the Choctaw reservation in the Indian Territory. Although he did not obtain any great personal satisfaction from his experience, he never doubted the need for such service, to enlighten those he would have regarded as living in spiritual darkness. And when he moved on to organize new churches in Minnesota, he had recruited two lady teachers to open a school designated as the Rochester Female Institute in 1866. While residing in Rochester, he served on the faculty of the school as a professor of higher mathematics and languages without salary. When he and his family moved to Denver, Colorado, in 1870, his responsibilities as superintendent of mission work in the Rocky Mountain West precluded any direct involvement in teaching. He did, however, find numerous ways to champion the cause of teaching young people in the West the moral and religious principles that would prepare them for productive positions in society.[4]

He used his newspaper many times, for example, to sing the praises of a proper education. It would be a rare occasion, indeed, when the *Rocky Mountain Presbyterian* did not include an article on the subject. A sample from the first issue, in March of 1872, illustrates the point. One article raised the question in its title, "How Shall We Educate?" For the author, the answer was really quite simple. Teach a child from infancy the Bible and the child would accept Christianity, thereby avoiding the fate of criminals in prison cells or on their way to the gallows who could attribute their unfortunate condition to early unchristian influences. Education for a child must be of a "proper character," the writer concluded, emphasizing moral as well as intellectual traits in order to strike a balance productive of "a useful and worthy member of society."[5]

Feature stories in Jackson's newspaper often provided examples to support the general theorizing about the attributes of an acceptable learning environment. A case in point was a lengthy article in the issue of March 1872, which described the goals of something called the American Railway Literary Union. This organization had been formed to "withhold railroad and steamboat facilities from the sale of immoral publications, and bring into competition with the vulgar trash, a more elevated and attractive style, discouraging the demoralizing and vile." Among the published endorsements for this project was a letter dated January 9, 1868, from General Ulysses S. Grant, who viewed the endeavor as "a most praiseworthy enterprise, and one which ought to succeed in working great good."[6]

Finally, a regular monthly feature in Jackson's paper was an article intended to provide a lesson in good Christian conduct for young readers. In the March issue, for example, there appeared the story of "A Brave Girl." Little Hattie had been making fun of the rather shabby bonnet worn by her friend Nellie. Defending her appearance, Nellie explained that her mother couldn't afford a better one, "and that is enough for me to know, to be satisfied with what I have." Hattie's vanity, according to the author, made her a "poor little mincing coward." On the other hand, "How much nobler is Nellie, who dares to follow her mother's counsels, though she may not appear quite so fashionable!"[7]

Echoes indeed of a long-gone era, an age of innocence wherein the struggle between virtue and wickedness could be expressed in a little morality play featuring the condition of a young girl's bonnet. One might wonder if this rather trite commentary in the *Rocky Mountain Presbyterian* may not have been scorned, perhaps even ridiculed, by a potential clientele whom Jackson had described in his solicitation for advertising as "the best class of people."[8] Certainly Jackson had no doubt that the selection of material for the columns of his newspaper was in perfect tune with the spirit of the time.

As part of a nostalgic reflection on the supposedly good old days of America's past, one might well include a picture of Sunday morning serenity, with all of the members of the family scrubbed and polished and in their places at church. Somewhere in that picture would be scenes from the always present adjunct to the morning worship service, the Sabbath school. Thousands of Tom Sawyers and Becky Thatchers must have been obliged to grapple with biblical verses and absorb morality lessons designed to build their characters. Presbyterians were certainly a part of that vision, and the church's position on the value of Sabbath school work was stated clearly at the New School General Assembly meeting in 1866. A report from a recently appointed Standing Committee on Sabbath Schools declared, "We believe that the Sabbath school is a nursery of the Christian Church, one bulwark of Christian doctrine, a promoter of Christian union, and the organizer of Christian labor. In other words, it saves the young, it secures the faith, it settles differences, and it develops power."[9]

Jackson would have agreed completely with this line of reasoning, and he gave his personal support to Sabbath school work whenever he could. On one occasion, on June 10, 1871, soon after he moved his residence to Colorado, he participated in a meeting of the Sunday School Institute of Colorado. The institute had been created two years previously in Central City, at a gathering designated as a Territorial Sunday School Convention. The delegates had hoped to have one or more meetings of the institute each year, but that had not occurred because the president of the interim committee charged with arranging the meetings had left the territory, taking with him all of the records from the organizing convention. On June 10, however, representatives from several of the Protestant churches in Colorado convened at the Methodist church in Denver to activate a Sunday School Institute. The gathering was honored by the presence of the renowned evangelist Dwight Moody, who was visiting in Denver. Moody led the opening devotional services and conducted what he called a "promise meeting," in which each delegate quoted some promise in scripture that had sustained him in times of trial. Another speaker then addressed the assembly, extolling the virtues of regular Sunday school attendance. He explained how the schools would not simply instruct young people in Bible knowledge, but would also "elevate the poor and ignorant children" by bringing them under religious influence. Since Jackson certainly espoused these same precepts, he gladly accepted an appointment on one of the committees formed by the institute to work for this good cause throughout Colorado.[10]

Jackson also devoted space in his newspaper to Sabbath school concerns. An article published in July of 1872 called for the Presbyterian Church officially to adopt the title "Bible School" for these organizations, "because it would serve at once to distinguish the true article from the base and spurious imitations which are springing up everywhere." According to the writer, "Roman Catholics, free thinkers, and infidels are organizing their Sunday Schools everywhere with great diligence." These wrong thinkers, the author concluded, could not establish authentic Bible schools, but if they attempted to do so, "the flaming sword of the spirit, which is the word of God, will consume their fine spun theories as the flame licks up the prairie grass."[11]

Among the many items appearing in the *Rocky Mountain Presbyterian* that encouraged Sabbath school attendance was an article in the September 1878 issue entitled "What Makes Boys Bad?" It conveyed a clear answer to the question. Four boys had recently placed stones on the New York City elevated railroad tracks, nearly causing a derailment. Three of the boys said they knew better, as they occasionally read Sabbath school publications, but they had been led astray by the fourth lad, who admitted that his reading was limited to the *Police Gazette* and *Boys and Girls Weekly*. The head of a New York correctional institution then warned all boys that the latter forms of reading material offered only wild and thrilling tales that would "unsettle their minds."[12]

Closer to home, in his own mission field, Jackson knew he could rely on his missionaries to provide Sabbath schools for their congregations, sometimes even before the formal organization of a church. A classic example occurred when a Presbyterian minister tried to establish a church in Miles City, Montana, in 1878. He reported his lack of success to Jackson:

> I have made the trip to Miles City and have returned. I did not organize a church because there was not material sufficient. Five church members in the whole town. These would have been sufficient had they been good ones. One was a Methodist, who had been bar-tender in a saloon. Two were Episcopalians, Ladies, a little doubtful in reputation, and two were Baptists, not willing to come in at once. I organized a Sunday School, with Mr. George M. Miles as Superintendent. He is a nephew of General [Nelson A.] Miles. . . . I have sent him material with which to carry on the school.[13]

By opening the doors of the Sabbath school to all children from both religious and nonreligious families in a community, a Presbyterian missionary could announce attendance figures that would appear to justify his efforts. Reporting on the "State of Religion in the Presbytery of Colorado" early in 1874, the committee appointed for that task noted good accounts from the Sabbath schools, with particular commendation for the gratifying results in the remote mining camp of Fairplay. Writing to Jackson at the end of 1873 about his experiences with the Fairplay school, the pastor, Delos Finks, explained how all of the children in the town, except for those in two or three families, were attending the classes he and his wife conducted on Sunday morning. He believed that children who did not receive decent treatment at home were beginning to respond to the uplifting lessons they learned in the school. "As we hold it in a school house where there is no discipline during the week it has been hard to discipline, but now with the indispensable assistance of my dear wife we get them quite respectable."[14]

Finks had touched upon a sensitive issue in his comments about his Sabbath school. In the Fairplay public school there was no discipline, in his opinion, and it was only by attending his class on Sunday morning that the children became "quite respectable." If that was the case, not only in Fairplay but also in many other frontier communities in the Rocky Mountain West, then perhaps the operation of a Presbyterian day school could be justified. In Jackson's mission field in the 1870s, several Presbyterian ministers who fancied themselves educators thought they perceived that pressing need, and they tried to operate "academies" in their communities. The label was often applied loosely to almost any kind of elementary or high school or combination of the two, and it was also not uncommon to find church schools structured for course work at the academy level but bearing names that included words such as "institute" or "seminary." A remarkable example of such a school existed in Montana. Of it, Jackson said: it "has already [1876] greatly raised the tone of morality and refinement among the settlers of a large area of country."[15]

The school mentioned by Jackson opened in the fall of 1872 in Bozeman, Montana. The teachers were the Reverend Lyman Crittenden and his daughter Mary. Jackson had selected Crittenden in the spring of that year to fill a vacancy at the church he had organized in Corinne, Utah, in 1870. Crittenden had hoped to encounter a congenial climate in Corinne, one that would improve a condition described by a later historian of the church as "nervous prostration."[16] Although Crittenden was already in his mid fifties and troubled by ill health, Jackson had decided to offer him the Corinne assignment because of his good work with churches in and around Pittsburgh, Pennsylvania. In Corinne, Crittenden carried out his responsibilities to his congregation for about four months. Then, when his health did not improve, he decided to accept an invitation from Will Frackelton to come to Bozeman and conduct "a Christian school of high order."[17]

The Crittendens opened their school in the Good Templars Hall in October, with an enrollment of five girls and four boys. They hoped to receive sixty dollars from each pupil for a full school year of ten months. Crittenden certainly needed the money. He owed about four hundred dollars for his moving expenses from Corinne and his purchase of some furnishings for the small cabin he had rented for his family in Bozeman. When he was forced to borrow another hundred dollars for his living expenses at a bank in Bozeman, he was dismayed to find that he would have to pay 2 1/2 per cent interest per month on the loan. Still, Crittenden was convinced that he had embarked on a worthy enterprise. Writing to Jackson at the end of 1872 with an explanation of the need for his school, Crittenden offered two reasons to justify its existence. It would attract students who might otherwise have been enrolled in the Catholic academy in Helena. And, although it was true that the citizens of Bozeman intended to build a so-called college in their community, that school would be simply a graded secular school, one that Crittenden could not regard "as a handmaid to our evangelical effort as a church in the territory."[18]

Early in 1873, the Crittendens were pleased when they learned that some Eastern women involved in home mission work were interested in their school. Cornelia Martin, who headed the New Mexico, Arizona, and Colorado Missionary Association, told Jackson that if Crittenden would select some land owned by the Northern Pacific Railroad for his school, she would exert pressure on railroad officials to donate that land for his use. Mrs. Martin was sure that she could also call on her friends at a publishing house in New York to contribute all the school books required for the Crittendens' classes. When Crittenden learned of this pledge of support, he wrote to a member of Mrs. Martin's society expressing his thanks for these generous offers. Confirming his intention of providing religious as well as secular instruction for his students, he assured the ladies, "Our school is opened in the morning by reading the Bible and prayer, and closed at evening by repeating in concert a passage of Scripture which has been read from the blackboard during the day." Crittenden was delighted to receive by return mail a check for three hundred dollars toward payment of his debt.[19]

Somehow, the Crittendens' school survived its first year of operation. After the summer vacation, it reopened in September of 1873 with fifteen pupils. Much of the teaching responsibility at that point fell on the shoulders of Mary Crittenden, as her father tried to fulfill the preaching assignments at the churches that had been served by Will Frackelton before his departure from the territory earlier in the year. As a preacher, Crittenden did not subscribe to any deviations from the orthodox doctrines promulgated by his church. "Mr. Crittenden is not what would be called a popular minister," another missionary in Montana noted, "but he is devout and earnest and sound. . . . He is far more useful than he would be were he to attempt the modern 'popular style.'"[20]

Crittenden's story of a journey in the fall of 1873 to the little outlying settlements emphasized the very real need for one or more new men in the field. On that trip of 120 miles, he visited the villages of Gallatin City, Willow Creek, and Hamilton. "I found persons on this trip," he lamented, "who had not heard a sermon in two and a half years, and two who said they had not heard a sermon in ten years." Although he pledged to try to sustain the vitality at these small churches, he regretfully admitted that he could not tell them when he could return again.[21]

While her father was circuit riding, Mary Crittenden conducted classes. One visitor to the school praised her for her achievements. "Possessed as she is of all of the qualifications to teach," the reporter noted, "she adds to it a profound sense of her obligations in a moral and religious sense, and we have rarely met with a school where so good an opportunity is offered to educate in a proper manner children who will assume in a few years the responsible duties of life."[22] As the study of music at the school was undoubtedly considered part of the "proper manner" of educating young ladies, Crittenden and his daughter were surely pleased with the arrival near the end of the year of a piano secured for their use by the Ladies Home Missionary societies in New York.[23]

Encouraging reports from the Crittendens at the end of 1873 turned, much to Jackson's surprise, to notes of despair early the following year. In April, Lyman Crittenden announced that he contemplated abandonment of the school in Bozeman. The general stagnation of business had caused many families to leave the area, and he saw little hope of recovery until the Northern Pacific Railroad resumed its construction toward Montana. Meanwhile, the Bozeman church was struggling and the little churches at Virginia City, Willow Creek, Hamilton, and Gallatin City, according to Crittenden, were dead. Expecting to leave early in June, Crittenden wondered if Jackson might have a place for him to relocate to in Colorado. This was not good news, of course, and when Cornelia Martin learned of Crittenden's intention, she expressed her disappointment in a note to Jackson. "We can never get public confidence or carry on our society," she complained, "unless we can show some perseverance in our christian enterprises."[24]

Providentially, several circumstances combined at this time to bolster Crittenden's commitment to persevere in the face of adversity. First, his friends in Bozeman surprised him with a gift of $112, which he could apply to his debts. Then, William Rommel, pastor of the church in Helena, visited Bozeman, and he argued persuasively that the Crittendens remain and renew their efforts to continue their school. Finally, an opportunity arose to move the school about twenty miles to a location between Bozeman and Helena near the little town of Hamilton. Crittenden decided to go ahead and relocate when the owner of the property under consideration offered an advantageous rental arrangement for a two-story log house on a 160-acre tract of land. With these incentives, Crittenden moved his family to the new location, and in the fall of 1874 he reopened the school as the Gallatin Valley Female Seminary, with an enrollment of nine young ladies between the ages of twelve and sixteen.[25]

The change to a school for girls apparently reflected a goal cherished by Crittenden since he had begun his career as an educator in Bozeman in 1872. He told Jackson in December of that year, "The school which I have as my ideal is a 'Female School,' a Christian family school. I would desire to begin with a capability to board comfortably 10 or 12 young ladies."[26] At the end of 1874, twelve girls were enrolled at the school, six as boarding students and six as day students who came on foot from two or three miles around or rode horseback from as far away as five or ten miles. Crittenden must have been pleased when the ladies in the East who had sponsored the school in Bozeman now declared, after learning of the move to the new location, "As a barrier to the pernicious influence of Catholic teachings, the importance of this school cannot be overestimated, and we expect to continue its support."[27]

The Crittendens completed the school year in their new quarters in the spring of 1875, but in the fall Lyman Crittenden announced another change of residence to a more commodious building a few miles distant. Mary Crittenden later recalled how morality and refinement were emphasized in the daily schedule of the school:

> Breakfast at six, family worship at 6:30, where the scripture lesson was always followed by a sacred song, accompanied by the piano, . . . [then] the long busy day in the schoolroom, where we gathered at 9:00, repeated our motto text for the day, always placed upon the board in readiness to greet the first pupil to enter the room, read our short scripture lesson and committed ourselves to an All-Father's guidance for the day. The noon luncheon partaken of by day scholars and boarders together in the school room, thus giving them the noon hour for chit-chat, the family gathering at the table at 5:30, recreation hour till 7, study in the school room till 9, then the reunion in the parlor for evening worship, with its scripture, hymn, and prayer.[28]

As classes continued at the school in 1876, its work received compliments from several sources. Writing to the secretaries of the Board of Home Missions in April, William Rommel said that he believed the Crittendens were "doing more to leaven Gallatin Valley with the gospel than all of the other denominations put together." He noted, however, the precarious state of Lyman Crittenden's financial situation. "The pitiful sum of $600 (about $300 in the states) was received by him last year," Rommel pointed out, "about enough for one man to starve to death on in genteel style."[29] Jackson traveled to Montana in the summer of 1876, and he included in his itinerary a visit to the Crittendens' school. When he returned, he announced that the school, though unpretentious in its exterior, was exerting an influence that many more wealthy schools could well envy. Jackson's newspaper also carried two congratulatory reports about the school. In the spring, the students gave a concert and exhibition attended by about two hundred people, who were impressed by the excellent discipline of the performers. And at the spring meeting of the Presbytery of Montana, the delegates resolved "that the Presbytery hears with pleasure of the growing prosperity of the Gallatin Valley Female Seminary [where] parents may safely intrust their children, confident that they will be faithfully instructed."[30]

The school's growing prosperity was evident in 1877. In the fall of that year Mary told members of the Ladies Board of Missions in New York that, in the previous three years, forty girls between the ages of seven and twenty had attended the school. More than two-thirds of that number were over twelve years of age, and most of them had remained at least one full school year. She hoped that the ladies would continue their support so that she would not have to abandon the work she had learned to love. Unfortunately, abandonment of the enterprise did occur in 1878. One of Jackson's correspondents in Montana told him that the school would open again in October. But Mary Crittenden had married in June, and her father was still giving much of his time to preaching. Too busy to keep the school alive, the Crittendens permitted the Gallatin Valley Female Seminary to become a memory, albeit a valued one for those who had been involved in its brief existence.[31]

While Mary Crittenden was conducting her school near Bozeman, Sheldon Jackson became involved directly in the first Presbyterian educational enterprise attempted in Colorado. After the first meeting of the Presbytery of Colorado in February of 1870, Jackson reported action taken for the creation of a Presbyterian academy. The action mentioned was apparently an announcement of intent only, as it was not until 1874 that actual planning began for a denominational school in the agricultural community of Evans, about fifty miles north of Denver. Evans, named for former territorial governor John Evans, was established in 1869 as the terminus, at that time, of the Denver and Pacific Railroad, which had been created to connect Denver with the Union Pacific line in Cheyenne. In 1871 continued growth for the fledgling community seemed assured when several hundred recruits for the St. Louis—Western Colony, a communal society, arrived to begin farming in the area. Confident that a Presbyterian church would secure a favorable reception from such an industrious and pious clientele, Jackson had organized a church with six members in Evans on May 14.[32]

The pastor of the Evans church, John F. Stewart, and Jackson made a critical decision early in 1874. They agreed to proceed with plans not for an academy, but for a full-fledged collegiate undertaking to be developed as a Christian school with ties to the Presbyterian Church. Jackson's decision to go along with the selection of Evans as the location for the school was influenced by a number of factors. Probably foremost in his considerations was an offer of forty acres in the center of town to serve as the campus for the institution. Stewart and the congregation of the Presbyterian church in Evans would also be available to provide the appropriate Christian influence for students. Finally, Jackson may have hoped that John Evans, who was known as a wealthy philanthropist with interest in higher education, would provide an endowment for the school, which would honor him by bearing his name.[33]

One might have asked if a Presbyterian school such as envisioned by Jackson and Stewart was really needed in Colorado when other Protestant denominations were moving ahead, at the same time, with plans to offer Christian educations at church schools in Colorado. For example, an Episcopalian school for young men had operated in Golden for several years, and its destruction by fire in 1874 was followed at once by an announcement that the school would soon reopen in Denver. And at a meeting in Denver in January, Congregationalists in Colorado had voted to establish a college under their auspices in Colorado Springs. Surely Presbyterian boys and girls could receive acceptable academic training at these locations. Jackson would not have seen it that way. Just as he insisted on organizing churches for Presbyterians in communities where other Protestant churches already existed, so his awareness of the other church schools in Colorado would only have spurred him on to provide an institution of comparable quality for young Presbyterians.[34]

The first revelation of Jackson's intentions appeared in a brief notice in the *Rocky Mountain Presbyterian* of July 1, 1874, which announced arrangements for the establishment of a Presbyterian college in Colorado and the opening of its "preparatory department" in the fall. On July 11 the county clerk of Weld County recorded articles of incorporation for the school, designated as Evans University. The new institution was now underway— on paper. Its objective, as stated quite simply in the articles of incorporation, was to educate young men and women in literature, science, and the arts. To provide the general public, however, with a more comprehensive justification for the university, one writer in Jackson's newspaper explained how the youth of Colorado could not depend on eastern colleges for their training because the expense incurred was prohibitive. Of course, the school would also welcome students from the East who "will be able to grow stronger in body, while prosecuting their studies in the pure invigorating climate of Colorado." The success of the university was ensured because "not less than four or five branches of the Presbyterian family are taking hold of this enterprise, resolved that it shall be vigorously prosecuted." Looking forward to the proposed opening day on September 28, this confident reporter believed that there would be "more than one hundred students gathered around its professors as soon as they are established and ready for work."[35]

Included with John Evans and Sheldon Jackson in the list of twenty-five designated trustees in the articles of incorporation were the names of several of the Presbyterian missionaries serving churches in Colorado. After preparing and filing the articles, Jackson then sought, in a rather extraordinary after-the-fact fashion, to obtain the acquiescence of those gentlemen to serve in that capacity. Responding to Jackson's request, the pastor at the Pueblo, Colorado, church accepted the challenge, but he asked, "Have you made a wise location, and have you made a good prospect of plenty cash?"[36] The minister serving at the Colorado Springs church asked for more information before consenting to act as trustee. He wondered if a college could succeed in Colorado if it had to depend on nebulous eastern aid. He also insisted that it was folly to talk of inducing students to leave eastern institutions to come to Colorado to study because if they could not carry on their studies at home they were probably too broken down to carry them on anywhere.[37]

Another trustee wondered if the school should be advertised as a university or college, with the thought that the latter more modest designation might be appropriate for the early stages of its growth. John Stewart, pastor of the Evans Presbyterian Church, did not agree. Charged with coordinating arrangements for opening the school in September, he strongly endorsed the term university to convey an impression of the highest level of scholastic endeavor. To further enhance the school's reputation as a top-quality educational institution, Stewart announced his intention of asking E. M. Rollo, principal of Maple Grove Academy of Stephentown, New York, and a man highly regarded by eastern educators, to head Evans University. Rollo tentatively accepted the offer and then complained to Jackson that he was completely in the dark on matters such as the nature of the school and the number of teachers. When he finally received more information from Stewart regarding his job, Rollo had to admit, "It is a little more crude than even the utmost stretch of fancy could anticipate. The real state of things is so much in contrast with the advertising of the school, that it excited more than a smile."[38]

Unfortunately, Evans University was not destined to achieve the great role in higher education anticipated by Jackson and those who had joined him in calling for its establishment. In one of Stewart's letters to Jackson, the pastor of the Evans church asked, "Have you ever felt Governor Evans' pulse on the subject of Evans University? The people in Greeley have it that he intends giving $50,000 to our University."[39] When the planners for the university finally got around to feeling Evans's pulse, they found that their predictions of his support were premature and, in fact, misconstrued. Evans revealed his intentions in an address to the Synod of Colorado meeting in Denver on September 24, when he called for support from all churches in Colorado for a Union University to be located in Denver.[40] The doors of Evans University did not open as planned on September 28. There was no further mention of its existence in the *Rocky Mountain Presbyterian*, and one can only conclude that the problems in financing and staffing the proposed institution encountered in the fall of 1874 had overwhelmed the best of intentions.

While Jackson and his missionaries were trying to provide appropriate opportunities for educating young people in the Rocky Mountain West, they were not ignoring the needs of the adult members of their communities. Lecture series, discussion groups, and reading rooms were all sponsored by the local Presbyterian churches. The pastor of the church in Georgetown, Colorado, in 1875 provided a typical example. He told Jackson of a course of lectures he was delivering on scriptural biographies. Encouraged by large turnouts for these presentations, he proposed to follow this sequence of commentaries with another on eminent women of the Bible. "I aim to make the lectures practical," he explained, "and I understand miners talk them over and acknowledge that the arrow comes home."[41] At Prescott, Arizona, in 1877, the pastor of the Presbyterian church announced creation of a literary society numbering forty members that met once a week for debates and recitations, while at the church in Del Norte, Colorado, early in 1876, Alex Darley reported growing interest in his "literary sociables."[42]

Alex Darley also ranked at the top of the list of missionaries who tried to supply wholesome reading material to isolated western communities. In the October 1875 edition of the *Rocky Mountain Presbyterian* there appeared a request from Darley for newspapers, magazines, and books for distribution among the miners in the nearby mountains. The response exceeded his expectations. He received over twenty boxes and barrels of reading materials, more than enough for his needs. He then challenged the citizens of Del Norte to open a public library, to be stocked from the remaining reading materials, with the assurance that he could provide a continuing supply from donors in the future. The town fathers accepted his proposal, and the San Juan Library Association opened its reading room in a public building in Del Norte on January 1, 1876. According to Darley, a "gentlemanly librarian" reported from thirty to one hundred readers in attendance daily. Acknowledging the obvious success, Darley described his experiment as a great blessing to Del Norte and the surrounding area and said that it had clearly proved itself "the means of the depletion of the saloon crowds."[43]

The leaders of the congregations in Jackson's mission field thus tried to respond to the Presbyterian minister who in 1874 had been concerned about the moral, educational, and religious future of this "backbone of the continent." None of the missionaries would have questioned the basic premise that those who moved to the Rocky Mountain West from the East must continue to have the opportunity to be properly educated and well informed. But what of the "exceptional populations"? That term was used in the 1870s by Presbyterians involved in home mission work to refer to those outside the Presbyterian fold. "Distributed in sections throughout the whole of this vast region," one of Jackson's friends declaimed, "there were unnumbered hosts of deluded Mormons, semi-Pagan Mexicans, sun-worshipping Pueblos, deeply degraded Eskimos, demon-worshipping Alaskans, with tens of thousands of Indians in reservations or roving wild over the plains and mountains."[44]

Of course Eskimos and Alaskans were not included in Jackson's superintendency when he moved to Colorado in 1870, but he soon realized that the benefits of a proper education were no less necessary for those who dwelled outside the mainstream of American society. The first such nonconformists targeted by Jackson were the "deluded Mormons" who, according to Jackson's friend, were subjugated by "one of the most cunningly devised systems of religious despotism which has ever been invented by the mind of man."[45]

11. Salt Lake City, view from Arsenal Hill in the 1870s, where Jackson orga-
nized the first Presbyterian church in this Mormon community in 1871. (Cour-
tesy, Utah State Historical Society, Salt Lake City)

Above:

12. *Corrine, Utah, in 1870 where one dejected observer noted: "In many places the name of Christ is never spoken, except with blasphemous lips." (Courtesy, Utah State Historical Society, Salt Lake City)*

Opposite above:

13. *San Francisco Street in Santa Fe (c. 1865) looking east toward the Catholic Church. (Courtesy, Museum of New Mexico, U.S. Army Signal Corps Collection, Negative No. 11330)*

Opposite below:

14. *Denver, Colorado, in the 1870s. On Jackson's first visit in 1870, he found that the "tidal wave of wickedness, the cesspools of iniquity, and the desperadoes that came in with the surging mass of gold-seekers have passed on. . . ." (Courtesy, Colorado Historical Society, Denver)*

Opposite above:

15. Black Hawk, Colorado. A visitor to Colorado in 1866 found Black Hawk a very crude settlement "where the sole pleasant object is the Presbyterian church, white, tasteful, and charmingly placed . . . above the chimneys and mills in the uniting ravines." (Anonymous, Mines and Mining Men of Colorado, *1893)*

Opposite below:

16. Cheyenne, Wyoming, in 1868. Jackson described it as "The Magic City of the Plains" in the following year. (Courtesy, Wyoming State Museum, Cheyenne)

Above:

17. Main street of Helena, Montana, in the early 1870s. In 1872, "The arrival of three Presbyterian ministers brought great joy to many loyal hearts. . . ." (Courtesy, Montana Historical Society, Helena)

18. Sheldon Jackson Memorial Chapel still stands in Fairplay, Colorado. When Delos Finks built this church in 1874, he selected a design that could well have been used for a church adjacent to the village green in any small New England community. (Author's collection)

*19. Krebs Memorial Church, Cheyenne, Wyoming. Erected in 1870 from compo-
nents prefabricated by a building contractor in Chicago. (Courtesy, Presbyterian
Historical Society, Philadelphia)*

Above;
20. First Presbyterian Church in Phoenix, Arizona, 1879. One reporter described this rather bizarre structure as "a booth covered with bushes. . . . It is named the 'Tabernacle.'" (Courtesy, Arizona Historical Society, Tucson)

Opposite:
21. Prospect Hill Monument, Sioux City, Iowa. Here Sheldon Jackson and his two companions vowed to "win the West for Christ" on April 29, 1869. (Author's collection)

THE PRESBYTERY OF

Prospect Hill

presents

"The Story of Prospect Hill"

22. *An appeal by Jackson in his newspaper for contributions from Sabbath schools to support home missionaries. (Rocky Mountain Presbyterian, February 1881)*

8 | Attacking a Formidable Fortress

*Mormonism is one of the most heathenish and anti-Christ-like
frauds on the face of the earth. It destroys the majesty of the
Godhead, robs Christ of his glory, substitutes wild fancies and
wilder dreams for the infallible word of God, introduces misery into
the family, and subverts the whole system of our Government.*

—The Rev. George W. Gallagher, Presbyterian Church,
 Ogden, Utah, November 1, 1878

When Sheldon Jackson decided to organize the first Presbyterian church in Utah at Corinne in 1870, his impressions of the Mormons
might have been derived, in part, from the report of a prominent leader of
his church who had visited Salt Lake City in 1869. Jackson had carefully
preserved the comments of the Reverend Frank Ellinwood, secretary of
the Board of Foreign Missions, who had written at length about his revealing experience. Looking back at the origins of the Mormon Church,
Ellinwood made no attempt to disguise his contempt for the founder, Joseph
Smith, and the despicable practice of polygamy. He described Smith as a
"blasphemous beast" who was "an imposter of the lowest order—ignorant,
loaferly [*sic*], drunken, licentious." Smith had not announced his revelation
on polygamy until years after the formation of his church, when "his criminal
relations with the wives and daughters of his own people had become so
notorious, that the authoritative annunciation of polygamy was his only
resource." Regarding the present status of polygamy in Utah, Ellinwood
had tried to ascertain the real views of Mormon women on this controversial matter. That turned out to be a difficult task, because the fearful women
would always try to defend polygamy in conversation with a Gentile, "yet
it weighs like a horrid incubus on their spirits. They seem to accept it only
as part of woman's disability, if not her curse."[1]

Naturally, Ellinwood deplored the dictatorial powers reputedly enjoyed
by Brigham Young. He was particularly amazed how the Mormon leader
could receive and manage all church funds without ever making any kind
of public report on receipts and disbursements. Still, the people apparently had the utmost faith in his proper administration of those accounts,
"and it must be admitted that the rare financial ability of Brigham Young

has done well for the church as well as for himself." When he had an opportunity to meet Young, Ellinwood perceived him as affable and dignified
with no outward indications in his look or manner of coarseness or sensu-
ality. Following this meeting, Ellinwood reluctantly concluded, "One thing
is certain: his people from the highest to the lowest have the most implicit
confidence in the sincerity of his belief, the honesty of his administration,
and the divinely directed wisdom of his counsels."[2]

When Ellinwood completed his observations on the Mormon dilemma,
he asked the ultimate question: what shall be done with Utah? Regarding
polygamy, Congress had already passed laws making the evil practice a
crime, but how could the crime be punished when the people of an entire
territory were the guilty parties? He had seen no symptoms of decay in
Mormonism, contrary to the views of some who were reluctant to honestly
face up to unwelcome facts. Actually, the ranks of the followers of Brigham
Young were continually augmented by boys and girls who were initiated
into the secret societies of the church "with strange mystic ceremony and with
most terrible vows and oaths." Ellinwood finally closed his commentary on
these issues with the fatalistic prediction, "Only He who in His own strong
way destroyed African slavery, can solve for us this next vexed question."[3]

After reading this disquieting analysis, Jackson may have perceived himself as the instrument of the Almighty who would take the first step, at
least, toward finding the answer for the "vexed question." And perhaps the
efforts of Edward Bayliss, the man selected to head the church in Corinne
in 1870, would be the leaven that would transform Mormon society. Certainly Bayliss began his work in Corinne with commendable zeal. He regarded as a high priority the creation of a Sabbath school to bring the
Gospel message to the children in the community. On the Sunday following his arrival in the town he organized a Union Sabbath school to accept,
for the time being, enrollment of children from any Protestant family in
Corinne. In a few weeks there were fifty-one scholars on the membership
roll, served by eight teachers, a secretary, and a superintendent. Announcing this gratifying result, Bayliss asked Jackson to send as soon as possible
some suitable books and tracts for the children's reading program on Sunday mornings.[4]

Bayliss also perceived an urgent need for a Presbyterian academy in
Corinne. He did acknowledge the presence of two small private schools in
Corinne, but he was particularly eager to start a Presbyterian school, which
he hoped could exert a considerable influence outside the classroom. Assuming that parents who would send their children to his school already
regarded the Presbyterian denomination with favor, then it must follow,
he told Jackson, that he could "readily at very little cost bind them to our

interests."[5] Plunging ahead boldly with his plan, at a meeting in Corinne in December of 1870 Bayliss announced his intention to call his projected school the Utah Presbyterian College. He would be president of the institution, and Jackson would serve as president of the board of directors. Bayliss called upon Sunday school children throughout the Presbyterian Church for support. Proclaiming his need for the staggering sum of twenty-five thousand dollars with which to erect his school building, he believed that if each child would contribute a dime the enterprise would prove a success. Since the dimes collected from this appeal would certainly not raise twenty-five thousand dollars, Bayliss told Jackson in December that he was preparing a lecture on "Life in Utah, Or Mormonism As It Was And As It Is." If all went as planned, he would present this exposé in the East early in 1871 to raise additional funds for his proposed college.[6]

At the end of January of 1871, Bayliss's plans received a setback. Speaking for the Board of Home Missions in New York, Henry Kendall emphatically told Bayliss to stick to his preaching in Corinne and abandon his nebulous college scheme. Drawing from first-hand knowledge of the climate in the East for fund-raising, Kendall believed that Bayliss's proposed lecture tour would not raise enough money even to pay his traveling expenses. Therefore, he should stay home and tend to the immediate needs of his little church, which would certainly die if he left Corinne for any length of time. Despite this admonition, Bayliss decided to go ahead and conduct his fund-raising expedition in the East. At the same time, he solicited funds in several publications of the Presbyterian Church. In one of those pleas for financial aid, he assured his readers, "Education and the Gospel go hand in hand; and it is our desire and aim to bring these powerful ameliorations to bear upon the ignorance, superstition, and fanaticism of the poor dupes of Brigham Young and his unscrupulous assistants."[7]

Bayliss did not receive the monetary support he had anticipated for his college. Influenced, perhaps, by this setback, he scaled down his plans. In a brochure prepared for his revised project, he now referred to the Rocky Mountain Female Academy, which would open in Corinne on September 4, 1871. He would be superintendent of this enterprise, and Miss Mary E. Heffleman, formerly head of the Young Ladies Athenaeum in Jacksonville, Illinois, would be the principal. Prospects for the endeavor were shattered, however, when Bayliss abruptly resigned his pastorate effective October 8, 1871. He cited as his reason his abandonment by the members of the home mission board, who had not paid him anything on his salary for the last nine months.[8]

A few years after Bayliss's departure, a missionary in a small town in central Utah had greater success in starting a Presbyterian academy. When Duncan McMillan arrived in the little town of Mt. Pleasant in March of

1875, he opened a school and started to preach to Mormons allegedly disenchanted with their church and its doctrines. McMillan apparently found some evidence of disaffection among the residents of Mt. Pleasant, and he described one of his experiences with an apostate Mormon in a touching story that he related to Jackson. "An old Methodist man who has been a Mormon for twenty-five years," McMillan noted, "came to me at the close of service last Sabbath with tears in his eyes and said: 'Your sermon came very near getting me, but when you sang old Coronation at the close that fetched me. I couldn't stand it no longer.'"[9]

McMillan opened his school in Mt. Pleasant at the end of April of 1875, and its enrollment continued to grow until an incident occurred on July 16 that threatened to terminate the enterprise abruptly. On that fateful day, Brigham Young and several apostles of the Mormon Church visited Mt. Pleasant to point out to leaders of the community the error of their ways in accepting a Presbyterian missionary as a teacher for their children. As McMillan recalled Young's remarks, the Mormon leader declared, "Keep your children away from that school. If God wants them to know grammar and arithmetic he can inspire them with that knowledge as well as with spiritual truth." Then, according to McMillan, who attended the meeting, Young "turned to me and denounced me as an imp of perdition, a minion of Satan, and a damned Presbyterian devil."[10] When Jackson later commented on the occasion in a Presbyterian publication, he related language allegedly used by Young in his attack on McMillan that portrayed the innocent young missionary as a "libertine" and a "whoremaster."[11]

Of course Jackson's extraordinary remarks were deliberately designed to portray the Mormon Church as not hesitating to use the basest tactics to destroy the reputations of good men who were fighting the good fight against overwhelming odds on an isolated battleground. Knowing that he could count on at least one audience that would be sympathetic, Jackson directed "An Appeal to Christian Women" in the April 1875 issue of the *Rocky Mountain Presbyterian*. In his comments, he asked for help "for your sisters in the harems of your own country. . . . Can you turn a deaf ear to the low wail of distress that comes from across the Rocky Mountains?" Referring then to the new mission school at Mt. Pleasant, he included in his article a letter from McMillan that he admitted had not been intended for publication. In it, in addition to calling for monetary support, McMillan had sought to emphasize the magnitude of his problem by describing the "poor, ignorant, deluded, degraded, priest-ridden serfs" who composed the population of Mt. Pleasant. As he described the situation, "The men stand about their customary loafing places with their hands up to their elbows in their pants pockets, their old hats on the backs of their heads, and their mouths open, utterly incapable of comprehending an intelligent thought; the women are literally servants of servants, and the children are legion."[12] Surprised by Jackson's unauthorized action, McMillan wrote to his superintendent, "Your April appeal might have done great harm here, but I carefully concealed the papers." He did assure Jackson, however, of his gratification in knowing that his comments would be copied extensively in eastern publications, as he had intended in the first place.[13]

To supplement his written appeals for financial aid, McMillan decided late in 1875 to make a trip, at his own expense, to carry his message directly to churches in the East. When his Mormon neighbors in Mt. Pleasant learned of his attacks on their religion in his addresses to eastern audiences, one of those offended by his remarks thought he knew the reason for the disparaging statements. That gentleman, who was one of the trustees for the public school in Mt. Pleasant, recalled how McMillan had approached him demanding a portion of the small fund allotted by the Utah legislature to the public school in order to subsidize his Presbyterian school. When the request was denied McMillan became very angry, according to this official, and during his eastern journey he spitefully circulated lies about the Mormon people, including one story of how he was obliged, while preaching in Utah, to hold the Bible in one hand and a pistol in the other to protect himself from attacks by Mormon assassins.[14]

While McMillan labored to raise funds for his school in Mt. Pleasant, which was soon designated the Wasatch Academy, he also developed the grand strategy of the Presbyterian Church for education in Utah. His plan, formulated (according to tradition) in 1875, included the establishment of academies in each of the important valleys in Utah, these to be surrounded by a group of primary mission schools, with the head of the system to be a collegiate institute that had opened in Salt Lake City soon after McMillan's arrival in Utah.[15] Josiah Welch, pastor of the Presbyterian church in Salt Lake City, had conveyed the news of the latter event to Jackson with the enthusiastic announcement, "Prof. Coyner and family have arrived, I tell you we have a prize in them. I predict that he will sweep everything before him."[16]

John Coyner, formerly superintendent of public schools in Rushville, Illinois, had been persuaded by Welch to give up a teaching job among the Nez Perce Indians in northern Idaho to come to Salt Lake City and start a school that they decided to name the Salt Lake Collegiate Institute. Coyner recalled that when he arrived, in April, a stranger had stopped him in the street. After ascertaining that Coyner did indeed plan to open a school, this gentleman pessimistically remarked, "One of three things is true. You have a fortune to sink, you have wealthy friends to back

you, or you came here to starve." Coyner remembered that he denied all of
the above, but he did believe that the remarks were not, under the circumstances, very inspiring.[17]

Coyner's school opened on April 12 in the basement of the Presbyterian
church. Twenty-seven pupils had enrolled, ranging from little children in
the A, B, C classes to older students taking course work in Latin, Greek,
and higher mathematics. Coyner's wife taught the primary grades, his
daughter taught the intermediate, and he taught advanced studies. Josiah
Welch served as president of a board of trustees composed of twenty-five
ministers and laymen of the church including Sheldon Jackson. Parents of
the students received assurances that all of the teachers (that is, the Coyner
family) had large experience in the graded school system of the East. Children enrolled from outside Salt Lake City could be placed under the special care of the principal, who would guard the habits and associations of
the young people as though they were members of his own household.[18]
Coyner also encouraged all students to join an "Abstainers League" by
making this promise:

> I pledge myself upon the honor of a true American citizen to en-
> deavor honestly, while connected with the Salt Lake Collegiate In-
> stitute, to abstain (1) from all intoxicating drinks as a beverage, (2)
> from the use of tobacco, (3) from the use of cards in the sense of
> gambling, (4) from the use of profane language, and will endeavor by
> all proper means to influence others to do the same.[19]

The results of the work at the institute during the first months of its operation showed promise. Writing for Jackson's newspaper in September,
Coyner boasted that the school had already "taken a front rank as a school
prominent in wholesome discipline and thorough instruction." Calling on
friends in the East, he hoped that many good Presbyterians would provide
scholarships of thirty dollars each, which would cover the cost of tuition
and books for a pupil for one year.[20] At the close of the first full school year
in June of 1876 Coyner reported an enrollment of 142 pupils, and he had
hopes that some of the bright young men who were exhibiting much religious interest in the weekly prayer meetings would someday become ministers. Coyner admitted that he did not always know where the money
would come from to meet the monthly bills, but somehow it came, and he
believed, quite sincerely, that "He who fed Elijah by means of the ravens
had something to do with it."[21]

At the end of 1876, Coyner told Jackson that his school was full, but
financial difficulties persisted because many of the students were "charity
scholars." Another problem facing Coyner was inadequate space for the

school. The church basement could no longer accommodate the number of pupils who wished to enroll. In a bold move, Coyner addressed this issue by starting construction of a new school building on a lot adjacent to the church. He had received pledges from businessmen in Salt Lake City and believed that the cost of the structure would be covered, but he was still faced with the challenge of finding one thousand dollars with which to furnish the building. Anticipating a large number of students when the building opened in September of 1877, Coyner told Jackson he would also have to hire three more teachers. If he could not secure these additions to his staff, he would be compelled to dismiss all charity pupils not on scholarships and arbitrarily reduce the enrollment to a number that he and his wife could teach. "I see my way clear in everything," he told Jackson, "except the salary of teachers. I do not see how I can support the teachers that I must have next year unless three of my teachers are commenced at $300 each, with this aid I can do a grand work."[22]

Help was on the way. While Coyner was writing this report in May of 1877 to Jackson, the General Assembly meeting in Chicago was taking action that would alter the scope of home mission work among the "exceptional populations" in the West. The members of the Presbytery of Utah could take credit, in part, for this breakthrough. At their meeting on February 8, 1877, those in attendance prepared an overture to the General Assembly. To achieve further progress in the growth of missions among the Mormons, Mexicans, and Indians, it was imperative, they asserted, that lady teachers and Bible readers be secured and placed in the Western fields. The General Assembly should therefore authorize the Board of Home Missions to commission these new employees "upon the proper request and recommendation of the Presbytery within whose bounds such work is required when the funds specially designated for such a purpose shall justify."[23]

This overture, along with a similar proposal from the Presbytery of Colorado and the adroit prodding of Sheldon Jackson and Henry Kendall, convinced the delegates at the General Assembly meeting to give their blessing, and John Coyner soon benefited from their action. He secured three lady teachers, hired by the mission board at salaries of three hundred dollars per year, for his Salt Lake Collegiate Institute, and his school continued to show commendable results. The school year closed on June 10, 1877, with an enrollment of 165 students, and the new school building was dedicated on August 22. A catalogue from the institution referred to the commitment of its leaders to develop a permanent scientific and classical school, based on the best school systems in the East, which would soon take its place among the colleges of the country. "Although the work is rapidly enlarging and requiring increased expenses," the catalogue stated, "they [school administrators] have faith in Divine Providence, that, as the work is His, He will provide all the needed means."[24]

Indeed, the good work was rapidly enlarging throughout Utah. In addition to the successes recorded with schools initiated by John Coyner in Salt Lake City and Duncan McMillan in Mt. Pleasant, other schools and churches sprang up throughout the territory.[25] One of the more interesting undertakings occurred at Ogden, a town located about thirty miles north of Salt Lake City, which grew rapidly when it became the junction point for the Central Pacific and Union Pacific in 1869. Writing to Jackson in the spring of 1876, a friend who had just concluded a business trip to the community described Ogden as "the most promising fruit in Utah, and if our church will, all she will have to do will be to 'go up and possess the land.'" Several of the residents would be eager to support a Presbyterian church, according to this reporter, if an acceptable man were sent. "They do not want a scrub," he noted, "but an earnest thorough worker."[26]

George Gallagher, who received the posting to Ogden early in 1878, was undoubtedly a "scrub." As a young graduate of Princeton, he accepted the challenge with some misgivings. He had heard that the Mormons in Ogden were immoral, intemperate, and opposed to religion in general. And, unfortunately, the non-Mormons residing there had been described to him as not much better. Still, he was ready to do his best in his new assignment. "The hard work and the immoral set I am going among do not appall me," he assured Jackson. "If God be for us, who can be against us?" With firm resolution, he then proclaimed, "I go to Utah with the intentions of living and dying there if need be . . . , and I hope I shall be able to do something towards rooting out Mormonism and towards introducing the Gospel."[27]

Gallagher and his wife reached Ogden on June 12, 1878. On the first Sunday after their arrival they started a Sabbath school that had attained an enrollment of thirty students when Gallagher reported to Jackson a month later. The young missionary's Sunday-evening worship services were also well attended, although the congregation must have been annoyed by the fumes of tobacco, beer, and cooking emanating from an oyster saloon next door. Gallagher went ahead and contracted for an organ to accompany the singing at these gatherings. He felt sure that he could obtain from collections the one hundred dollars, along with interest at 2 percent per month, on or before the twelve-month period stipulated in his purchase agreement. He did admit that he was presently financially embarrassed, and the living quarters occupied by the young couple must have been rather crude. "My wife and myself have had some good laughs over the extent of our furniture," he told Jackson, "however we are willing to work away and hope for better things bye and by."[28]

In his letter to Jackson, Gallagher also noted, "The Princeton ladies have promised to fit up the school and we have no misgivings on that score."[29] He did not reveal the identity of the "Princeton ladies," but presumably they were women whose support he had secured while completing his studies at Princeton Seminary. The school mentioned in his comment was the Ogden Educational Institute. Gallagher had a prospectus printed for this proposed institution in the summer of 1878. In that publication, it was announced that the school was scheduled to open on September 16 in a rented hall in Ogden. The principal and vice-principal were the Rev. G. W. Gallagher and Mrs. G. W. Gallagher, respectively. The school would be divided into primary, intermediate, grammar, and academic departments. Tuition charges varied from one dollar per month for the primary department to two dollars per month for the academic department. Piano lessons of forty minutes' duration could be obtained for a payment of fifty cents. A broad array of course offerings ranged from "First Reader" and "Printing on Slates" in the primary department to "Natural Philosophy" and the "Constitution of the U.S." in the academic department. Gallagher did not comment on events associated with the school in subsequent correspondence with Jackson, but apparently the doors opened as scheduled. An article in the *Rocky Mountain Presbyterian* in November of 1878 mentioned a day school operated by Gallagher in Ogden with twenty students in a second-story hall: "very inconvenient, and rented at $200 per annum, mostly paid for by the missionary."[30]

George Gallagher may have been a "scrub" when he arrived in Ogden, but he soon displayed the qualities of "an earnest and thorough worker." While the Ogden venture and other new missionary enterprises in Utah showed promise late in the 1870s, churches organized by Jackson earlier in the decade had experienced varying degrees of success and, in some cases, the loss of the resident pastor. Of course the church in Salt Lake City received much attention and support. After the tragic death of Josiah Welch early in 1877, Robert McNiece, a graduate of Princeton Seminary, arrived in the territorial capital in June of that year to take charge of the church. Judging from a later recollection of the young man as "a born warrior, whose heroes in the church militant are Paul, Luther and Knox," the congregation in Salt Lake City could surely count on vigorous leadership in the days ahead.[31]

Less pleasing was the news from the church in the mining camp of Alta, located about twenty miles southeast of Salt Lake City. In the summer of 1873 Jackson had organized a church in the town and entrusted its future to James Schell, who had recently graduated from the Union Theological Seminary in New York City. At first, Schell's reports to Jackson were brimming with enthusiasm. He announced completion of a modest church building on October 5. The facility included a basement reading room that was attracting the interest of the miners. "We feel proud of it [the church]," Schell boasted, "and think it might compare favorably for beauty and situation with the famous temple of Solomon."[32] Early in 1874, Schell was delighted when some of the citizens in Alta raised two hundred dollars to purchase a fine Mason and Hamlin cabinet organ to accompany the singing on the Sabbath. Then, in the fall of 1874, Schell resigned abruptly, without disclosing his reasons for abandoning his post. In the ensuing months, Presbyterian missionaries from other churches in the vicinity occasionally preached at Alta until the summer of 1878, when a disastrous fire destroyed most of the buildings in the town, including the little Presbyterian house of worship. Writing later about that calamity, one of Jackson's colleagues provided an apt assessment of the unfortunate events. "Like most of the mining camps," he recalled, "its day was brief, and at length the little church which had stood for all that was good and true amid abounding evil, died, like the town in which it was located, for lack of population."[33]

Lack of population was one of the factors contributing to the decline of another of the churches organized by Jackson early in the 1870s. After Edward Bayliss left Corinne in the fall of 1871, the congregation there was without a leader until the summer of 1874, when Samuel L. Gillespie, with his wife and child, arrived to take charge of the church. Gillespie, a Civil War veteran and a graduate of Princeton Seminary, had recently returned from an assignment at a mission station in West Africa. The Gillespies were pleased with their warm welcome from the Presbyterians in Corinne, and for several years Samuel was content with serving this church and preaching periodically in neighboring communities.

One of his outreach assignments was at Brigham City, an agricultural center located only a few miles from Corinne. The two towns were very different indeed. Corinne still retained a reputation as a predominantly Gentile community, but Brigham City was known as a stronghold of Mormonism. Gillespie may have been captivated with the greater challenge to his ministry offered in the latter town, because his concerns turned more and more to planting the standard of Presbyterianism in the hostile environment at Brigham City.[34]

Like many of the Presbyterian missionaries in Utah, Gillespie believed that opening a school in a Mormon settlement was the key to gaining a foothold there. In September of 1877 he told Jackson that the liberal element in Brigham City was desirous of his beginning a school there at once. Taking the initiative, he and two of his friends gave their personal notes for the down payment on a building in Brigham City that could be used for classes during the week and worship services on the Sabbath. Then, noting how the decline of Corinne had eroded the base of his financial support, Gillespie decided to move his residence to Brigham City. Sadly, Corinne had never fulfilled the expectations of its founders. When the managers of the Union Pacific Railroad decided to make nearby Ogden the division point for its operations in that part of Utah, the population of Corinne noticeably diminished. Now the few remaining Presbyterians in the moribund community were obliged to mourn the loss of their resident pastor.[35]

Duncan McMillan, meanwhile, had enlarged the scope of his activities in Utah. He became actively involved in finding teachers for schools in Utah, after the General Assembly in 1877 authorized the Board of Home Missions to commission applicants. Reporting in his newspaper on McMillan's work in Utah, Jackson credited the zealous missionary with securing "a widely extended influence through a large section of the Territory."[36] McMillan had, in fact, expanded his role beyond his position with the church and school he had established in Mt. Pleasant. Leaving his school in the capable hands of a lady teacher whom he had recruited from the community, he traveled extensively, preaching and assisting in the organization of new churches and schools in promising locations throughout Utah. Unfortunately, for a brief period of time in 1878 his assumption of this supervisory role caused friction with the Board of Home Missions, and Jackson found himself caught in the middle of an unpleasant situation.

A letter from Henry Kendall to Jackson in March of 1878 revealed the essence of the problem from the board's point of view. "How did you find D. J. McMillan?" Kendall asked. "Is he sick, or mad, or what is the matter? The women and the men [new teachers] are getting out of all manner of patience with him. He takes no notice of any of them, does not even account for moneys received." And, later in the year, Kendall noted that the work seemed to be going well in Utah, "except McMillan has 50 applicants and can't make up his mind which three to choose for his teachers."[37] While Kendall fretted about McMillan's apparent disregard for the principles of sound administration, the harassed missionary complained to Jackson about the board's refusal to provide adequate financial support for his endeavors. He told Jackson that the secretaries of the board seemed to have a low estimate of his services. "I am a mere foundling, as they seem to think," he lamented, "unworthy of the bread I eat." Continuing, he addressed the specific issue of his wages. "My salary is small, barely sufficient," he observed, "yet the Board has never paid or offered to pay one dollar of my travelling expenses. . . . I am today bankrupt, disgraced before the eyes of the Church."[38]

Thankfully, this storm soon subsided. McMillan presumably found ways to make ends meet, and Henry Kendall spoke no more of his inadequacies. Jackson's interests throughout this controversy lay in continuing to enhance the image of McMillan as a heroic figure combating the forces of evil on the battleground in Utah. The tales of derring-do published by Jackson to create this impression were often flamboyant, to say the least. One of the more blatant articles on the subject related a story about McMillan thwarting the intentions of a would-be Mormon assassin.[39] A spokesman for the Mormon Church felt obliged to offer an angry rejoinder. Writing in the *Deseret News*, a Mormon newspaper published in Salt Lake City, the respondent spoke of "A Sample Presbyterian Bait":

> That our readers may know what kind of bait the Presbyterian preachers, now on a money gathering tour in the East, use to catch silver and gold scaled gudgeons [small fish], we clip the annexed paragraph from an exchange. It was solemnly told for truth by Gallagher of Ogden, and is endorsed by Coyner of Salt Lake. There is no need for us to say that it is untrue from beginning to end, nor to express our utter contempt for the clerical scoundrels, who impose such absurdities on Christian people for the purpose of getting money, to aid them, as they pretend, in their hazardous labors among the terrible Mormons who never attempted to harm a hair of their ignoble heads.[40]

Of course, part of Jackson's responsibility, as superintendent of Presbyterian mission work in Utah and throughout the Rocky Mountain West, was getting money to support the forces in the field. He was particularly concerned with obtaining funds with which to erect church buildings for Presbyterian congregations in Utah. In one appeal in a Presbyterian newspaper, for example, he explained how twenty-five thousand dollars could be raised for the contemplated church structure in Salt Lake City "if one out of every fifty of the female communicants of the Presbyterian Church, as a Christmas offering to the Saviour, will each contribute five dollars to build a church that will act an important part in rescuing their sisters from the degradation of Mormonism."[41] Jackson's targeting of the female membership of his church for contributions was a carefully calculated maneuver. Assuming, no doubt correctly, that Presbyterian women could readily identify with a campaign to liberate their sisters in Utah, he supplemented his own appeal for aid with a supplication from the female members of the Salt Lake City congregation. Calling for donations from "The Ladies of the Presbyterian Church," these women had prepared an open letter "to our sisters in the Church in behalf of the poor deluded and downtrodden women in Utah. Hundreds of them have been the unwilling slaves of Mormonism. They now hail the present movements here as the morning star announcing their deliverance."[42]

Not surprisingly, when news of these actions reached Salt Lake City, spokesmen for the Mormon Church responded angrily. In a communication to the *Deseret News*, one correspondent, writing as "One of the Deluded Women," sought to correct the erroneous impressions presented by the Presbyterian ladies on the role of women in Mormon society. "When *women* undertake a system of misrepresentation," this writer argued, "are we not able ourselves—is it not our right and duty, to pull down the covering of falsehood with which they seek to envelop their would-be righteous enterprise[?]" If the church building scheme were successful, then "not one honest 'Mormon' woman would ever be found within its walls."[43] And the editor of the *Evening News* deplored the obvious concentration by the Presbyterians on money in their campaign. He pointed out "that the remarkable results manifest all around us have been effected by the 'Mormons' without the intervention of begging letters, but by the faith, energy, and persevering industry of the people themselves."[44]

Jackson did not express his personal views on these often bitter exchanges, but he continued to find ample ammunition for the salvos of propaganda depicting the evils of Mormonism that he fired regularly at eastern audiences to stimulate fund-raising. There is no record of the precise amount of money he obtained for this particular cause, but one of his efforts in 1877 resulted in a windfall of four hundred dollars. In a letter addressed to the "Ladies of the Presbyterian Churches of Brooklyn, New York," he began with his understanding of a rumored part of the Mormon faith known as "blood atonement." He charged that there was not a town in all of Utah that had not been repeatedly "stained with the blood of those who becoming obnoxious to the ruling powers of the Church were murdered at the command of the Church." Elaborating, he insisted that if Mormons showed any signs of apostatizing, it became the duty of their friends to kill them. "This doctrine has borne legitimate fruit," he claimed, "in hundreds of murders."[45]

Jackson dwelled at length on the subject of polygamy. He felt that the great mass of Mormon women suffered the same form of hopeless degradation that their sisters did in the harems of Turkey. A rebellious woman who tried to escape from Utah would be pursued, and "before she would get many miles, she would be shot and her body left to feed ravens and wolves." Polygamy was bad enough in itself, but he went on to show that permissive abandonment to masculine lust brought with it the even greater sin of incest. He charged that a man prominent in the Mormon church had his own sister among his wives, and another man, "a bishop's counselor, begat a child by his own daughter, she being at the time the third wife of another man." The only hope of removing that "foul blot," according to Jackson, and freeing the thousands of deluded victims was the establishment among them of Presbyterian mission churches and schools. He ended his appeal with the assurance that liberal donations from Eastern purses would support "leavening influences" in Utah, and would "save the tens of thousands of girls that are coming on to a marriageable age from this soul-destroying degradation of polygamy."[46]

Jackson must have regarded the response to these revelations as gratifying indeed. The secretary of the Board of the Brooklyn Woman's Home and Foreign Missionary Society replied that his communication was read before that body "in secret conclave," and it presented a frightful picture of degradation without parallel in history. As for the poor women and children, the ladies presumed "that they never smile, but wear perpetually that hopeless, sunken, wretched look that seems like a pathetic appeal to the God of justice to come and liberate them." This correspondent assured Jackson that all of the ladies were deeply affected by his story, and that they had four hundred dollars in their treasury that would now be directed to the support of a Presbyterian school in Utah.[47]

Jackson and all who were deeply concerned with the Mormon issue could regard the Presbyterian presence in Utah as firmly established by the end of the 1870s. Statistics compiled by the Presbytery of Utah at the end of the decade certainly seemed to support such a conclusion. Reporting to Jackson in 1879 on these gratifying figures, Duncan McMillan confirmed the existence in Utah of eight churches, ten ministers, twelve mission schools, sixteen teachers, 786 mission school students, and 872 Sabbath school scholars.[48] In an attempt to analyze all of this impressive data, Robert McNiece, pastor of the church in Salt Lake City, preached a Thanksgiving sermon on November 25, 1880, that he entitled "God's Wondrous Works in Utah." As he surveyed the impact of the Presbyterian missionary efforts among the Mormons, he concluded, "There are evidences of a wonderful moral progress in Utah." Much of that progress, in McNiece's opinion, could be attributed to the success of Presbyterian schools in Mormon communities. "As I like to put it," he explained, "these schools constitute the skirmish line. Back of this line are the Christian churches with the resistless artillery of the Gospel. And back of all is the Grand Army of all the Christian hosts in America, before whose mighty tread all forms of civil and religious error and oppression are fleeing away."[49]

The Mormon Church, in the Woodruff Manifesto in 1890, officially abandoned its sanction of polygamy among its members. Robert McNiece would surely have regarded that action as a symbol of "moral progress." Preeminent among the Presbyterian propagandists on the polygamy issue was Sheldon Jackson. Were the conditions of Mormon women in Utah as bad as Jackson proclaimed? He related to the women in Brooklyn, for example, his charge that life in a polygamous household "in hundreds of cases has unseated reason and in others driven to suicide."[50] If challenged to provide evidence to sustain his claim of "hundreds of cases," Jackson would probably have replied, quite simply, that his statement was supported by "common knowledge." Angry at Jackson's reckless approach to eastern audiences, one Mormon writer reflected on a speech by Jackson to an audience of women in St. Louis. The commentator insisted, "Jackson drew largely upon his imagination, and told some pious and pathetic stories of manufactured horrors." Concluding with an assessment of Jackson's influence on his female audience, the irate author noted, "No wonder that such travelling clerical imposters as Jackson can move them to tears and wheedle the dollars out of them while they weep."[51]

Jackson was undoubtedly adept at "wheedling the dollars" out of the purses of prospective donors in the East. Gradually, by the end of the 1870s, this money-raising function became his primary role in connection with the growth of the Presbyterian schools and churches in Utah. That was because problems demanding his attention had arisen with another segment of the "exceptional population" in his superintendency. Jackson could not ignore a report in 1874 from the General Assembly's Standing Committee on Home Missions citing a great need for financial support in New Mexico, "where a superstitious native population of 100,000 need the gospel to save their souls and to fit them for American citizenship."[52]

9 | Combating the Legions of a "Foreign Pope"

*Almost before we know it there will rise up among us Romish
States with no public schools, no free Bibles, no free speech, and
desiring the glory and prosperity of a foreign Pope far more than
that of the United States.*

—JULIA M. WRIGHT, "CHILDREN'S LETTERS,"
Rocky Mountain Presbyterian, SEPTEMBER 1876

In 1848 at the conclusion of the war between the United States
and Mexico, the victorious nation received, as part of the spoils of war, the
area that would later become the state of New Mexico. The acquisition of
this new territory presented issues that many in the United States viewed
with alarm. Under the terms of the Treaty of Guadalupe–Hidalgo, which
ended the war, former citizens of Mexico who chose to remain in the area
could share eventually in "the enjoyment of all the rights of citizens of the
United States," and they would be "secured in the free exercise of their
religion without restriction."[1] For the many Americans who were devoutly
Protestant in their religious beliefs, these stipulations must have raised
several questions. Could Mexicans really become "Americanized" by the
simple stroke of a pen? Was their faith in the Catholic Church so firmly
entrenched as to be beyond the hope of salvation by the Protestant message? When Sheldon Jackson set out from Denver on his first visit to the
Presbyterian mission field in New Mexico in 1870, he may have pondered
these same concerns. He could have obtained guidance from the accounts
of William Kephart, pastor of the Presbyterian church in Cheyenne, Wyoming, describing his experiences in New Mexico in the 1850s.

Kephart retained vivid impressions of his tour of duty in Santa Fe from
1850 to 1853 as a representative of the American Missionary Association.
He had distributed Bibles printed in Spanish, which, according to Kephart,
the people received joyfully. As soon as he left their homes, however,
Kephart believed that the recipients burned his gifts because they had been
threatened by the Catholic priests with excommunication if they retained
them. Kephart encountered aggressive opposition to his efforts in 1851,
when Bishop Jean Baptiste Lamy arrived in Santa Fe to supervise the ac-

tivities of the Catholic Church in New Mexico. This dynamic leader immediately inspired the priests under his jurisdiction to renew their efforts to prevent the intrusion of competing denominations in the area. When Kephart left New Mexico, he lamented the loss of a great opportunity to strike a telling blow against the dominant influence of Catholicism. He was convinced that the victory of the United States over Mexico in the war had given to Protestantism the same kind of prestige in New Mexico that the conquest of the Aztecs by Cortez had given to Catholicism. But the Protestant denominations did not exploit this favorable situation by sending in their missionaries in large numbers. As a result, in Kephart's opinion, the respect or awe with which the people of New Mexico had regarded their conquerors as a superior race had soon given way to disgust and contempt, to the point that they had become more than ever attached to their old Catholic faith.[2]

The mission field for Presbyterianism in New Mexico lay fallow for over a decade following Kephart's departure in 1853. Finally, late in 1866, David McFarland arrived in Santa Fe to open a mission station. The Old School Board of Domestic Missions had recruited McFarland for the purpose from his position as principal of the Mattoon Female Seminary in Mattoon, Illinois. He organized the First Presbyterian Church of Santa Fe with twelve members on January 13, 1867. Eager to provide an alternative to Catholic parochial education for children in Santa Fe, McFarland soon opened a school that he later called the Santa Fe Collegiate Institute. His wife, Amanda, joined him in the spring of 1867, and he received additional assistance for his remote outpost when Presbyterian women in Auburn, New York, who organized themselves as the Santa Fe Missionary Association in 1867, sent Bibles and religious tracts. Cornelia Martin, who headed the new missionary association, had received notice of McFarland's needs from letters written to her by her daughter Eveline Alexander, wife of an army officer in New Mexico at the time. In the fall of 1867, the ladies in New York also raised enough money to employ Charity Ann Gaston, a young lady who had previously taught Choctaw Indians in the Indian Territory.[3]

Pleased with his work to date, McFarland hoped to secure formal recognition for his efforts from the Old School General Assembly. In a bold stroke indeed, he asked and received permission from that body in June of 1868 to form a Presbytery of Santa Fe from "such churches as may be found in New Mexico."[4] Of course his was the only Presbyterian church in New Mexico, so he had to call on qualified parties throughout the territory to provide the quorum for an organizational meeting of the rather extraordinary presbytery on December 14, 1868. Attending this gathering, beside McFarland, were the chaplain of the army garrison at Fort Craig,

New Mexico; a missionary working for the Board of Foreign Missions on the Navajo reservation at Fort Defiance, Arizona; and a ruling elder from McFarland's church in Santa Fe. The delegates carefully adopted standing rules from the official *Presbyterian Form of Government* for the conduct of their presbyterial meetings. With only four delegates it was somewhat difficult to fill the many committee responsibilities, but each man simply accepted numerous positions. Acknowledging "superstition, licentiousness, intemperance, profanity, Sabbath breaking, and intense worldliness" to prevail to a fearful extent in New Mexico, the churchmen nevertheless closed their exercises by confidently predicting, "The Spring of Christian civilization is teeming with bud and blossom, for a glorious and fruitful Autumn."[5]

McFarland and his colleagues were pleased when, in the fall of 1869, they could welcome another member to their little presbytery. In October, John Annin, who had served as pastor at a church in Lake City, Minnesota, arrived in New Mexico to organize a Presbyterian church in Las Vegas, a ranching community about fifty miles east of Santa Fe.[6] In Las Vegas, Annin found a friend and supporter, one who shared his Presbyterian beliefs. José Ynes Perea, who was born in 1837 into a wealthy Catholic family in New Mexico, was converted to Protestantism while attending a school in New York. When he returned to New Mexico he developed financial interests in several sheep ranches and a trading post at Las Vegas. When he learned of Annin's arrival, he courageously offered his services to the missionary as a traveling evangelist to carry the Word to ranches and small communities in the vicinity of Las Vegas. Perhaps inspired by Perea's offer, which he gladly accepted, Annin organized a Presbyterian church with six members in Las Vegas on March 21, 1870 with six members. José Perea was unanimously chosen from the small group to serve as ruling elder. At the same time, Annin opened a little school that he called the San Miguel County Educational and Literary Institute.[7]

Jackson was aware of many of these events when he set out on his first trip to New Mexico in August of 1870. Henry Kendall had provided him with explicit instructions. In order for the home mission board to plan intelligently for future expansion in the territory, Jackson was to identify the communities with the greatest potential for growth. Knowing of Jackson's inclination to react positively to even the smallest Presbyterian presence in a small frontier town, Kendall emphatically told Jackson "to give us all the facts on both sides—you are to discount the extravagant utterances of sanguine settlers and speculators and make up your own judgment and transmit the same to us." Jackson could tell the Presbyterians whom he encountered in New Mexico what he would recommend and what he hoped the board would do, but final decisions would be made by the mission board. Also, any commitment to provide additional resources for New Mexico would be directed primarily to the anticipated influx of Presbyterians because "the Spanish population cannot compare in importance with the English speaking people."[8]

When Jackson arrived in Santa Fe, after a tiring stagecoach ride from Denver, his conversations with David McFarland might have included comments about strange religious practices conducted by some of the Catholic residents of northern New Mexico and southern Colorado. Jackson had learned of these ceremonies in a letter he received from a friend in southern Colorado who provided a vivid description of a commemoration of Easter he had witnessed:

> They set up a Cross about a quarter of a mile from the house; had one of them carry the Cross there; they then stripped one of their number on a very cold day entirely naked except a breech cloth, had an ox chain fastened to each foot or ankle, and led him blindfolded to the Cross and back. They then had a kind of paddle that seemed to be made of canvas filled with gravel, or something that was very heavy and whipped themselves on the bare back until their backs were in a gore of blood. It was the hardest sight I ever saw. When I talked to them they said the Priest told them to do it. I have heard and read much of doing penance but never saw anything like this before. These people seem to have no moral sense.[9]

What this gentleman had witnessed was a ceremony of the Brotherhood of Our Father Jesus, commonly known as the Penitente Brotherhood, which had originated in the Southwest early in the nineteenth century. Although never officially sanctioned by the Catholic Church, these rites were certainly regarded by Jackson and the other Presbyterian missionaries in the area as only one more shocking example of the kind of depraved society that was sure to evolve under the influence of a false religion.[10]

Jackson came away from Santa Fe and Las Vegas convinced by David McFarland and John Annin of the need not only to sustain the existing mission stations but also to expand the field of endeavor by posting men to other promising locations in the territory. When he reported his findings and recommendations to Henry Kendall, he must have assumed that the board secretary would try to implement his proposals as far as monetary resources would permit. To his complete dismay, he learned from Kendall of the board's decision to abandon all home mission work in New Mexico. The board members acknowledged the importance of the work in that region, but, in view of the limited resources, available funds would accomplish much more elsewhere. Perhaps the Presbyterian Board of Education could be convinced to support McFarland's little school in Santa Fe, but Annin would be withdrawn if no other agency could be persuaded to underwrite his efforts.[11]

Jackson was, of course, shocked. He was determined to do whatever he could to save the little churches and schools in New Mexico, but at the end of 1870 he did not help his cause when he contributed to an incident that incurred the wrath of some of the residents of Santa Fe. On December 20, David McFarland reported the actions of some evilly disposed persons who had created great excitement in the community by publishing one of Jackson's letters in a local newspaper. Jackson had written the letter for publication in the *New York Evangelist* in an attempt to raise money for McFarland's little school. Describing his visit to Santa Fe in August, he spoke of the "low hovels, dirty children, and barking dogs of the poor" in a city that seemed foreign "and in some measure hostile to the genius of American institutions." He hoped some good Christian woman would endow the school in Santa Fe "as a memorial of her gratitude to Him, who has caused her to differ from these poor degraded, superstitious Mexican women" whose daughters "have nothing before them but a life of ignorance and shame." Understandably indignant at this unflattering description of his city and the "Mexican" women residing therein, the editor of the Santa Fe newspaper condemned Jackson as a "hypocrite and a blackguard." The furor caused by Jackson's faux pas soon subsided, but, in retrospect, he must have regretted this incident at a time when the very existence of the Presbyterian churches in New Mexico was endangered.[12]

If the shock waves from this regrettable incident reached the rooms of the Board of Home Missions in New York, they apparently had no effect on an earlier board decision that had surely pleased Jackson. Soon after Henry Kendall's announcement in September of the termination of support for the churches at Santa Fe and Las Vegas, Jackson must have presented a strong case to the board members for postponement of that drastic action. In response, at the end of November, the board renewed commissions for David McFarland at Santa Fe and John Annin at Las Vegas for an additional six months.

Encouraged by this reprieve, McFarland acted in December to formalize the existence of his little school, previously designated the Santa Fe Collegiate Institute, by incorporating it under the laws of the Territory of New Mexico as the Santa Fe University, Industrial and Agricultural College. Including a pledge to provide to all classes of society the opportunity to obtain the very best intellectual and practical education, the charter also allowed McFarland and the other trustees to issue and sell one hundred dollar shares of stock to a maximum of $500,000. McFarland announced the anticipated opening of the university on January 2, 1871. With these decisive actions buttressing his own support for the New Mexico missions, Jackson surely hoped that the mission board members in the days ahead would reconsider their decision on the importance of this mission field.[13]

In the ensuing months, the movement by the home mission board to terminate operations at Santa Fe and Las Vegas subsided, and Jackson was undoubtedly relieved early in 1872 when he learned that Henry Kendall had changed his mind about the value of the work in New Mexico. The board secretary no longer spoke of abandoning the missions there, and he now proposed to place a much higher priority on strengthening the churches in the Presbytery of Santa Fe. The abrupt change in his attitude can be attributed directly to a threat from another denomination. "I made a call on Bishop [George M.] Randall, who is stopping in Brooklyn only an evening or two ago," Kendall wrote in haste. "He gave me his report. Get it Jackson and read it. He proposes to take New Mexico. He evidently thinks the [Episcopalian] Canonicals and vestments will do it! Well, let him try!"[14]

Jackson contrived a way to visit New Mexico again in the fall of 1872. The stated purpose of his trip was to preach and hold a Communion service for a small group of Christians at Fort Garland in southern Colorado. While there, in late September, he decided to do some sightseeing. Learning that Indians at the Taos Pueblo, located in northern New Mexico about eighty miles south of Fort Garland, would soon celebrate a great annual feast to St. Jerome, their patron saint, he borrowed a cavalry horse and set out. He later wrote at length about this journey, with vivid descriptions of the colorful countryside and with his impressions of the people he saw, who were harvesting grain in a crude manner that brought to mind the biblical stories of reapers in the fields. Arriving at the pueblo, he secured accommodations in the nearby village of Taos with Mrs. Charles Bent, widow of the first American territorial governor of New Mexico, who had been killed in a local rebellion in 1847.[15]

After viewing the festivities, Jackson returned to the neighboring non-Indian community. There he was dismayed by the shameful conduct of some of the visitors and residents who, as he reported, persisted in their merrymaking into the wee hours:

> The crowd surged back to Taos to consume the night at the fandango and gaming tables. After supper, the tables were removed, and dancing commenced. The fiddler occupied one end of the hall, and the barkeeper the other. Every one that danced was expected, at the close of each set, to patronize the bar. Some of the women took their full share of "Taos lightning" [potent home brew], and, as might be

supposed, the whole company became uproarious before morning. Both sexes smoked incessantly. When a woman rose to dance she handed her cigarette to a friend. While the Mexican women were smoking, drinking, and dancing with American men, the Mexican men were in adjoining rooms gambling; and so ended the "most holy feast of St. Jerome."[16]

To judge from Jackson's comments, Taos was certainly one of the places in New Mexico where a Presbyterian missionary would find a fertile field in which to plant the seeds of salvation. The man who was eventually selected as bearer of the Presbyterian message to the citizens of Taos obtained his assignment in a rather roundabout fashion. James Roberts arrived in Santa Fe in the fall of 1872 with a commission from the Board of Foreign Missions to open a school at one of the Indian pueblos in New Mexico. After his graduation from the Western Theological Seminary in Allegheny, Pennsylvania, Roberts had taught school from early in 1869 to the spring of 1872 for the Navajo Indians at their agency in Fort Defiance, Arizona. His lack of success at that assignment compelled the foreign mission board to relocate him. Roberts selected the Taos Pueblo in which to exercise his pedagogical skills, but at the end of 1872 he decided to give up Indian work and try for a school in the town of Taos itself. He and his wife had received encouragement in that venture, as he told Jackson, from a small number of parents in the town who wanted to have their children educated in his school because they believed that the Catholic priests desired to keep the people in ignorance.[17]

Roberts opened his school on May 1, 1873, with five pupils, and by midsummer fourteen students had enrolled. Encouraged by what he perceived as a positive response to his message, on November 15, 1874, Roberts organized a church in Taos with ten members, all of whom except Mrs. Roberts were "Mexicans." Regarding this event as a substantial achievement, Jackson reported in his newspaper, "The work at Taos is very encouraging indeed."[18] James and Martha Roberts might not have used the word "encouraging" to describe one aspect of their situation in Taos in 1874. Financially, they were, in effect, orphans—unclaimed by either of the missionary boards of their church. As a teacher at an Indian school with a commission from the Board of Foreign Missions, Roberts would have been paid six hundred dollars per year by the federal government. But as he was no longer teaching at an Indian school, that source of income was not available. He hoped, therefore, that Jackson would intercede with the Board of Home Missions to obtain an appointment for him that would provide a salary for his work at Taos. Jackson may have tried to respond to his request, but a year later the matter was still unresolved. In July of 1874 Martha Roberts, with a note of despair, simply asked Jackson, "Now, brother, what are we to do?"[19]

Jackson could tell Mrs. Roberts only to stand firm and have faith that all would be well in God's own good time—or words to that effect. He did decide, however, to make another trip to New Mexico in the summer of 1875 to personally assess the status of the Presbyterian mission stations there. He was also inspired by a request from Cornelia Martin, his friend in New York whose women's society had continuously supported mission work in New Mexico, to visit as many military posts in the territory as his schedule would permit. Hoping to obtain the names of women who would take the lead in opening the way for further mission work, Mrs. Martin promised to raise two hundred dollars towards Jackson's travel expenses if he would gather the information.[20]

Jackson began his long journey on July 5. The Denver and Rio Grande Railroad carried him from Denver to the end of its track at Pueblo, Colorado, where he continued south by stage over Raton Pass into New Mexico. At Las Vegas, he found John Annin enjoying the new structure built to house his church and school. A local newspaper had lauded Annin's achievements: "On a meager allowance from the Presbyterian Board of Missions, he offers the best years of his existence to the noble cause of instructing the future fathers and mothers of our community."[21] Jackson surely appreciated Annin's achievements, but he warned, in his later account of his journey, that Catholic opposition to the mission was still so prevalent that the Annin family was not yet "fully free from the dangers of violence at the hands of a fanatical mob."[22]

At Santa Fe, the news was less encouraging. In the spring of 1873, David McFarland's health had deteriorated to the point that he decided to leave Santa Fe to accept a teaching post in the warmer climate of San Diego, California. Jackson thought that he had found someone to fill the vacancy when he persuaded Melancthon Hughes, one of the three pioneer missionaries recruited by Jackson to work along the Union Pacific Railroad in 1869, to return to the West to take over the Santa Fe church. Sadly, Hughes served only a few months in his new position before his unexpected death on November 18. At the end of 1873 there had been only one encouraging bit of news from Santa Fe. Although McFarland's so-called Santa Fe University, Industrial and Agricultural College had apparently expired after his departure, one of the elders of the church had opened another school that already exhibited, according to one observer, "the most flattering prospect of success. It is the only school of the kind here, and is very greatly needed."[23]

While the school may have continued to serve its purpose, the vacancy in the position of resident missionary of the church in Santa Fe continued into 1874. Martha Roberts, writing from Taos, described the unfortunate situation to Jackson in July. "You know doubtless what a great injury to mission work the abandoning of the mission at Santa Fe has been both in the territory and also in missionary circles in the East," she wrote. "Those who gave to the Santa Fe mission regard it as a failure and do not care to help others in New Mexico."[24] Mrs. Roberts was worried, of course, about the impact on continuing contributions for the Robertses' work in Taos. She was premature, however, in her description of the Santa Fe mission as failed and abandoned. The problem in that city was finally resolved in December of 1874 with the arrival of George G. Smith to try to revive interest in the dormant church. A graduate of Western Theological Seminary in Pennsylvania, he had served during the Civil War in the Union Army as adjutant in a regiment of black soldiers. He found only one person remaining in Santa Fe who acknowledged communicant membership in the congregation, but he applied himself vigorously to his rebuilding task. In the summer of 1875, the success of his efforts was apparent, and when Jackson visited him he concluded that Smith was "securing a strong hold upon all the classes in Santa Fe."[25]

Continuing his trip, Jackson stopped next at Taos for a brief visit with the Roberts family. Although James and Martha Roberts must have conversed with Jackson about the still unsettled question of a regular salary for James Roberts, Jackson made no mention of the matter in his report of his journey. Perhaps drawing on their own resources, along with occasional donations from individuals interested in their work, the dedicated missionaries were determined to maintain the Taos mission. Jackson did call on all friends who had stood by Roberts in the past to increase their support because the mission was bearing fruit. For example, Roberts had secured a plot of five acres on the edge of town where he hoped to erect a building that would serve as both church and school for the small congregation. Meanwhile, he continued the operation of his school in a small rented building. Commenting on conditions in the school, Jackson observed, "In those few children, in that low room with a dirt floor, we saw in training the future teachers of New Mexico, when her common schools are rescued from the control of the Sisters of Charity."[26]

Returning from Taos to Santa Fe, Jackson continued his travels south, passing through Albuquerque and Socorro until he reached Las Cruces near the Texas border. From Las Cruces, he took a stage to Silver City in the southwest corner of the territory. It was on that portion of his journey that he visited Fort Craig and Fort Selden, both located along the Rio

Grande River, and Fort Bayard near Silver City. By including those forts in his travel plans, he fulfilled his commitment to Cornelia Martin to evaluate the status of Christian enterprises at military establishments. He found that the garrisons were, quite simply, without the Gospel. There were some followers of Christ at these posts, but the entire chaplaincy system of the army needed overhauling, in Jackson's opinion, to ensure that religious privileges would be available to all of the soldiers and their families at these isolated duty stations. "Oh when shall the time come," Jackson pleaded, "when the American Church, so abundantly able, shall at last give gospel privileges to her own sons and daughters in her own land?"[27] From Silver City, Jackson retraced his route until he reached his home in Denver after twenty-four days of strenuous travel.

Jackson wrote at great length in his newspaper about his impressions of New Mexico. Of course he concluded his account with an appeal for additional support from those members of his church in the East who had not yet committed a portion of their resources to the western mission field. He warned of dangers sure to be encountered when an illiterate people received the right to vote without any real comprehension of the responsibility associated with this privilege:

> New Mexico has 100,000 American citizens, of whom not more than one in thirty can read or write their own names, and a large majority of whom are sunk in the most abject superstition. They already have the ballot. Shall they have the gospel? They are knocking at the door of Congress to be admitted into the sisterhood of States. Shall they be evangelized? Reader, are you doing all you can to sustain and encourage the Church in this great work? Have you given all that you should this year to Home Missions?[28]

With this rousing conclusion to the story of his grand tour, Jackson left no doubt about his own conviction that the time was at hand when the achievement of his objective to in the West for Christ, at least as it applied to New Mexico, now hung in the balance. If his readers did not respond favorably to his entreaties, then his dire prediction of the erosion of the national spirit by the infusion of a debilitating strain into the life blood of the body politic would surely come to pass. While he could only wait to see if his passionate appeal would bring the money sorely needed for this portion of his mission field, the missionaries in New Mexico carried on as best they could.

An admirable example of persistence in the face of adversity in New Mexico could have been found in the career of José Ynes Perea, an elder in John Annin's church in Las Vegas. In his history of the Las Vegas church,

Annin proclaimed, "I am confident that he [Perea] will labor up to the full measure of his power for the enlightenment, elevation & emancipation of this, his benighted, degraded & enslaved people."[29] Members of the Presbytery of Santa Fe licensed Perea, along with three other young men of Mexican ancestry, as evangelists in November of 1877. Perea preached at numerous locations in northern New Mexico until the summer of 1878, when he accepted an offer to assist the Presbyterian missionary to the Indians at the Zuni Pueblo, located in the western part of the territory near the border with Arizona. While there, he married Susan Gates, a young lady who was teaching at the mission. After spending a few months at this assignment, the Pereas moved, first to the little town of Canyon, New Mexico, near the Jemez Indian Pueblo, and then to Corrales, New Mexico, located about fifty miles south of Santa Fe, where José began an extensive correspondence with Jackson.[30]

In several communications from Corrales to Jackson in 1879, Perea described the Spartan life he and his wife endured. They had managed to secure a rundown building to serve as a residence and a school house. The cost of repairs on the structure exceeded the Perea's savings, and José was obliged to go into debt to make the dwelling livable. When they were settled into their house, José devoted his time to evangelistic work among receptive families in the vicinity while Susan conducted the school. Although, according to José, the Catholic priests in the area were exhorting the people not to send their children to the Presbyterian school, by the end of the year seventeen students were attending. Boasting of this achievement, José assured Jackson that the pupils "are of the best families in town, they are bright children and learn well."[31]

Truly, there were many bright children in northern New Mexico who were obtaining both secular and spiritual training in Presbyterian schools as the decade of the 1870s drew to a close. Much of the impetus for the enlargement of this work came, as it did in Utah, from the action taken by the General Assembly in 1877 authorizing the Board of Home Missions to secure teachers for the "exceptional populations" in the West. The first of this new group of educators assigned to New Mexico received their commissions at the end of 1877.[32] While these teachers were on their way to New Mexico, the mission board secretary had to deal with another problem that had repercussions for the New Mexico mission field. In the summer of 1877, Henry Kendall asked Jackson, with no attempt to disguise his displeasure, "What on earth is A. M. Darley doing with the Mexican people?"[33] Alex Darley had, in fact, decided that his real calling to redeem nonbelievers in southern Colorado lay in working with "Mexicans." To reach them, he began to preach at scattered settlements in the Conejos Valley, just south of his headquarters at Del Norte, Colorado, in June of 1877.[34]

Obviously, Henry Kendall was not delighted with this surprising turn of events, and others of Darley's colleagues in the region were not pleased with the new and unauthorized arrangement. James Roberts, for example, working out of his mission station in Taos, New Mexico, had regarded the area entered by Darley as his own responsibility. He had organized a small church at the town of Cenicero in September of 1877, and although the church was actually in Colorado he believed that the whole district, just across the border from New Mexico, was properly under the jurisdiction of the Presbytery of Santa Fe. On one occasion, Roberts went so far as to accuse Jackson of exercising partiality in the dispute. "Your special friend and favorite Mr. Darley," he angrily proclaimed, "has done us, and we think the cause, much harm in presuming to come into a church organized by us, belonging to our Presbytery . . . , going from house to house, baptizing infants not a week old, and making regular appointments and preaching at regular intervals during the week while at the same time I had my Evangelist there preaching every Sabbath."[35]

Regrettably, the warnings expressed by Darley's critics concerning his work among the "Mexicans" proved to be correct. It seemed that all of his well-meaning efforts were marked by turmoil. One of his friends disclosed that a Catholic priest called together his parishioners after one of Darley's visits to their town and undid all of the good work by collecting and burning the Bibles Darley had distributed. "I have nothing to say against the form of religion which this priest is supposed to represent," the reporter stated, "but such an enemy to free knowledge somehow suggests the days of the rack and thumbscrew."[36] And when James Roberts succeeded in obtaining several teachers to open schools in southern Colorado in 1878, Darley apparently tried to become a self-appointed supervisor of their activities. When Henry Kendall learned of this maneuver, he told Jackson that placing Darley in control of the school work could never be condoned. "No one doubts Darley's energy," Kendall wrote, "but I think every man who knows him, doubts his prudence."[37]

During all of this wrangling, Jackson did try to help the cause, in general, by utilizing the columns of his newspaper to attack the enemy, as he had in the campaign against the Mormons. Children of families who subscribed to the *Rocky Mountain Presbyterian* often received revelations about the evils of Catholicism in the columns of the newspaper. Jackson's favorite author of children's homilies was Julia Wright, who had acquired a reputation throughout the church as a purveyor of uplifting messages for young people. In her "Children's Letters" published by Jackson in September of 1876, Mrs. Wright warned her young readers:

Do you know that in Rome they have a great map of all our country? On it they have marked all those parts that were settled, explored or claimed by Romanists—as Maryland, Florida, Louisiana, the Mississippi, etc. If ever they get a chance they mean to claim all this back. . . . As population and our industries move westward, along with them will go this Church, building her cathedrals, nunneries and schools, and getting a strong hold of the new population; seizing on the children (very fond of getting children is this Church), and almost before we know it there will rise up among us Romish States with no public schools, no free Bibles, no free speech, and desiring the glory and prosperity of a foreign Pope far more than that of the United States.[38]

Mrs. Wright concluded this extraordinary declamation with a challenge. "If we expect our country to be worthy of her high place and calling," she admonished, "and to have a future creditable to her heroic past, we must make it all Protestant and righteous."[39]

Jackson assumed, of course, that residents of New Mexico hoped to move someday soon from territorial status to statehood. He wanted readers of his newspaper to understand, however, that the "Mexicans," who constituted a great majority of the population, were hardly ready for this significant step. In an article he published entitled "Ought New Mexico Be Admitted To The Union?" the anonymous author noted, "Nearly all the natives of New Mexico are Roman Catholics. Therefore the masses are deplorably ignorant. The Roman Church abhors the idea of education for the common people." Presumably, by keeping the people ignorant, the priests could extract money from them for performing every sacrament of the church. "The avarice and extortion of their church," the writer continued, "are a by-word among multitudes of Romanists in New Mexico." Finally, New Mexico should not be granted statehood too soon because "under an administration of affairs by the Roman Catholic clergy, there would be ruinous regression. I put the fact in plain words—STATE GOVERN-MENT WOULD BE, FOR SOME TIME TO COME, GOVERN-MENT BY THE CHURCH!"[40]

On at least one occasion, the sometimes preposterous statements in Jackson's newspaper regarding the status of the people of New Mexico drew an angry reply. When he printed an article extracted from the popular periodical *Harper's Weekly* on "New Mexico: Its Peoples and Customs" in 1877, an irate response appeared in the *Albuquerque Review*. The writer began by declaring, "That *Rocky Mountain Presbyterian* is a funny paper. If it ain't funny, its a big liar, for it tells lies as big as your printing press. Though I must acknowledge they are harmless for they are Presbyterian lies." Referring to the item in question as "filthy and vile," the commentator quoted some of the statements which he regarded as disgusting:

> "The New Mexicans are impoverished and ignorant people." They are "feebly indolent," blind slaves of crude superstitions, taxed beyond their means to support a tyrant Church. Their fidelity and patriotism is called in doubt for, we are told "it is not denied that in event of another war with old Mexico, many of them would be found leaning toward, if not actually engaged on, the side of their quondam [former] compatriots."[41]

Distraught at what he regarded as "a hurricane of fibs and abuse," the respondent concluded that this was surely not the best means to secure the good will of New Mexicans toward the Presbyterian ministers stationed in their communities, but "it will go far to make the Ladies Missionary Societies out East believe in the zeal of these most sincere missionaries, and induce them to continue to send them money."[42]

In his final comment, this perceptive analyst had cut directly to the core of the whole issue. The kind of distorted rhetoric employed by Jackson and others who wrote for his newspaper was deliberately designed to touch the heart strings, and loosen the purse strings, of potential donors in the East. It was simply understood that massive financial support would be needed to redeem the "Mexicans" from a condition perceived by the missionaries as degraded and immoral. One Presbyterian historian, who wrote about the home mission work of his church at this time, concluded that among "Mexicans" idleness was widespread and the men were shiftless and lazy. They suffered from extreme poverty because they failed to appreciate the value of money and its proper use. Another writer, who had served as a Presbyterian missionary in New Mexico, agreed. In a book, which he entitled *Our Mexicans*, he said that the average "Mexican," doubtless affected by the climate of the Southwest, had little ambition, and "as a race they seem to be fond of putting off any task as long as possible."[43]

Still, it was not a lost cause. In the eyes of Jackson and those who supported him, the work of the Presbyterian missionaries among the "Mexicans" would yield good citizens, Presbyterian in their affiliation and 100 percent American in their loyalties. They would be thrifty instead of spendthrift, diligent instead of lazy, sober instead of intemperate, moral instead of profligate, and, all in all, a reasonable facsimile of the ideal Presbyterian American.[44]

In any event, as the decade of the 1870s drew to a close, the good work among the "Mexicans" in New Mexico and southern Colorado could well have been described as being in a state of disarray. At Santa Fe, George

Smith had departed from his brief tenure as pastor of the church to accept an assignment to the congregation in Helena, Montana. At Las Vegas, one member of the church told Jackson that things were in a very bad state indeed. John Annin had "got into a rut that he will never get out of. In other words, would not a change be better both to him and to the cause?"[45] Annin's protégé José Perea was still financially distressed as he tried to serve as a traveling evangelist working out of Corrales, New Mexico. When he received his commission from the mission board for 1880, he was dismayed to learn that it was for six months only, with a salary of $375. Apparently he was expected to support himself for the other half of the year from whatever outside employment he could obtain. "I think you must see at once," he lamented to Jackson, "the sore tribulation into which my family and I are cast. . . . I do not know where or how I could get anything to do to support my family. I had never thought that such a thing could be done in our church, and so it has found me entirely unprepared."[46]

In Taos, James Roberts received good news when the mission board finally decided to place him on its payroll at the end of 1877 with an annual salary of one thousand dollars. The board also commissioned his wife to teach in the school at Taos for three hundred dollars per annum. Roberts's rival Alex Darley did not fare as well with the board. In the fall of 1878, he had persuaded the Presbytery of Colorado to authorize him to give his entire time to mission work among the "Mexicans" in the San Luis Valley in southern Colorado. The members of the mission board refused, however, to put their stamp of approval on that action, influenced, perhaps, by Henry Kendall's personal aversion to giving Darley free rein. When one of Darley's friends learned of this rejection, he told Jackson that a great wrong had been done, not only to the courageous man but also to "the Mexicans in not giving them a man peculiarly qualified to be their leader in getting out of the dark bondage of Romanism."[47]

Jackson's own role in regard to liberating people from the "dark bondage of Romanism" remains hard to define. In some respects, he seemed to regard New Mexico as almost a semiautonomous province within the broader scope of his mission field. That might be explained by the fact that the Presbytery of Santa Fe was already in place when he first arrived on the scene in 1870. And he had nothing to do with the selection of the principal characters in the cast of missionaries who guided the course of events there. David McFarland and John Annin were already on the scene when Jackson appeared, and James Roberts's activities in the area were originally directed by the Board of Foreign Missions. One aspect of the work in New Mexico, however, could be attributed to Jackson's initiative. A statistical report in

the minutes of the meeting of the General Assembly in 1880 showed eleven
school teachers employed by the Board of Home Missions in the territory.
The report also noted that three additional Presbyterian teachers were
working at the Indian Pueblos of Laguna, Zuni, and Jemez. The presence
of this trio of workers at those particular locations stemmed from Jackson's
daring move to intervene in the lives of still another segment of the "exceptional population" in the West.[48]

10 | A Clarion Call to "Uplift the Heathen"

Resolved: That the [General] Assembly views with deep concern the unevangelized condition of the aboriginal population of our land, and deprecates the increasing tendency among many of our citizens to treat them as a race to be exterminated, rather than as the proper objects of Christian effort, to be thereby civilized and gathered into the fold of Christ.

—GENERAL ASSEMBLY MINUTES, 1870

Strictly speaking, Presbyterian mission work during the 1870s among the Indians living in the Rocky Mountain West was none of Sheldon Jackson's business. The responsibility had been placed in the hands of the Board of Foreign Missions by an action of the General Assembly in 1837, because relations between the tribes and the United States were established by treaties, just as the country dealt with other foreign nations. And, of course, the Indians did speak languages other than English. Jackson's awareness of this division of authority did not deter him, however, from gathering information on the Indians within the boundaries of his superintendency, or from forming opinions about their association with their white neighbors.[1]

Jackson's early impressions of western attitudes toward the Indians could have been derived from his first trip to southern Colorado early in 1870. In his report on the journey, he mentioned passing several earth forts and blockhouses "suggestive of Indian depredations." He also heard a harrowing tale about a previous Indian attack on a stagecoach traveling along his route. Fortunately, the passengers, mounted on the horses which had been drawing the stage, reached the safety of a neighboring fort "amid a shower of arrows and bullets." From these observations, Jackson concluded, "The frontier settlers see no romance in the Indian. To them they are an unmitigated nuisance."[2]

Other Presbyterians who commented on western opinions of their Indian neighbors agreed with Jackson's appraisal. One visitor to Colorado in 1870, detecting a great diversity of opinion on this issue between East and West, decided:

> Those who live among them [Indians] are unanimous and emphatic in their expressions of contempt for the race and in their testimony of their inhumanity towards their women, their laziness, treachery,

166

dishonesty and abject degradation. Honest toiling farmers whose subsistence is obtained with care and diligence, who, with their families, live in hourly danger from these sneaking robbers and murderers, see with a dissatisfaction that is not concealed, the government rewarding these crimes by subsidies increased from year to year.[3]

The delegates to the General Assembly in 1870 were not at all inclined to develop a position paper on the so-called Indian problem based on uncharitable western viewpoints. On the contrary, they reacted, like many Americans at the time, to a widespread demand following the Civil War for reform of the Office of Indian Affairs. Responding to these pressures, President Grant was preparing a new federal program designed, in part, to offer the great churches of America the opportunity to select good Christian laymen from their denominations to serve as government agents on Indian reservations. Exhibiting a reluctance to take a stand on what was, essentially, a political issue, the final wording of the resolution adopted by the assembly delegates on this topic simply stated:

That the Assembly views with deep concern the unevangelized condition of the aboriginal population of our land, and deprecates the increasing tendency among many of our citizens to treat them as a race to be exterminated, rather than as the proper objects of Christian effort, to be thereby civilized and gathered into the fold of Christ and the Assembly hereby authorizes the Board of [Foreign] Missions to put forth its utmost efforts to accomplish this humane and benignant purpose.[4]

The Office of Indian Affairs proceeded to initiate the so-called Grant Peace Policy in 1870. Each participating religious denomination received an allotment of Indian tribes, with authority to recommend good Christian laymen for federal appointments as agents at the reservations. It was hoped that the churches would also find the ways and means to then assign missionaries to open churches and schools at the agencies. With agents and missionaries working harmoniously together to "uplift" their Indian wards, surely great things could be achieved in the days ahead. The Presbyterian Church enthusiastically embraced this program, and the Board of Foreign Missions accepted nine Indian agencies in the initial distribution. An article in a Presbyterian periodical in October of 1870 entitled "New Hope For The Indians" announced the inauguration of this new partnership of church and state. The writer predicted great success for the new policy in the days ahead "with upright and benevolent men as Indian agents, with the friendly influence of the Indian Department, fostering education, and favoring missionary labors."[5]

Sheldon Jackson's own impressions of the Indians in his mission field were shaped, in part, during his visit to the Taos Pueblo in 1872. Arriving during the annual feast of St. Jerome, the patron saint of the pueblo, Jackson witnessed the festivities from a vantage point on the roof of one of the tallest buildings, where he could look down on the central plaza, crowded with brightly dressed Indians. The events commemorating the saint's feast day began with High Mass, celebrated in the pueblo church. This solemn ceremony was followed by a procession of the participants, who carried sacred images of the Virgin Mary, St. Jerome, and the infant Jesus. The Indians then placed these figures in a booth erected on one side of the plaza where, according to Jackson, the Indians believed they could watch the events that followed. The festivities in the afternoon included colorful Indian dances, foot races by runners who were naked but for a breech-cloth, and efforts to climb a tall greased pole crowned with prizes such as a live sheep, bottles of wine, and melons. Disturbed by what he must have regarded as a profane distortion of a supposedly religious ceremony, Jackson concluded his report with thoughts about the religious expectations for the Indians in the several pueblos of New Mexico. "As the Jews of old looked for a Messiah that should deliver them from Roman bondage," he noted, "so let these Pueblos receive the gospel at the hands of the 'white men from the East.'"[6]

There were nineteen Indian pueblos in New Mexico at the time of Jackson's first visit to Taos. These communities had existed for many years prior to the arrival of the famous expedition of Francisco Coronado in 1540, which brought with it missionaries of the Catholic Church. For some reason, Jackson became captivated with the affairs of the Pueblo Indians, perhaps because these people were both Indians and Catholics. While he showed little interest in the plight of the Sioux Indians in Montana or the Ute Indians in Colorado, and in the 1870s he had only peripheral interest in tribes in Arizona, he would soon take it upon himself to intervene in efforts to bring his version of the Christian message to several of the pueblos in New Mexico. He acknowledged that these Indians did attend mass in what he called "a Romish church" in each pueblo, but he gave little credence to any claim that these were, in fact, bona fide Christian observances. "Upon the arrival of the Spaniards," he announced after his visit to Taos, "these Indians were nominally converted to Roman Catholicism, but in reality their paganism was only baptized."[7]

Soon after Jackson's departure from Taos the first Presbyterian missionary arrived in the area, intending to open a school for children in the pueblo. After three years of unproductive efforts to conduct a school and preach the Gospel for the Navajo Indians at their agency in Fort Defiance,

Arizona, James Roberts was reassigned in the fall of 1872 by the Board of Foreign Missions to teach at the Taos Pueblo. In a moving report on his activities, he described his stubborn efforts to teach the Indian children:

> I go each fine day to the Pueblo or Indian village, and sit down on the ground, Indian like, on the sunny side of the old church, and sing hymns and songs until the young men and boys collect around me, and then I cease singing and teach them: no roof over me but the canopy above, no floor but that furnished by mother earth; no place, nor wood for fire; of course, I do not deem it proper to continue teaching more than an hour at a time, but some of the young men and boys are very anxious to learn to read English.[8]

Citing opposition from Catholic priests in the area, James Roberts soon abandoned his efforts to teach at the Taos Pueblo, and he opened a school for "Mexicans" instead in the nearby non-Indian community of Taos in the summer of 1873. While Roberts was retreating in the face of the enemy, another opportunity presented itself for the Presbyterians to move into the Pueblo Indian mission field. The agency for those Indians, located in Santa Fe, had been awarded initially to the Christian Church under the terms of the Grant Peace Policy. That relationship ended in the spring of 1873 when the agent appointed on the recommendation of the small denomination resigned from his position. The Board of Foreign Missions of the Presbyterian Church then accepted an offer from the Commissioner of Indian Affairs to add the Pueblo Indians to its list of agency responsibilities. The first agent appointed on the recommendation of the foreign board did little to distinguish himself in his work with the pueblos during his brief tenure of office from July of 1873 to November of 1874. His successor, however, was destined to play an important role in the development of agency policies, and in the involvement of Sheldon Jackson with several pueblo communities.[9]

Benjamin Thomas, an ardent Presbyterian, came to the Southwest from his home in Indiana at the end of 1870 to try to improve his health. He found employment as agency farmer at the Navajo Agency in Fort Defiance, Arizona, until the end of 1872, when he resigned to become agent for the Southern Apaches at Tularosa, New Mexico. He held that position until he learned of the vacancy at the Pueblo Agency in Santa Fe in the fall of 1874. With the approval of the Board of Foreign Missions, Thomas received the appointment as agent to the Pueblo Indians, and he assumed the duties of his new office on November 30, 1874. One of his immediate objectives was to visit the pueblos to evaluate the status of the schools started by his predecessors, and his assessment must have been a topic of conversation between Thomas and Sheldon Jackson when the latter visited Santa Fe in 1875.[10]

Jackson learned from Thomas that only seven schools were operating among the nineteen pueblos in the territory, and none of the teachers were Presbyterian missionaries. Jackson would not have viewed that situation as compliance with the mandate of his church to educate and uplift these Indians. When he then visited several of the pueblos along his route, he received impressions that reinforced his opinion about the regrettable religious beliefs and practices of these unfortunate people. When he revisited the Taos Pueblo, for example, Jackson received permission to descend into what he called a "heathen temple." He entered this circular building, which had no windows or doors, by a ladder placed through a hole in the flat roof. A crude altar had been erected on the earthen floor of the structure, and according to Jackson those residing nearby believed that the Indians still occasionally sacrificed children here to their pagan Gods. Exhibiting cultural traits supposedly of Aztec origin, the Indians always designated one of their number to ascend to the loftiest housetop in the pueblo at sunrise each morning to see if Montezuma was coming to restore his great kingdom. "And as they watch the rising sun," Jackson declaimed, "let them behold the more glorious rising of the Sun of Righteousness. And this call comes to the Presbyterian Church."[11]

As always, the Presbyterian Church was hearing an assortment of calls, amplified by Sheldon Jackson, from various parts of the Rocky Mountain West. Jackson's concerns, however, focused on the communities of Laguna, Zuni, and Jemez. In 1876 his call to assist the Indians of the Laguna Pueblo, located in New Mexico about forty miles west of Albuquerque, brought forth a gloomy prediction from one observer. Any Presbyterian missionary arriving at Laguna would find, in his opinion, Indians who "were destitute of all religious instruction."[12] If that statement was true at Laguna in 1876, it could not have applied to the situation there two decades earlier. In 1852, Samuel Gorman, a Baptist missionary, had settled at Laguna to conduct religious services and operate a school for the Indian children. When Gorman departed in 1859 to accept a position as pastor of the Baptist church in Santa Fe, he left behind a legacy of strong support among many of the Indians for his Protestant message. When those Indians succeeded in electing a majority of the tribal leaders, the ones who wished to retain their old ties to the Catholic Church had moved to a site several miles from the pueblo.[13]

That was the situation encountered by the first teacher assigned to the Laguna Pueblo in 1870 after implementation of the provisions of the Grant Peace Policy. For several years, reports on that gentleman's work indicated that he was achieving some success. Prospects for the school at Laguna deteriorated, however, when Ben Thomas arrived as agent for the Pueblo Indians in the fall of 1874. He found that the school had been shut down for several months. When the teacher reopened the school, he conducted it until July 10, 1875, when he closed it for the summer vacation. At the end of the year, however, the school was still not open, and Thomas concluded in a report to the Board of Foreign Missions, "The present teacher there is not doing half what might be done."[14] This unsatisfactory situation would have been on Jackson's mind as he prepared for a trip to New Mexico early in 1876. Assured that the Protestant faction was still in charge of pueblo affairs, he must have viewed Laguna as the most favorable starting point for an eventual network of Presbyterian missions and schools that would serve all of the pueblos of New Mexico.

When Ben Thomas decided to discharge the teacher at Laguna at the end of 1875, he sought the advice of Sheldon Jackson as he considered a replacement. Jackson's recommendation of John Menaul for the teaching position at Laguna was based on his awareness of the man's exemplary record in mission work. After training for the ministry at Princeton Seminary, Menaul had studied for a year in the medical department of the University of Pennsylvania. His first mission assignment was on the island of Corisco off the west coast of Africa where he served from December of 1868 to April of 1870. Suffering from deteriorating health and despondent over the death of his wife, he had decided to return to the United States. He found employment as physician at the Navajo Agency at Fort Defiance, Arizona, and at the Southern Apache Agency in New Mexico, but he felt that his real calling was to the preaching and teaching ministry. In January of 1876, he visited friends at the Allegheny Seminary in Pennsylvania, where he wrote to John Lowrie, secretary of the Board of Foreign Missions, "It may surprise you to hear from me at this place. I have been here for two weeks, and intend to be here until God, in his good providence, gives me something to do."[15]

God's providence was soon revealed through the instrument of his good servant Sheldon Jackson. Knowing that Menaul was unemployed, Jackson queried the home mission board about the possibility of convincing the missionary to take a position at the Laguna Pueblo. Cyrus Dickson, one of the board secretaries, told Jackson that the board members would be pleased if Menaul could be useful at the pueblo, but since they had no authority to intervene in the selection process, they could not become involved. Interpreting this response, perhaps, as a go-ahead, Jackson arranged for Ben Thomas, with Menaul's approval, to make the appointment at Laguna. Menaul was placed on the payroll of the Office of Indian Affairs at a salary of fifty dollars per month, which would be supplemented by a pledge of support in the amount of five hundred dollars per year from the ladies home mission society in Albany, New York.[16]

With all of the preliminary work now successfully completed, Jackson and John Menaul, Ben Thomas, and George Smith, pastor of the Santa Fe Presbyterian Church, set out from Santa Fe for Laguna on March 23, 1876. At their destination, communicating with the Indians required rather complex linguistic arrangements. One interpreter would translate the visitors' comments into Spanish, and another would then transform the Spanish into the native tongue of the Indians. Jackson and each member of his party began by preaching short, simple Gospel sermons to their attentive audience. Jackson informed the Indians that he had brought a minister to live among them and teach them about Jesus their Savior. The Indians responded with expressions of joy, according to Jackson, and the governor announced, "Now they could learn of God and his law; now they could learn to be good; they would do as the good men had told them; it was all good—very good." Concluding his story, which he published in the *Rocky Mountain Presbyterian*, about these moving events, Jackson could not refrain from making his customary appeal for more financial support for home missions. "When will the Church realize," he declaimed, "that tens of thousands in our own land have never even heard that there was a Savior? If the Church will increase her offerings . . . then the gospel can be sent to every tribe and kindred in our borders."[17]

Jackson could not become personally involved with carrying the Gospel to every tribe in the West, but he did find opportunities in the days ahead to bring the message of his church to two other Indian pueblos in New Mexico. He made three trips to New Mexico in 1877. On each occasion, his commitment to extend the influence of his church among the pueblos was strengthened. On his first trip early in 1877 he directed his attention to conditions at the Zuni Pueblo in western New Mexico near the border with Arizona. Ben Thomas divulged the basis for Jackson's concern in a letter to the Board of Foreign Missions on February 5. After praising John Menaul's work at Laguna, Thomas announced, "Rev. Sheldon Jackson has a movement on foot to place a man with the same qualifications on the same basis at the Pueblo of Zuni. This must be carried out if possible, the more surely because the Mormons are creeping into that place and will soon have possession of the place and the Indians."[18] Thus inspired, Jackson arranged a journey for the spring of 1877 to New Mexico and Arizona that would include stops at Zuni and other pueblos and Indian agencies along the way. His traveling companion was a man who had already attained a reputation as a perceptive observer and recorder of life in the Rocky Mountain West.

William H. Jackson had achieved renown as the official photographer for the government surveys of the West led by Ferdinand Hayden after the Civil War. In Washington, D.C., during the winter of 1876–77, Sheldon Jackson told William of his intention to visit New Mexico in the spring of 1877. Sheldon invited William to join him, and the latter quickly agreed when he learned of the extent of Sheldon's proposed itinerary.[19] Sheldon met William in Pueblo, Colorado, on March 22, and they continued on together to La Veta, Colorado, the end of track at that time of the Denver and Rio Grande Railroad. From there they traveled by team and wagon to Taos and Santa Fe, where they turned west for a long and arduous trip to Fort Wingate, New Mexico. From there, the two Jacksons proceeded to the Zuni Pueblo, located near the Arizona border.[20]

The Jacksons were well received at Zuni. At a council with the governor of the pueblo and other leaders of the tribe, Sheldon Jackson received assurances that the Indians warmly approved of the establishment of a mission school for their children. Land would be made available for a mission building, and the tribal council would see that the children were regular in their attendance at school. Gratified by these promises, Sheldon and his traveling companion continued their journey into Arizona, where they stopped briefly at the Navajo Agency at Fort Defiance before moving on to the Hopi villages located atop several high mesas about eighty miles west.

When the travelers left the Hopi villages, they retraced their route, starting on the homeward leg of their journey. William Jackson left the party in northwestern New Mexico to visit and photograph Indian ruins in the Chaco Canyon. Sheldon Jackson, meanwhile, hurried on to attend a meeting of the Presbytery of Colorado on May 9 in Colorado Springs. He told those attending the meeting of his experiences among the poor Indians who had no knowledge of Christ, and one reporter recalled that Jackson shocked his audience by displaying "a number of hideous and veritable specimens of idols" he had collected from the pueblos.[21]

The results of the great trip varied sharply for William and Sheldon. Commenting on William's role in the expedition, one reporter in an eastern newspaper observed how he had secured a complete set of photos of the remarkable scenes encountered by the travelers, and that these pictures would soon be available in published form. Regrettably, that goal was not realized. William had taken nearly four hundred exposures with a new form of dry film, instead of relying on the old wet plate method that had been so successful for him on previous occasions. He was surely discouraged, to say the least, when all of his efforts to develop the film failed. Scholars studying the history of the West can only regret that an extraordinary opportunity to view the land and the people was lost forever.[22]

Sheldon Jackson did secure a residual benefit from this trip, which aided him in his goal to bring the gospel to the Indians he met on his journey. At one point, as he was traveling between Santa Fe and Fort Wingate, he recorded in his journal, "In camp at Rio Puerco we found Agt. B. M. Thomas."[23] Ben Thomas then accompanied the party to the Zuni Pueblo, and he and Jackson came away from that experience with the shared conviction to open a school at the pueblo as soon as possible. Thomas had previously told Jackson of his interest in this project, and he had assured him of his expectation to have six hundred dollars available for the year July 1, 1877, through June 30, 1878, with which to pay the salary of a school teacher at Zuni. Thomas then left the responsibility of recruiting for the position in Jackson's hands. In a later communication to Jackson, Thomas went even further. He told Jackson of his willingness to discontinue the schools at six other pueblos where Thomas had appointed teachers, with the exception of the school conducted by John Menaul at the Laguna Pueblo. The other five teachers to be discharged were not Presbyterians; Jackson could find replacements to reopen the schools with the understanding that the Board of Home Missions would provide additional financial support to augment the six hundred dollar annual salary per teacher from Thomas's agency payroll.[24]

It would appear that Ben Thomas was prepared, in fact, to create a predominantly Presbyterian presence in the pueblo schools by quietly manipulating the system. Under the terms of the Grant Peace Policy, an Indian agent could be appointed on the recommendation of the religious denomination assigned the responsibility for a particular tribe. The agent could then hire one or more teachers, depending on the funds available, to open schools at his agency. There was no stipulation in these arrangements that the teachers be from the same church, or from any church for that matter. Staffing with members of a single denomination was not prohibited, and Thomas would have considered his intentions responsive to the spirit of the celebrated Peace Policy. Any course of action, he might have believed, that would provide the Indians with the teachings offered in a good church school would surely contribute significantly to the goal of uplifting them. There is no existing record of Jackson's response to Thomas's overture, but he did move quickly to recruit a teacher for the Zuni Pueblo, which had never had a resident teacher. He revealed his strategy in the August 1877 edition of his newspaper with the statement that Dr. and Mrs. Henry K. Palmer had been commissioned to commence a school at the Zuni Pueblo, where the Indians "are worshippers of the sun and moon, like the Baalites of old."[25]

The Palmers were members of the First Presbyterian Church in Colorado Springs, Colorado, where Dr. Palmer conducted a medical practice.

He and his wife had previous missionary experience working for the Board of Foreign Missions in India. Palmer arrived at Zuni on October 22, 1877, following the route Sheldon Jackson had taken earlier in the year. He opened his school with ten pupils a few days later.

He soon formed an opinion about the challenges he faced. "I do not believe that a more needy field exists in the world," he reported in the *Rocky Mountain Presbyterian*, "and the work is that of the most heathenish of people.... There are at least 1,300 souls in this Pueblo, and no one else has ever attempted to gather them as a portion of Christ's harvest."[26] Mrs. Palmer joined her husband on November 28. Her initial impression of the Zuni people was not favorable. "They have stolen my coffee pot," she complained to Jackson. "They are all, men, women and children, full of vermin. The women are the most disgusting women I have ever met in their appearance."[27] Mrs. Palmer thought, however, that she could discern a way to raise up a generation of educated Zuni women. The solution, she suggested, was "a boarding school, into which we could gather the most promising girls and keep them under Christian influence, away from their homes, for a few years."[28]

While the Palmers were trying to adapt to their lives at Zuni, Sheldon Jackson was working on plans for a school at another of the pueblos. His involvement in this new project originated from his second trip to New Mexico in the fall of 1877 when, according to a friend, he was "favored with more agreeable company than usually fell to his lot on missionary journeys."[29] This "agreeable company" included Mrs. Jackson and Henry Kendall and his wife. The home mission board secretary had finally consented to accompany Jackson on this tour of inspection, although he hoped that the rigorous travel schedule would not be too hard for the ladies. With Jackson's assurance that their wives would find the conditions tolerable, the party set out from Denver early in September. They visited James Roberts and his family in Taos, and then they moved on to Santa Fe, where Ben Thomas made his agency wagon available for the continuation of their trip. Their next stop was the Laguna Pueblo. John Menaul later recalled that the time spent with his distinguished visitors was pleasing and profitable. The travelers also visited the pueblo of Jemez, located about forty miles west of Santa Fe. There they found that a small school that had operated briefly was now without a teacher, an unfortunate situation that Jackson was determined to address as soon as possible. The Jacksons and Kendalls returned to Denver in mid October, and when Jackson commented on their experiences in his newspaper, he spoke highly of Henry Kendall's conduct on the journey. "If the church could have seen," Jackson noted, "how gracefully the senior secretary of home missions can handle a frying pan before a camp fire, eat off a tin plate seated Indian fashion, and when night comes roll up in a blanket and sleep on the ground without a tent, the coyotes barking around the camp, they would recognize the same vigour that is everywhere manifest in home missions."[30]

Certainly Jackson exhibited considerable vigor in his commitment to fill the vacancy at the Jemez school. Soon after his return to Denver, he wrote to Dr. John M. Shields, a member of the Presbyterian church in the small town of Covode, Pennsylvania, offering him the Jemez teaching position. Shields accepted, and when he and his family arrived at Jemez on March 6, 1878, his impressions of the Jemez Indians were similar to those formed at Zuni by Dr. and Mrs. Palmer. Writing later in two "Home Mission Letters to Children," he noted how the Indians all had vermin on their bodies, "and some will even appropriate to their own use things that do not belong to them." He believed, however, that the Indians were just as good, by nature, as other people, "but they are ignorant and thick darkness is resting upon them." At the school he had opened on March 18, some of the children came to classes completely naked. Mrs. Shields began to make dresses for the little girls, and "you just ought to see how good they seem to feel with a nice clean dress, and fixed up like little girls ought to be."[31]

While John Shields labored in Jemez to put his house in order, Jackson made his third trip in 1877 to New Mexico. His purpose on that occasion was to attend a meeting of the Presbytery of Santa Fe, scheduled to convene in Taos on November 9. The delegates there prepared a resolution to the Board of Foreign Missions stating, in part, "That the Home Board having undertaken with vigor the work of Evangelization in this territory, it [the Presbytery of Santa Fe] has placed all the work within the bounds of this Presbytery, among both Mexicans and Indians, under the care of that Board."[32]

This action, presented as a fait accompli, calling for a transfer of authority from one board of the church to another, was not accepted with equanimity by the Board of Foreign Missions. John Lowrie, secretary of that board, wrote to James Roberts, who had signed the resolution as moderator of the Santa Fe Presbytery, requesting clarification of intent. Roberts hastened to inform Lowrie that the delegates to the presbytery meeting had been assured by Sheldon Jackson, who was present, "that the measure was entirely in harmony with the wishes of the Foreign Board."[33]

The latter assumption was manifestly incorrect. Relations between the two boards on the matter of supervision of missionary work among the Indians were decidedly inharmonious, a fact that Jackson knew very well. He was determined, however, to force the issue on this controversial topic. The members of the Board of Foreign Missions were well acquainted with

Jackson's intent. "We understand that our friend, Rev. S. Jackson and others," John Lowrie had written earlier to Ben Thomas, "are doing everything in their power to have this work placed by the General Assembly, or by the Presbyteries, in the hands of the Home Board."[34]

Indeed, delegates to the annual meetings of the General Assembly at this time were acutely aware of this power struggle. Jackson had assumed a leadership role in the drive to place the American Indian mission work in the hands of the Board of Home Missions early in 1877. In his view, any form of mission work within the United States should quite logically be directed by the Board of Home Missions. Not so, said the Standing Committee on Foreign Missions of the General Assembly. A report from that group at the annual meeting in 1877 asked the commissioners to recall that the great work of foreign missions in the Presbyterian Church in the United States began with efforts to evangelize the native Indians. "That mission was, and is," the report stated, "the tap-root of this wide spreading tree that now overshadows nations with its branches." A legacy of many years of successful work by the Board of Foreign Missions among the Indians who "sit in darkness and the shadow of death," should not be lightly laid aside, the report concluded, "for the experiment of an untried superintendence, which, if successful, promises no superior efficiency."[35]

The battle lines had now been drawn. The General Assembly tactfully decided to postpone any decisive action by referring the matter to a joint committee of members from each of the mission boards for further study. Those who may have hoped for a clear-cut decision one way or the other on this matter from the joint committee were surely disappointed. Reporting in the spring of 1878, the committee members decided, essentially, that no jurisdictional changes were warranted at present. If and when the time should arrive when a transfer of responsibility for Indian missions was deemed appropriate, that action could be taken only by the General Assembly with the sanction of the whole church. In the meantime, the committee report concluded, "We deprecate as suicidal to the common cause everything that tends to produce or foster a hostile rivalry between Home and Foreign Missions."[36]

Jackson's failure to obtain official sanction from the leaders of his church for the home board to take responsibility for all Indian mission programs did not deter him from continuing his personal crusade to strengthen and expand this work in New Mexico. Once again, the Presbytery of Santa Fe added its endorsement to his endeavors by appointing him a committee "to solicit special funds for the erection of mission chapels and premises among the Pueblo villages of New Mexico."[37] In September of 1878, the rather unusual one-man committee made another trip to New Mexico to visit the pueblos of Jemez, Laguna, and Zuni. At Jemez, Jackson, assisted by John Shields and José Perea, who served as interpreter for Jackson on this journey, organized a church with six members on September 8. Jackson was especially pleased when this solemn ceremony was enhanced by the singing of special hymns by three little girls from the audience. Moving on to Laguna, Jackson, Perea, and John Menaul organized a church on September 15 for a few of the residents who, according to one reporter, had given up their "heathen dances" and had exhibited good evidence of having become Christians.[38]

At Zuni, the outlook for the school and mission station was less encouraging. In April of 1878, Henry Kendall in New York had received a terse notification from John Menaul revealing that Henry Palmer was on his way back to his former home in Colorado Springs to die. Reporting on this tragedy in his newspaper, Jackson explained, "Exposure incident to the establishment of a new mission rapidly developed lung disease and compelled the relinquishment of the work that was opening up with great promise."[39] Jackson moved quickly to find someone to take Palmer's place, and when he visited Zuni in September he could tell the tribal leaders that Dr. Taylor Ealy, with his wife and two small daughters, would soon arrive to carry on for the fallen Palmer. Ealy had tried to conduct a school and mission station at Lincoln in southeastern New Mexico earlier in the year, but an outbreak of violence between two rival factions in the town had compelled him to seek employment elsewhere. Jackson left José Perea at Zuni to help the Ealys get established, and he came away from the Pueblo feeling confident that the residents would give a warm welcome to the new missionaries when they arrived in October.[40]

Following his journey to New Mexico in September, Jackson wrote several lengthy articles in the *Rocky Mountain Presbyterian* about his travels. Adhering faithfully to his charge from the Presbytery of Santa Fe to raise funds for mission structures in the pueblos of New Mexico, he always included in his narrative a story carefully calculated to bring contributions from eastern philanthropists for the Indian missions. For example, describing his visit with the Shields family at Jemez, he wrote, "This noble family is living in one of these uncomfortable old buildings, full of poisonous insects, where, during my stay, a centipede dropped from the grass ceiling. Hasten to gather the funds for the Pueblo mission buildings, that this and the other families may have comfortable, healthy homes."[41] He also targeted the children of the church at large as potential donors with creation of a Children's Church Building Stock Company. This innovative enterprise offered certificates of stock at ten cents a share to all young people who would contribute part of their savings to the worthy cause of erecting mission premises where, as Jackson explained, Christian teachers could tell Indian children about the Savior. And to make sure that his readers comprehended the magnitude of the task before them, he proclaimed, "The centuries of labor of the Roman Catholic Church among them [the Pueblo Indians] has been a complete failure, and it remains for the Presbyterian Church to take hold of them at this late day and instruct, elevate and Christianize them."[42]

Jackson may have concluded at the end of the 1870s that the process of instructing, elevating, and Christianizing the Pueblo Indians by Presbyterian missionaries was progressing as well as could be expected. If that was his appraisal of the situation, it was certainly shared by Abraham Earle, a prominent resident of New York City, who visited several of the pueblos in 1879. Earle's inspection tour was mandated by the Board of Indian Commissioners, of which he was a member. The board had been created by President Grant in 1869 to monitor expenditures of the Office of Indian Affairs. In his report on this journey, Earle had many words of praise for the Presbyterian mission stations at Laguna, Jemez, and Zuni. He noted that each of the devoted teachers at these three pueblos was also acting in the capacity of physician. That was not a coincidence. When Jackson had called for applicants to fill the teaching positions at these pueblos, he had included the stipulation that the prospective missionaries have some knowledge of medicine.[43]

Jackson visited the New Mexico pueblos again in November of 1879. At Zuni he was impressed by the work of Taylor Ealy, who had graduated in 1874 from the University of Pennsylvania with a degree in medicine. He found Ealy, who had replaced the departed Henry Palmer, erecting what he regarded as a suitable dwelling for his family. Ealy shared the teaching responsibilities with his wife and a young lady who had arrived in the summer of 1879 from Pennsylvania to assist at the mission station.[44]

Jackson stopped at the Jemez Pueblo after leaving Zuni. He knew that John Shields had endured much discouragement and travail over the course of the last year. Tragedy had struck the Shields family in the first week of November of 1878, when Mrs. Shields died of typhoid fever. Announcing her death to Jackson, Shields lamented, "Mrs. S. told me to bury her here and stay with these people. . . . The boys and I are keeping house and doing the best we can, but oh, it is very lonely and we miss Mama so much."[45] In June of 1879, however, two young women from Pennsylvania arrived at the pueblo to serve as teaching assistants in Shields's school, and Jackson was surely pleased when he was asked to conduct a marriage ceremony for John Shields and one of the young ladies on November 10.[46]

With the situation at Jemez stabilized for the time being, Jackson continued his journey. For some reason, he did not include the Laguna Pueblo in the itinerary for his trip in 1879. Perhaps he was pressed for time. He did know from several reports that John Menaul was doing a fine job at that mission station. The physician employed by the army at Fort Wingate, New Mexico, for example, had told Jackson, "He is a peculiar genius, can preach, teach and practice medicine, build a house, weave a carpet or a blanket, build a mill, and alter a Springfield rifle to a breech loader, and other such mechanical work so that he is a desirable acquisition to any community that is taking its first steps in civilization."[47] Another visitor to Laguna, who also described Menaul as a genius, had noted, "He has a printing office at Laguna, and is engaged in translating American schoolbooks for the benefit of the heathen."[48]

Confident that the good work initiated at the three pueblos was in good hands, Jackson embarked on a new program in 1880 directed toward the education of Indian children. Early in the year, he secured permission from Carl Schurz, secretary of the interior, to take fifteen Navajo, ten Pueblo, and five Hopi children to the industrial training school for Indian children that had opened the previous year in abandoned army barracks at Carlisle, Pennsylvania. At least one of the men whom Jackson had secured to open schools at the Indian pueblos in New Mexico viewed this new development with high regard. Writing to Jackson from the Jemez Pueblo, John Shields proclaimed, "If we just had these dear children away from this Sink of Abomination and iniquity [Jemez Pueblo] we might soon see them clothed and in their right mind and sitting at the feet of Jesus, meek and lowly, and ready to learn of him instead of Montezuma.[49]

Jackson traveled to New Mexico and Arizona in June and July to try and fill his quota of young Indian scholars. With the help of Ben Thomas he was successful in securing the ten Pueblo children, but at the Navajo and Moqui agencies in Arizona he failed to obtain the parental permission required for the trip. After delivering the ten Pueblo boys and one other lad identified only as an Apache boy to the authorities at Carlisle, Jackson soon decided that he would try again when he learned that he could draw on a larger area for his recruiting efforts. In August of 1880, the Dutch Reformed Church transferred the Indian tribes in Arizona that had been assigned to their care under the Grant Peace Policy to the Presbyterian Church. Interpreting the action as an opportunity to enlarge the area of his campaign to obtain students for the Carlisle School, Jackson set out on another recruiting journey at the end of December of 1880.[50]

There was one notable difference between Jackson's first and second expeditions to New Mexico and Arizona in 1880 and 1881. On the second trip, his wife, Mary, accompanied him, with the thought that she could assist in the care of the children, some of whom, on this occasion, would be

girls. Jackson was successful in securing the number of children he had
hoped for from the Pima, Papago, Maricopa, and San Carlos Apache agencies in Arizona. Stories were circulating during their travels about Indians
on the warpath attacking stagecoaches, but the Jackson party was not mo-
lested. Returning, they safely reached Albuquerque, where they were joined
by ten girls and boys from the Indian pueblos of New Mexico who would
accompany them early in February to the Carlisle School and to the Hampton Institute in Virginia, another government boarding school that accepted Indian students.[51]

During Jackson's recruiting trips for Carlisle and Hampton, he and Ben
Thomas had been instrumental in coordinating the partnership of the Interior Department and the Board of Home Missions in the opening of the
Pueblo Indian Industrial School near Albuquerque. The school opened on
January 1, 1881, and at the end of the year the superintendent reported an
average enrollment of thirty-six students.[52] In 1881, Jackson added a school
for Indian children in Arizona to the roster of institutions sponsored by
the Presbyterian Church in the Southwest. At the Pima Agency, Charles
Cook, a Methodist who had been involved in mission work in Chicago,
had operated a school as a government teacher on the agency payroll from
January of 1871 until September of 1878. Jackson met him when he visited
the agency in January of 1881. He persuaded Cook to become a Presbyterian and conduct a mission and school for the Pimas sponsored by the
Board of Home Missions.[53]

At the end of 1881, Jackson could look back with mixed feelings on the
results of his efforts during the past decade in behalf of the Indians of his
superintendency. In his mind, he had at least made a start, in certain selected areas, in fostering moral, intellectual, and spiritual growth in most
Indians. The Presbyterian Indian mission school was intended as the primary instrument of change in this uplifting process. One eastern writer
who assessed Jackson's work found it very commendable. "It is hoped," he
ventured, "that the grand solution of the Indian question has been found
in their [Presbyterian] educational system."[54] Not everyone, of course,
shared this sanguine hope for solution to a problem that had defied the
best intentions of many white Americans since the origins of their nation.
One westerner offered a different appraisal of church schools for Indians
in the West. "Schools were established," he insisted, "and usually presided
over by the wife, sister, or daughter of the agent who sat in front of empty
desks and their labors consisted chiefly in making out elaborate reports
and sending them to Washington."[55] In Presbyterian eyes, this gentleman
was surely a wrong thinker. If the number of good Indians who were ground
from the Presbyterian educational mills was small, then the fault was to be

found not in the process but in an unfortunate paucity of Presbyterian human and financial resources.

In any event, Sheldon Jackson had already decided on a course of action that would drastically alter his connection to the development of Presbyterianism in the Rocky Mountain West and the fate of Indian schools sponsored by his denomination. He would continue to strive for the growth of schools in the Southwest. But he would also permit his interest in Indian schools to carry him far from his headquarters in Denver, Colorado. As early as 1877 he had felt compelled to bring the message of Presbyterianism to a still more distant unchurched wilderness. "Rev. Sheldon Jackson is at Ft. Wrangle [Wrangell], Alaska," a reporter noted in the *Rocky Mountain Presbyterian* in September of 1877, "establishing a Home Mission Station among the whites and Indians at that place."[56] By 1881 Jackson was prepared to move on to accept new challenges in his quest to win the West for Christ. He gradually relinquished his role as superintendent of Presbyterian Missions in the Rocky Mountain West, and, according to one of his colleagues, "although he knew it not then, the rest of his active life was to be devoted to the education and evangelization of the people of this far-away northland."[57]

11 | A New Field for Conquest

The Secretaries of the Board did not fully approve of my action,
but as the step had been taken, they concluded to accept the
situation and enter the Alaska work.
—SHELDON JACKSON, N.D.

Delegates to the General Assembly of the Presbyterian Church
who met in Pittsburgh in May of 1878 were surely pleased to note in a
report on the "State of Religion" that their church was now established in
all the frontier states and territories of the Union. "The past year has seen
an advance along the whole line," the document proclaimed. "Many a battle
has been fought and won above the clouds in the Rocky Mountains and
Sierras. . . . Even to far off Alaska the banner of the cross has been carried."[1] The intrepid standard bearer who had established the outpost in
Alaska was Sheldon Jackson. Henry Kendall and Cyrus Dickson, the secretaries of the Board of Home Missions, revealed the reason for Jackson's
presence in the area in a letter to the secretary of the interior soliciting
funds for Presbyterian mission schools in Alaska. The board secretaries
explained how they had received a petition in June of 1877 from Fort
Wrangell, Alaska, pleading for a school and teachers. The call appeared so
urgent "that Dr. Sheldon Jackson, Superintendent of our missions and
educational work in the territories visited Alaska."[2]

The statement by Kendall and Dickson really deserved clarification in
several areas. The petition mentioned by the board secretaries was a letter
written by a soldier stationed at Fort Wrangell. He had directed the letter
to General Oliver O. Howard, commandant of the Department of the
Columbia in the Pacific Northwest. The general, in turn, forwarded the
document to a Presbyterian missionary in Portland, Oregon, who gave it
to the commissioner from the Presbytery of Oregon to take to the General
Assembly scheduled to meet in Chicago on May 17, 1877. When he met
Sheldon Jackson at the assembly meeting, the delegate from Oregon gave
the letter to Jackson, who promptly had it published in a Chicago newspa-

per and various Presbyterian periodicals. He then forwarded the original letter to the Board of Home Missions, expressing his hope that a Presbyterian missionary could be sent to Alaska as soon as possible.[3]

Kendall and Dickson had also stretched the truth a bit in the wording of their comments to the secretary of the interior. Alaska was certainly not included within the boundaries of Jackson's superintendency at the time. And Jackson's charge from the board for his journey in the summer of 1877 did not mention Alaska. He was expected to evaluate the status of Presbyterian mission work only in Idaho, eastern Oregon and Washington, and Nevada. Commenting on his deviation from the board's directive, Jackson confessed that he had added Alaska to his itinerary without orders from or the knowledge of the Board of Home Missions, but that he was beyond the means of communication and felt he must act on his own responsibility. "The Secretaries of the Board did not fully approve of my action," he admitted, "but as the step had been taken, they concluded to accept the situation and enter the Alaska work."[4] While Jackson probably did perceive the need for schools in Alaska, as implied in the letter from the secretaries, he had another reason for his action. He had learned that Episcopal and Catholic missionaries were actively exploring the field, and his intervention, he explained, also "prevented the Methodists from occupying the ground."[5]

Whatever the motives for making the unauthorized change in plans, Jackson set out on his extraordinary journey early in July of 1877. He traveled by train to northwestern Utah, where he transferred to a stagecoach that carried him to Boise, Idaho, where he conducted the first Presbyterian worship service in the territorial capital on Sunday, July 15. He continued his travels on the following day, passing through Walla Walla in southeastern Washington. He reached the Columbia River at a point where he could board a river steamer, which took him downstream to Portland, Oregon. There he met Amanda McFarland, wife of David McFarland who had founded the church at Santa Fe, New Mexico, in 1867. When the McFarlands left Santa Fe in 1873, they had gone to San Diego, California, where David had hoped to establish a female seminary. The enterprise was short-lived, however, and he and his wife moved again to teach at the Nez Perce Indian reservation in northern Idaho. David died there on May 13, 1876, and Amanda moved to Portland, where she met Jackson and courageously agreed to accompany him to Alaska with the intention of remaining to conduct a school at Fort Wrangell.[6]

Jackson's selection of Fort Wrangell, located along the coast of the southern panhandle of Alaska, was not made by chance. He knew that a native who had been converted to Christianity several years earlier at a Methodist mission in British Columbia was conducting a school of sorts there.[7] When Jackson and Amanda McFarland landed at Fort Wrangell on August 10, after a scenic voyage from Tacoma, Washington, they found the young Indian teacher willing to work with Amanda to enlarge the schoolwork under Presbyterian auspices in Fort Wrangell. Amanda could not have been pleased with the school facilities she inherited. A dance hall had at first been rented for this purpose, but the building had been relinquished and the students were now meeting in a dilapidated log house. She bravely accepted the challenge, however, and she and her Indian assistant were determined to keep the school open.

Jackson did his part after his return to Colorado by widely publicizing the need for missionaries and money to support the good work in Alaska. The Board of Home Missions reacted positively to these concerns near the end of 1877. John G. Brady, a recent graduate of Union Theological Seminary in New York City, was assigned to establish a mission and school at Sitka, the territorial capital of Alaska. At the same time, the board commissioned another young seminary graduate to work with Amanda McFarland at the little mission station at Fort Wrangell.[8]

In the ensuing months, Jackson continued his fund-raising campaign for the Alaskan mission field. By the summer of 1879 he had secured three thousand dollars for construction of mission buildings at Fort Wrangell, and at the end of June he set out once more for the far North. He was accompanied by his wife, Mary, and by Dr. and Mrs. Henry Kendall. When they reached Fort Wrangell, the mission board secretary apparently made a profound impression on some of the Indians. In his report, Jackson noted, "One after another of their chiefs and leading men called to see him and express their pleasure at his visit; one with great earnestness remarked that he had not slept all night for joy."[9] The culmination of this inspiring trip occurred on August 3, when Jackson and Kendall participated in a service organizing a Presbyterian church for Fort Wrangell. At the end of the year, after the Jacksons and Kendalls returned to the States, Amanda McFarland reported a joyous Christmas celebration in her school, complete with the singing of carols and a visit by Santa Claus. She was also pleased to announce that services on the Sabbath were well attended. "It was very inspiring," she told Jackson, "to see so many of these poor creatures with their blankets and painted faces crowding into the church."[10]

With mission stations in place at Sitka and Fort Wrangell at the end of 1879, Jackson was ready to begin a new decade with a personal commitment to concentrate his time and efforts on Alaska. One clear signal of this realignment came in 1880 with his publication of *Alaska and Missions on the North Pacific Coast*. In that volume he described effusively the new treasure box of natural resources waiting to be opened by courageous American pioneers. He also emphasized the pressing need for schools and churches to ensure that what he considered a proper Christian society would evolve from the intermingling of native inhabitants and new arrivals from the States.[11] This and other indications of Jackson's diminishing concern for the Rocky Mountain West brought some angry declamations from missionaries in that area. At a meeting of the Presbytery of Santa Fe in the fall of 1879, for example, those present reminded Jackson that "the souls of the people in New Mexico were as precious as the souls of Alaska."[12] And at a meeting of the Presbytery of Montana in February of 1880, the delegates prepared a report for the Board of Home Missions that reviewed all of the old complaints about Jackson's alleged lack of interest in their problems. The members of the Presbytery resolved "that the Presbytery is strongly and unanimously opposed to having the Rev. Sheldon Jackson, synodical missionary, Synod of Colorado, devote any part of his time or attention to working within the bounds of this Presbytery."[13]

Clearly the time had arrived for the Board of Home Missions to re-evaluate Jackson's position. The board members decided, as a first step, to subdivide Jackson's old superintendency. At the end of 1880, Duncan McMillan agreed to give up his work with the church and school at Mt. Pleasant, Utah, and to move to Salt Lake City, where he would assume the duties of synodical missionary for Montana and Utah. In the summer of the following year, the pastor of the church in Boulder, Colorado, received authorization to serve as synodical missionary for Colorado and Wyoming. That left Jackson with a new commission, dated October 1, 1881, to oversee the work in New Mexico and Arizona. Candidly analyzing this sequence of events, one of Jackson's colleagues concluded, "With the modest title of 'Missionary' on the face of his commission—which meant to one reading between the lines—*missionary at large*, he looked after the interests of New Mexico and Alaska."[14]

A change in responsibilities was also accompanied by a change of residence for Jackson and his family. Their decision at the end of 1881 to move to New York City was justified, in the opinion of a family friend, because "of the exceptional opportunity this afforded to scan the whole field from this central watch tower behind the lines."[15] Jackson also decided at this time to present his newspaper to the Board of Home Missions. The title was changed from the *Rocky Mountain Presbyterian* to *Presbyterian Home Missions*, and it became the official organ of the Board of Home Missions, with the understanding that the work of the Woman's Executive Committee of Home Missions would be emphasized in its pages. An interpretation of these events could only have led to one conclusion. Jackson might be nominally involved in other mission fields, but, to all intents and purposes, his attention would now turn to the far Northwest.[16]

Jackson made another trip to Alaska in the summer of 1881. He established several mission stations among the native tribes in southeastern Alaska, and he managed to secure missionary families to staff these new outposts. He named one of the new locations Haines, honoring Frances Haines, his good friend and the secretary of the Woman's Executive Committee of Home Missions.[17] In the following year he returned again with five thousand dollars, which he had raised to assist John Brady at Sitka in a school-building project. Brady had abandoned his missionary assignment at Sitka at the end of 1878, but he returned in May of 1879 to seek his fortune as a private businessman. He retained his strong support, however, for Presbyterian missionary efforts in the area, and he sponsored an industrial school for boys at Sitka, in November of 1880, in an abandoned building belonging to the government. Unfortunately, the building burned to the ground on January 24, 1882. When Jackson arrived with his funds early in September, he and Brady worked diligently to erect a new structure on a plot of ground donated by Brady. When Jackson departed later in the fall, he could look back with satisfaction at an imposing school building that was known locally by several names, including the Sheldon Jackson Institute.[18]

The record of Jackson's activities in 1883 contains some incidents that can only be described as bewildering. In the previous year, the home mission board had provided an annual salary of twenty-five hundred dollars for him, with the notation in the board minutes that it would "allow him to remain in New York to help in the office until the Board became thoroughly acquainted with all the details of conducting *Presbyterian Home Missions.*[19] In January of 1883, the board continued its affirmation of this role for Jackson with a commission designating him business manager of his former newspaper at a salary of two thousand dollars, one quarter of which was to be provided by the Woman's Executive Committee of Home Missions. These actions seemed designed to find a niche for Jackson at the headquarters of the Board of Home Missions in New York, but in the fall of 1883 he and his family moved once again, this time to Washington, D.C.[20]

This latest relocation may not have come as a great surprise to those who knew Jackson best. There was simply no way for this dynamic individual to devote the remainder of his active years to an office job in New York. His overwhelming concern was to spread the word about the needs of the Alaska mission field. One of his friends who was very impressed by Jackson's efforts in this behalf estimated that the indefatigable publicist delivered approximately nine hundred addresses about Alaska from 1878 to 1884.[21] But what necessitated a move to Washington late in 1883? Jackson himself might have replied, quite simply, that decisions regarding Alaska's future were finally receiving serious consideration in the nation's capital. He had already been called upon to testify on several occasions before congressional committees on issues pertaining to Alaska, and he now had hopes that 1884 would be the year when a bill providing a system of government for the territory would finally be enacted.[22]

Previous attempts to pass a so-called organic act for Alaska had all failed, but at the end of 1883 prospects did appear brighter because a prominent senator had taken a personal interest in the matter. Taking advantage of his position as chairman of the Senate Committee on the Territories, Benjamin Harrison, an ardent Presbyterian, introduced an Alaska bill in December of 1883. Jackson, who was a good friend of Harrison's, lobbied energetically in Washington early in 1884 for passage of the legislation. Finally, after some revisions, President Chester Arthur signed the long-awaited organic act into law on May 17, 1884. Jackson was undoubtedly pleased with the educational section of the act. Provision would be made for the education of children without regard for race, and twenty-five thousand dollars would be appropriated for that purpose.[23]

Following passage of the Alaska act, Jackson decided to take a break from the pressures of Washington politics. In what might have been termed a working vacation, he utilized a tactic that had once served him well in Colorado to spread the word about the natural wonders of Alaska. At the conclusion of the annual meeting of the National Education Association in Madison, Wisconsin, in July, Jackson led an excursion of approximately 150 delegates on a tour of southern Alaska. And, armed with a new commission from the Board of Home Missions to serve as missionary to the congregation at Sitka, he managed to combine business with pleasure on the journey. After the excursionists returned to the States at the end of August, he stayed on in Sitka to organize the First Presbyterian Church of Sitka and the Presbytery of Alaska. The latter entity represented missionaries and teachers at six mission stations in southeast Alaska. At the end of the year, one of the summer excursionists, acknowledging Jackson's efforts in their behalf, told the tour leader, "You have done more than all others to bring the land and its people to the thought of the world."[24]

In 1885, the man regarded by many as "Mr. Alaska" received recognition for his services in a manner regarded, perhaps, as commonplace in the national political arena. Responsibility for the administration of funds appropriated for education in Alaska had been placed with the Bureau of Education in the Department of the Interior. The commissioner of education was John Eaton, a good friend of Jackson's and a fellow Presbyterian. He announced that, effective April 11, 1885, Sheldon Jackson would be the general agent of education for Alaska on the government payroll in the Bureau of Education at an annual salary of twelve hundred dollars. For Jackson's career, his acceptance of this position could only be regarded, in terms of its far-reaching consequences, as equivalent to his decision in 1868 to supervise the extension of Presbyterian missionary work in the Rocky Mountain West. Jackson intended, of course, to work hard to bring good schools to all children in Alaska, but he was also determined to do his best to ensure that the principles of "good government" espoused by those he considered right-thinking Americans would be adopted by the new set of territorial officials appointed under the terms of the organic act of 1884.[25]

It was the latter fixation that brought embarrassment, to say the least, to Jackson in Alaska. When he arrived in Sitka with his new commission in May of 1885, he was—arrested! Apparently some of the government officials, who had recently taken office with typical political patronage appointments, did not relish the thought of having a powerful and conscientious churchman interfering in the way they intended to run the territory. The petty indictments against Jackson charged him with obstructing a public road in an expansion project at the Sitka Industrial School. Jackson obtained his release on bail, and when the news of his incarceration reached Washington, the outcry against what was viewed as an injustice eventually resulted in the dismissal of Jackson's accusers and the dropping of all charges by a new territorial judge.[26]

With that obstacle removed from his path, Jackson embarked energetically on a program to bring the blessings of a proper education to the young people of Alaska. During the summer months he traveled extensively throughout his school district, often escorting teachers whom he had recruited in the States to their remote duty stations. On at least one occasion, when he became incommunicado on these long journeys, he received a rebuke from Henry Kendall for not responding to requests for information from the mission board secretary. "I followed you," Kendall wrote later, "with your load of schoolhouses and school teachers . . . out from Seattle into the great wide ocean, and waited to know what I should hear next. I would not have been surprised to hear that you were climbing the frosty north pole."[27] Jackson never reached the pole, but on July 20, 1890, he did succeed in placing a teacher with the Eskimo community at Point Barrow, the northernmost settlement on the Alaskan coast. It was on that trip that Jackson received the impression that the Eskimos living in Arctic Alaska were in danger of extinction because their traditional food sources were becoming depleted. He envisioned a solution to this problem that, ultimately, gave another spin to the wheel of fortune determining his fate.[28]

In his annual report to the commissioner of education covering his trip in 1890, Jackson urged the introduction of domestic reindeer into northern Alaska. "To do this," Jackson asserted, "will give the Eskimo as permanent a food supply as the cattle of the Western plains and sheep of New Mexico and Arizona do the inhabitants of those sections."[29] Early in 1891 an attempt was made to obtain congressional funding for this purpose, but the proposed legislation did not pass. Undaunted, Jackson called for private donations to purchase reindeer in Siberia and transport them across the Bering Sea to Alaska. With $2,146 raised to implement his program, Jackson sailed to several coastal villages in Siberia in the summer of 1891 aboard the U.S. revenue cutter Bear. He procured sixteen reindeer and placed them with Eskimo caretakers at an island off the coast of Alaska. In the following year, another attempt to get federal funding failed, so Jackson returned to Alaskan waters, once more on the *Bear*, with money remaining from the sum he had collected the year before. He succeeded in purchasing 175 reindeer, which were settled on the Alaskan mainland at a point close to Siberia along the Bering Strait. Impressed by these successes, Congress finally appropriated six thousand dollars in 1893 for Jackson to continue his work with the reindeer, and a much publicized moment in Alaskan history was under way.[30]

Jackson continued to merge his interest in reindeer with his responsibilities as general agent for education in Alaska as the nineteenth century drew to a close. There were those who regarded his activities as exceeding, by far, his role as an agent for education. That notion seemed confirmed by a notorious event that occurred in 1898. At the end of the previous year, a report had reached Washington of a large number of miners on the verge of starvation in the remote Yukon Valley of Alaska, where gold had recently been discovered. In Washington, Congress provided a relief fund of $200,000, with a substantial portion of that amount earmarked for acquisition of reindeer from Lapland, the far-northern area of the Scandinavian peninsula in Europe. Reindeer from that region were stipulated, as they were said to be trained as pack animals and, presumably, could form the nucleus of a relief expedition to the endangered miners. Since Sheldon Jackson had attained a reputation as a man knowledgeable about reindeer culture in Alaska, his superiors ordered him to go to Lapland, secure the reindeer, and bring them back to the United States.[31]

Jackson set out from New York on his incredible journey on December 25, 1897. When he reached the target area in Lapland on January 13, 1898, he managed to obtain 538 reindeer, 418 sleds, 511 sets of harness, and sixty-eight Lapp drivers with their wives and children. Jackson and his companions then endured a rough voyage across the Atlantic, arriving finally in New York at the end of February. At that point Jackson's responsibility with the project ceased, and he returned to his home in Washington only to learn that the starving miners had managed to obtain sufficient food for their needs until spring. The movement of the reindeer across the continent continued, however, and Jackson now received orders to travel to Seattle to resume command of the expedition. He rejoined the group in Seattle on March 16, and he shepherded the company as far as Skagway, the port of entry to the gold fields in Alaska. He left his charges in the care of an assistant and he returned, once again, to his home in Washington. The reindeer caravan continued on to its destination, but by the time it finally reached the mining district there were only 141 reindeer remaining out of the original 538.[32]

Many of the critics of government policy in Alaska regarded the reindeer relief plan as a fiasco from start to finish. One of Jackson's colleagues insisted that the disaster should not be attributed to Jackson who, after all, was simply carrying out the mandate of Congress in the matter. This same gentleman admitted, however, that the incident was often quoted "as an illustration of the folly or useless extravagance of those who were responsible for the introduction of the reindeer industry among the Eskimos."[33] Jackson's detractors found added fuel for their critical observations when his old friend, the former Presbyterian missionary John Brady, became governor of Alaska in 1897. Charges of a Presbyterian dynasty that used unethical, and perhaps illegal, practices to direct all aspects of Alaskan affairs were not uncommon. Following one particularly vicious series of accusations, one of Jackson's friends noted, "While these foolish and baseless charges were thus set aside, and utterly failed of their avowed purpose, they did nevertheless influence many people who were ignorant of the facts."[34]

One of the many people who became influenced, finally, by the increasing output of the rumor mills was President Theodore Roosevelt who, in 1905, yielded to pressure from several sources and appointed a special investigator to look into the matter. Frank Churchill, an employee of the Interior Department, traveled to Alaska to gather data for his report, which was published in the Senate Executive Documents series on June 12, 1906. In what appeared to be a thorough examination of the status of Alaskan schools and the reindeer industry in the territory, Churchill drew some unflattering conclusions. He found that Jackson seemed to show undue favoritism for church schools in Alaska. And, although Jackson did encourage several denominations to conduct schools, there was a feeling that "denominational favoritism has prevailed" when numerous Presbyterians showed up on the government payroll. As for the reindeer issue, Churchill pointed to blunders that came from a lack of business experience by those who administered the program. He also detected a danger, in terms of conflict of interest, in Jackson's continuing to draw a salary from the Board of Home Missions while he was employed by the government. Concluding his comments, Churchill found no reason to suspect Jackson of dishonesty or malfeasance. "His health is far from good, and . . . possibly his judgement has in consequence been impaired."[35]

Jackson's friends rallied to his support in the wake of these accusations, but both he and John Brady realized that their influence in Alaskan affairs had been undermined beyond repair. Brady resigned as governor in 1906, and two years later Jackson ended his affiliation with the Bureau of Education. He was very ill at that time, as Frank Churchill had intimated in his report, and the death of his beloved wife, Mary, on August 28, 1908, surely added to his anguish. On January 9, 1909, he wrote to George Darley in Colorado announcing his intention to attend the General Assembly meeting in Denver in May. He thought that it would be an appropriate time for a reunion of as many of the old pioneers as could be present.[36]

Jackson was not destined to attend that gathering. Seriously ill, he moved from his residence in Washington, D.C., to Asheville, North Carolina, where he spent what were to be his last days counseling the students at the Asheville Schools, which were sponsored by the Woman's Board of Home Missions. On April 26 he entered the Asheville hospital for surgery to try to correct a condition causing him almost constant pain. He died on the Sabbath, May 2, 1909, and was buried in the cemetery of his home town, Minaville, New York. Of the many letters he received during his life commending him for his achievements, he may have taken greatest satisfaction from the comments of a friend writing on November 26, 1881: "I do not always sympathize with so-called 'persecuted men,'" his admirer noted, "but somehow my cauld Scotch heart has always warmed to you. . . . Go ahead and in Christ's name unfold the blue flag all over the continent and by and by the grand old orthodox war horses that clamp the bit at your mention will bless the good Lord that Sheldon Jackson lived and labored and cavorted as he did."[37]

Conclusion

I have known Americans to form associations to send priests out into the new states of the West and establish schools and churches there; they fear that religion might be lost in the depths of the forest and that the people growing up there might be less fitted for freedom than those from whom they sprang.
—ALEXIS DE TOQUEVILLE, *Democracy in America*, 1835

It would be a herculean task to recount the fortunes of all of the missionaries who served with Sheldon Jackson in the Rocky Mountain West during the 1870s; however, a brief review of the later careers of some of the most prominent figures will help complete an account of the spread of Presbyterianism in the West. Some of Jackson's comrades-in-arms moved on to other assignments after his departure; others continued to labor in the region for their church.

In Montana, James Russel, who had moved from Deer Lodge to take charge of the church in Butte in 1879, resigned in 1884 when his health failed. He obtained employment in various capacities working for the city until his death in Butte on March 21, 1928. Lyman Crittenden, who had been associated with the Gallatin Valley Female Seminary until it closed in 1878, continued to serve as pastor to several churches in the territory until his death on June 12, 1892 in Belgrade, Montana. The depressed economy in Montana revived when the directors of the Northern Pacific Railroad decided to resume construction in the territory in 1880. A report from one of the Montana missionaries in that year announced, "The outlook at this time is very encouraging. We have more men than ever before."[1]

The outlook in Wyoming at the end of the 1870s was not particularly encouraging, but at least the churches built along the Union Pacific Railroad line at Cheyenne, Laramie, Rawlins, and Evanston still existed. Presbyterianism in Colorado, on the other hand, flourished, and in 1880 the General Assembly agreed to divide the Presbytery of Colorado into the Denver Presbytery (for churches in the northern part of the state) and the Pueblo Presbytery (for those in the southern portion). From the ranks of the young seminarians Jackson recruited for Colorado early in the 1870s,

Henry Gage and Delos Finks were still serving churches there at the end of the decade. Gage, who had arrived in Colorado City in 1870, was pastor of the church in Pueblo, Colorado, and he continued in that position until he moved to Los Angeles in 1886 for reasons of health. Finks, who had accepted the Fairplay church in 1873, was employed at the Fort Collins, Colorado church in 1880. In the following year, he moved to Denver where he served churches until 1885. Troubled, then, by deteriorating eyesight he labored as a traveling lecturer for the Board of Home Missions until his death in Maine on August 15, 1913. The veteran Lewis Hamilton, who had preached to miners in the Denver area during the great gold rush year of 1859, continued to serve congregations throughout the state until he died tragically when struck by a train while changing cars in Pueblo, Colorado on December 7, 1881.[2]

The work of the Darley brothers, Alexander and George, greatly impacted Colorado Presbyterianism in the late 1800s. Early in 1880, the always obstreperous Alex decided to ignore previous mission board admonitions and proceed with his plan to devote his entire time to "the Mexican work" in southern Colorado and northern New Mexico. His endeavors, in what he considered a supervisory role, continued to incur criticism from other Presbyterian missionaries. One of his colleagues reported to Jackson that there was "dissatisfaction at every step—evangelists out of humor—one with this and another with that—three teachers disgusted with him and laughing at his wild remarks."[3] Reacting, finally, to this opposition, Darley moved his residence to Pueblo, Colorado where he published religious tracts and a newspaper in the Spanish language along with a book decrying the evil practices of the Penitentes in the Southwest. According to Mrs. Darley, their publishing work was "our chief minister, as the general preaching work, at our suggestion, is in Mexican hands, and we stand back of them to render literary help. . . . So the Mexicans today have the word."[4] In 1907 Darley and his family moved to the Philipines to reside with a son living in Manila. Alex died there in 1912, and his obituary in a Philipine newspaper acknowledged his achievements in the statement, "Besides the great benefit of his life's example, we have preserved to future generations his mature thoughts expressed in form and style characteristic of the man."[5]

George Darley temporarily relinquished his missionary work in Colorado in 1880, when ill health and financial difficulties compelled him to leave Lake City to serve a church in Nebraska. From there, he accepted an offer from Jackson to take an assignment in Alaska, but *en route* in the fall of 1881 he changed his mind and returned to Colorado to fill a pulpit vacancy at the Del Norte church. During his tenure there, he was instrumental in the founding of the College of the Southwest, which opened its doors in September 1884. One of the school's goals was to graduate a number of "Mexicans" who would carry the Presbyterian message to others of their ethnic background throughout the Southwest. Darley served as president of the college, until he suffered a nervous breakdown in 1888. He then left Del Norte with his family, and for the remainder of his life ministered to churches in Fort Morgan, Denver, Delta, and Ouray in Colorado, and in Springville, Utah. He was employed by the church in Walsenburg in southern Colorado when he died on February 21, 1917. In his book *Pioneering in the San Juan,* he called for missionaries in the West "who can endure hardness, face dangers, take the chances, attempting even impossibilities, not counting even their lives dear unto them, if thereby the church can be advanced."[6] Many of his friends would have agreed that George Darley certainly possessed those attributes, and that his contribution to the advancement of his church was noteworthy.

In Utah in the spring of 1880, reports on the status of Presbyterianism praised past achievements and predicted still greater advances for the future. Eight churches had been organized, and fifteen day schools had been established in which twenty teachers were instructing nearly a thousand pupils. Four more ministers and eight additional teachers were also expected. The big gun in the Presbyterian offensive against Mormonism in the 1870s had been Duncan McMillan. He served briefly as synodical missionary for Utah and Montana after the dismantling of Jackson's superintendency at the end of 1880, but he then accepted employment as president of the College of Montana, a Presbyterian school which opened in Deer Lodge in 1883. He held that position until 1890, when he was appointed secretary of the Board of Home Missions. When he died in 1939 at age of ninety-three, there were few in his church who could match his long record of meritorious service.[7]

In Salt Lake City, the Collegiate Institute opened and headed by John Coyner in 1875 struggled after he relinquished his position in 1885. Near the turn of the century, however, Sheldon Jackson took a personal interest in the school. Jackson used his influence to raise funds for the institute, for which the trustees honored him by changing the name of the school to Sheldon Jackson College. In 1902, however, Jackson agreed to a request from the brethren in Utah to change the name, once again, to Westminster College. Although the Mormon Church officially relinquished its endorsement of polygamy in 1890, and Utah was admitted as a state of the Union in 1896, Jackson never wavered in his opposition to what he perceived as the Mormon menace. Addressing the General Assembly in 1902, he warned, "If the Mormon system prevails, the 'president, prophet and revelator' of the Church of the Latter Day Saints will be in the White House in Washington, congress will be disbanded and the twelve apostles of the Mormon Church will dictate the laws and govern the land."[8]

The result of Jackson's work in New Mexico is often understood in terms of the labor of the missionaries he recruited to serve at the Indian Pueblos of Laguna, Jemez, and Zuni. At Laguna, John Menaul persisted diligently in his teaching and preaching to the Indians, and he turned out many tracts and textbooks for his school until he and his family moved to Albuquerque in 1889. There he took charge of the recently organized Spanish Presbyterian Church and produced an extraordinary number of religious publications from his printing press. He retired in 1904 to Hinton, Oklahoma, where he died January 9, 1912.

John Shields, another of Jackson's missionaries, labored at the Jemez Pueblo and at other locations in New Mexico and Arizona until 1908, when he returned to Jemez to reside until his death on May 23, 1915. At Zuni, Taylor and Mrs. Ealy were heartbroken when their little baby boy died suddenly on June 4, 1880. A year later the Ealys decided to leave the Zuni mission and return to their former home in Pennsylvania, where Ealy entered into medical practice with his father. The schools, opened by the Presbyterians with great expectations, eventually closed—the last one at Laguna in 1902. Education for the Indians at the three Pueblos was later resumed in the form of government day schools without religious affiliation.[9]

Ben Thomas, Jackson's ally at the Pueblo Indian Agency in Santa Fe, weathered the storm of criticism directed against him at the end of 1879. In the following year, a thorough investigation of his activities exonerated him from all but the most trivial of the charges. He continued to serve as Pueblo Agent until 1883, when he accepted an offer of employment as register in the Tucson, Arizona, Land Office. Returning to Santa Fe in 1886, he conducted a dental practice until 1889, when President Benjamin Harrison appointed him secretary of the Territory of New Mexico, a position he held until his death in Santa Fe on October 2, 1892. Rivalry between the Board of Home Missions and the Board of Foreign Missions for control of mission work among the Indians continued throughout the 1880s. The General Assembly in 1884 finally directed the foreign board to transfer its Indian mission stations to the home board. The wheels turned slowly, however, in Presbyterian governance, and it was not until 1893 that this transfer was complete.[10]

The fortunes of the off-reservation Indian schools Jackson had sponsored fluctuated after he undertook mission work in Alaska. At Albuquerque the Presbyterian Church conducted the Pueblo Indian School in a contractual relationship with the Department of the Interior until 1886, when the government assumed complete control of the operation. Presbyterians in Albuquerque, however, were determined to have a separate Indian school. With the support of the Board of Home Missions, they opened another Indian school which, by the turn of the century, also accepted Hispanic students. This highly regarded secondary school continues to function today as the Menaul School, named for John Menaul's brother James, who came to Albuquerque in 1881 to take charge of the church Jackson had organized in 1880. Charles Cook, who opened a Presbyterian school in 1881 at the Pima agency in Arizona, conducted a small school in his home in 1890 to train Pima young men for the ministry. From this modest beginning grew the Cook Christian Training School, established in Tucson in 1911. The school was relocated to Phoenix two years later and moved again in 1965 to a campus in nearby Tempe, where today, as Cook College and Theological School, it is a well-known and respected institution for Indian students.[11]

As for the men who had been most prominently associated with Jackson in his work among the "Mexicans" in New Mexico, John Annin's departure from the area coincided closely with Jackson's diversion to another mission field. Undoubtedly aware of the prevalent desire in his Las Vegas church for a change in pastoral leadership, Annin resigned in the spring of 1880 and moved to Rolla, Missouri, where he served a congregation until his death on June 4, 1903. When his successor arrived in Las Vegas in June 1880, he found, according to one resident of the area, only five active church members and the mission school grounds being used as cattle pens. The new pastor managed to instill new life into the church, however, and a new church building was erected and dedicated on a new site in October 1881. At Taos, James Roberts relinquished his post soon after Annin's departure. Troubled by ill health in 1881, he moved to Anaheim, California, where he assisted in the organization of a church and taught a school. He died there on May 7, 1886.[12]

José Perea had been understandably dismayed when his annual salary was drastically cut by the mission board to only $375 at the beginning of 1880. His spirits rose again, however, when he learned later in the year that his salary for 1881 would be restored to a more respectable figure of nine hundred dollars. Meanwhile, John Shields had taken it upon himself to act as mentor for Perea and another young evangelist. Occasionally the teacher was exasperated with the lackadaisical attitude his pupils had toward their responsibilities. "They both mean well," he reported to Jackson, "but have the miserable Mexican way of doing business. A careless way, and it is almost impossible to get them to keep appointments or come to time sharp. I think both are beginning to see that their way is a very poor one."[13] Presumably Perea did benefit from Shields' tutelage, as he

had the distinctive honor in September 1880 of becoming the first Hispanic in
the United States to be ordained as a Presbyterian minister. He then served a
small church near Albuquerque until his retirement in 1905. When he died on
July 17, 1910, he was eulogized as a man who could suffer persecution for his
faith and still "exult in the hope of the glory of God."[14]

Sheldon Jackson concluded his remarkable career as an employee of the
federal government following his appointment as general agent for education in Alaska in 1885. His interest in the work of the Board of Home
Missions never diminished, however, and he must have been saddened to
learn of the death of his old friend and supporter Henry Kendall on September 9, 1892. Kendall had continued to serve as a secretary of the mission board until his death, and a statistical evaluation of his achievements
shows his success in this position. More than three thousand churches were
organized during his administration, and as secretary he signed more than
forty thousand commissions, or more than half of all the commissions issued by the board during its entire history from the time of its organization in 1816.[15]

There yet remains the challenge to interpret the impact of Sheldon Jackson and his church on the settlement of the American West following the
Civil War. Turning first to the Rocky Mountain West, some historians
assert that Protestant churches in that area generally became noticeably
different from their eastern counterparts. For example, Walter Prescott
Webb, distinguished historian of the American West, believed that there
was an "institutional fault" that divided the United States from north to
south along the 98th meridian, roughly bisecting the state of Kansas. He
argued that Protestant churches established beyond that line in the late
nineteenth century became more radical as they moved west: they tended
to drift away from adherence to the values long regarded as commendable
in proper eastern society.[16]

Taking issue with Webb's contention, other scholars have concluded
that conservatism and continuity loomed larger than radicalism in the history of early western Protestantism.[17] Which of these seemingly contra-
dictory viewpoints best describes the kind of Presbyterianism that evolved
during Sheldon Jackson's superintendency in the 1870s? On the whole,
the views expressed by the latter group of historians seem to have caught
the spirit of Rocky Mountain Presbyterianism at that time.

One might challenge Walter Prescott Webb's perception of a trend to
radicalism in religious denominations as they moved westward. That development, he believed, was exemplified by their tendency to abandon formal rituals.[18] His contention does not wear well on the frame of western

Presbyterianism. There was no exhibition of a leveling influence in the Presbyterian Church on the frontier. Leaders of the western church did not become radicals. They came from the ranks of the professionally trained ministry, and they were not inclined to challenge the tried and true precepts of their faith. They were quite sure that they belonged to an upper, and better, class of society. Rather than abandon themselves to an existence that would dilute their own superiority, they believed that it would be much better for their communities if those beneath them would strive—guided by Presbyterian principles—to elevate themselves as near the top of the social structure as their talents, ambition, and ethnic background might carry them.

If western Presbyterianism was not a deviant offspring of the parent church, then what was it? Certainly prominent in its characteristics was a sense of mission to win the West for Christ. The Presbyterian missionaries also believed that there would be a corollary benefit derived from this great achievement: good Christians would also be good Americans. It would have surprised the missionaries if they had been asked to define the latter term. To them it was self-evident that there was only one road to progress and perfection, and that was the American way, with its enlightened political system.

That conviction was evident in the deliberations at the convention called in Denver at the end of 1875 to draft a constitution to change the political status of Colorado from a territory to a state. Religious issues raised in the wording of the proposed document were debated vigorously. Some prominent Catholics, for example, objected to a clause prohibiting the use of public funds for the support of churches and church schools. Authors of the constitution, who were predominantly Protestant, simply cited the traditional adherence to the principle of division between the interests of church and state. The constitution was overwhelmingly approved in a final vote taken on July 1, 1876, and, on August 1, President Grant issued the necessary decree, making Colorado the thirty-eighth state of the Union. Reflecting on this momentous occasion, one of Jackson's friends proudly proclaimed, "When Colorado was admitted to the Union with fitting ceremonies and celebrations as the Centennial State, the Presbyterian Church was one of the most potent influences for good within its widely extended borders."[19]

The Presbyterian Church in the West, as a "potent influence for good," did exhibit concern for two of the so-called social evils that flourished in many western communities. Presbyterian missionaries could be counted on to support campaigns for temperance and against prostitution. There were numerous occasions when Jackson's men in the field wrote to him about lecture series they had presented decrying indulgence in alcoholic beverages. These reports invariably concluded with the gratifying an-nouncement that many of those in attendance then had come forward to "sign the pledge."[20]

Presbyterian pastors would usually participate in movements to combat prostitution. On at least one occasion, this involvement brought a violent reaction from those targeted. At Cheyenne, Wyoming, in the spring of 1873, Jackson learned to his sorrow that the veteran missionary William Kephart had resigned his post and returned to the States. Kephart's deci-sion to withdraw was apparently influenced in part by bitter feelings that developed in the community following his efforts, and those of Josiah Strong, pastor of the Congregational church, to wage war in the pulpit and the local press on prostitution in their city. In retaliation, some of those regarded by the missionaries as bad elements among the residents of Chey-enne allegedly started a fire that badly damaged parts of the city.[21] The principles espoused by these western, Presbyterian reformers were not re-gional in origin. On the contrary, they were in direct accord with the posi-tions of their national church.

Even if it is agreed that conservatism and continuity constituted the essence of western Presbyterianism, another question still remains to be addressed. Was the crusade of the Blue Banner in the Rocky Mountain West in the 1870s a success? The use of such a term to characterize the results of a religious movement is tenuous at best, but something might be said in that vein to complete a picture of western Presbyterianism that is as objective as possible. The Rocky Mountain West was not conquered for the Blue Banner. Dreams of total victory were never realized. Still, it could be said that the home missionaries did satisfy some westerners by their presence: building churches, preaching sermons, and administer-ing the sacraments of their faith. On the other hand, some Americans at the time surely rejoiced that God, in his infinite wisdom, did not allow the West to be totally Presbyterianized. Certainly more than one westerner would have joined with Granville Stuart, a colorful Montana pioneer, when he admitted, "Am glad I do not have to attend church and sit on a bench two hours listening to some fellow telling us how much hotter it would be somewhere else, and that we are heading for that particular spot. We may miss some of the good things of life by being out here, but we escape some mighty disagreeable experiences."[22] Stuart would have found it hard to picture a more depressing and unstimulating society than the one called for in the Presbyterian rheto-ric on the frontier, and he and others might not have perceived them-selves as transgressing too far into blasphemy by thanking God for letting the West be at least a little wild.

Presbyterian missionaries in the Rocky Mountain West did achieve limited success in some of their educational endeavors. They were disappointed, of course, when mission schools conducted for children of white Protestant families were, with only a few exceptions, short-lived and sparsely attended. The Presbyterian schools did, however, serve as gadflies to local, territorial, and state governing bodies that sometimes appeared to be lax in their support for high-quality public education. And Presbyterian schools for the so-called "exceptional populations" in the West did receive much attention and support in the late nineteenth century. Teachers in these many schools labored diligently to prepare their students for what they understood to be the commendable goal of adapting to the advanced civilization of white Protestant society. Colin Goodykoontz, in his excellent study of home missions on the American frontier, concluded that mission schools did give young people in many communities an understanding of the need for a better education, and they were a positive influence on western society.[23]

While some Presbyterian missionaries were gratified by achievements at their schools, others were frustrated when they experienced only minimal results or actual failure in organizing and sustaining churches in the Rocky Mountain West. An unfortunate corollary to that problem was a tendency to equate failure with conspiracy. When things went wrong at a remote outpost, it seemed easy to take solace in the thought that sinister forces had combined to keep the Presbyterians from reaching their goals. When Jackson and his missionaries wrote such letters and articles for readers in the East, they did their cause and their country a disservice. An influential Presbyterian layman in the East, for example, might also have held high political office. One must wonder whether irrational decisions regarding national policy stemmed, in part, from the outrageous propaganda pouring from the pens of western Presbyterians who saw Mormon and Catholic conspiracies to take over the country.

Sheldon Jackson's work in Alaska might be regarded as an extension of his role in the Rocky Mountain West. That is, he accepted the responsibility to begin establishing churches and schools there for the "exceptional population." His motivation was the same as it had been in New Mexico: to "uplift" those whom he regarded as "degraded heathen." His comprehension of his position in Alaska soon broadened, however, as he came to see what he regarded as incompetence in high places in the territorial government. Much of his earliest criticism in that regard focused on the position taken by local officials on the importation and sale of alcohol in Alaska. Whereas these gentlemen called for a licensing system for liquor sales, Jackson was vocal in his demands for total prohibition. Here was an opponent who would not be content merely to organize churches and schools.[24]

After Jackson moved to Washington, D.C., and received his appointment on the government payroll as general agent for education, he was to have acted as a general agent, not a Presbyterian agent. His area of concern was, presumably, limited to education. He did apply himself vigorously to his assigned task, and a report issued in 1905 that showed fifty-three schools established throughout Alaska seemed to confirm his success. Some of his critics, however, insisted that he devoted much of his personal attention—and the distribution of federal funds and philanthropic contributions—to mission schools for the Alaskan natives as opposed to common or day schools for the growing number of white communities in the territory. That was understandable, perhaps, when the white settlers insisted on applying a principle of education long revered in the States, local control of schools. Frank Churchill's observation in his report to President Roosevelt on Jackson's tenure in office—that Jackson's work with the schools retained "many of the methods used by him when representing the Presbyterian Board"—may not have been far from the mark.[25]

If Jackson did show more regard for mission than public schools, did he favor Presbyterian schools above those of other churches? Certainly there were a number of denominations involved in Alaskan education. Frank Churchill verified that fact when he reported that "nearly every color of religious faith is represented in some way in the schools or missions in Alaska."[26] Apparently Jackson did support this multidenominational participation in education. As early as 1880, he had attended a meeting in New York City with Henry Kendall and representatives of the Methodist and Baptist churches, to establish operational zones for all of the denominations that sought to bring schools and churches to Alaska. The allotments made at that time gave the southern and most populated area to the Presbyterians, with the remainder of the territory divided among the Episcopalian, Baptist, Methodist, Congregationalist, and Moravian churches. The Roman Catholic Church also entered the field, with missions along the Yukon River. When Jackson later met a priest from one of these outposts, he told a friend, "My heart went out to him as a brother."[27] In the absence of any real evidence to the contrary, it does appear that Jackson's opposition to interdenominational comity in the Rocky Mountain West may not have carried over to his actions as general agent of education in Alaska.[28]

As to Jackson's involvement in the introduction of reindeer into Alaska, one of his colleagues insisted that it "has been justly described as one of the most noteworthy events of the nineteenth century."[29] Frank Churchill did not agree. In his report on the issue, he stated that the concept itself was worthwhile, but that the many blunders encountered in implementing the plan came, quite simply, from a lack of business experience among the churchmen involved. And the plan itself, according to Churchill, was not original with Jackson: it had been advocated earlier by officers of the U.S. Revenue Cutter Service.[30] Taking issue with the assertion that there was a dire need for reindeer with which to save the Eskimos from starvation and extinction, more recent studies have suggested that Jackson did not comprehend that the Eskimos had actually adapted very well to a life that may have appeared impoverished only to him. Further, the coming of the reindeer had no significant impact upon the death rate among the Eskimos.[31] In retrospect, it might have been wiser for Jackson to distance himself from the issue at the time. He had never been content, however, to accept narrowly defined limits to his responsibilities, and the courage he displayed and the hardships he endured during the reindeer enterprise have never been questioned.

Finally, to understand Sheldon Jackson as an individual, one would have to try to develop a composite picture. He was undoubtedly the nonpareil among the propagandists who sought to convince easterners, particularly the women of his church, of the urgent need to contribute money to the cause of winning the West for Christ. The distorted rhetoric he employed for that purpose was not modified when he shifted his concern to Alaska. In his book on Alaska published in 1880, for example, he wrote graphically of young native girls who were doomed to lives of toil "and low sensual pleasure." Crushed by what he described as "a cruel heathenism," Jackson concluded "that many of them end their earthly misery and wretchedness with suicide."[32] One might have attempted to justify Jackson's exaggerations by simply asserting that the ends justified his means. Surely he did mean well, his supporters would have argued, and there was no denying that many who knew of his exploits approved of his efforts to improve the lot of the "exceptional populations" in the Rocky Mountain West and Alaska.

But surely the language used by Jackson to describe the native inhabitants of the lands where he labored could only be interpreted today as stemming from racist impulses. Not really, argues Michael Coleman, in his definitive study of the attitudes of Presbyterian missionaries toward American Indians in the nineteenth century. Finding little evidence of explicit or even implicit racism in thousands of documents of missionary correspondence, Coleman offers ethnocentrism as a more meaningful description of the views of the churchmen. Although speaking of "inferior" peoples, the missionaries invariably believed that the Indians could be "elevated" or "uplifted." Although these words today suggest attitudes of arrogance, condescension, and paternalism, they were not, according to Coleman, used with racist implications. This same reasoning can be applied to the Presbyterian view of the "Mexican" population in the Southwest. Terms like "depraved" and "degraded" appear repugnant when encountered by readers more than a century later, but they should be considered in the context of the time. With that in mind, the missionaries could well be regarded as sincere humanitarians who wished to be of benefit to those who, in their eyes, were "living in darkness."[33]

Perhaps there is no tried and true interpretive formula that can be applied to Sheldon Jackson and his legacy.[34] A negative analysis does not take into account the lasting impression that Jackson made on his church and the society in which he functioned. It was his advocacy, above that of all others, that led finally to recognition of women as important participants in the home mission work of the church. While the ladies who headed mission boards in the East coordinated fund-raising campaigns, many other courageous women served the cause as missionary wives or schoolteachers at far-flung mission stations. Pressure applied by Jackson was also instrumental in securing in 1884 the sensible reassignment of all missions conducted by the church among the Indians from the Board of Foreign Missions to the Board of Home Missions.[35] And in Alaska, as well as the Rocky Mountain West, Jackson exhibited great interest in the field known today as cultural anthropology. In the *Rocky Mountain Presbyterian*, he published many articles on the culture of Indians in the Southwest. In Alaska he organized a Society of Natural History and Ethnology in Sitka, which assisted him in the sponsorship of a museum for native artifacts on the campus of the Sitka Industrial School.[36]

Jackson's own honor's list continued to grow in the waning years of his life. He had received an honorary degree of Doctor of Divinity from Hanover College, Indiana, in 1874, and in 1897 his alma mater, Union Seminary in New York, conferred upon him the degree of Doctor of Laws. He must have been very proud also in 1897 when his peers selected him as Moderator of the General Assembly. In Alaska, the school established as the Sitka Industrial School is today known as the Sheldon Jackson College.[37] Regrettably, Mary Jackson did not receive any tangible rewards for her exemplary role as wife and mother in the Jackson household. One of Jackson's friends, commenting on Mary's role in the Jackson saga, provided a thoughtful observation that could well have applied to the careers of all of the wives of missionaries at the time. "Of Mary Jackson's part in the great work to which her husband was so fully committed," this writer observed, "not much has been written, except in the book of remembrance on high; but in the administration of this service, so faithfully rendered in the Master's name, it may truly be recorded of her: 'She hath done what she could.'"[38]

Finally, in evaluating Jackson's career, one might be tempted to weigh his achievements in the Rocky Mountain West against his Alaskan exploits. Ted Hinckley, who has written extensively on Jackson's work in Alaska, concluded that Jackson's significance, above all else, should be measured by his role as an advocate for programs designed to create what he regarded as a civilized society in that territory.[39] On the other hand, those who recall the events of his tenure as superintendent of Presbyterian mission work in the Rocky Mountain West might insist that he deserves just as much credit for his pioneering efforts there. Sheldon Jackson himself surely believed that he had fought the good fight, to the best of his ability, on all of the several battlefields where he had encountered conditions dangerously detrimental to the fulfillment of America's enlightened destiny. Although Jackson died just before the meeting of the General Assembly of his church in 1909, the delegates there surely would have found the works of Sheldon Jackson, in all of his capacities, to have been commendable in their sight, and worthy of the highest accolades.

Appendix I

Rules for Missionaries of the Board of Home Missions

1. The grand object of the Missionary should be to build up the kingdom of Christ, by constant and prayerful labor for the conversion of the unregenerate, the edification of Christians, and the training up of the children of the Church.

2. As soon as may be, the Missionary is to organize, in every suitable locality on his field, where one does not exist, a church, which is to be placed at once under the watch and care of the Presbytery to which it naturally belongs, in connection with the Grand Assembly.

3. As soon as possible, the Missionary will endeavor to secure the erection of a suitable house of worship for each congregation.

4. He will organize a Sabbath School in each suitable locality, and cultivate the benevolence of his people by inducing them to contribute to religious and benevolent purposes as they may have ability; seeing also that each congregation take up an annual collection for the Board.

5. He will make a quarterly report of his operations to the Board.

—SHELDON JACKSON BIOGRAPHICAL FILE, PRESBYTERIAN HISTORICAL SOCIETY

Appendix II

A Typical Solicitation for a "Missionary Box"

Mr. Jackson: Winona, Minnesota, Sept. 12, 1864

As you have kindly volunteered to make our wants known to the proper source, I present them herewith. As the most needful, I mention flannel, *real* flannel. Fifteen or sixteen yards is as small a quantity as is necessary to clothe the female members of our family with undergarments of that material. The cold, keen winds make it necessary as a preventative against neuralgia and rheumatism. It is necessary both to health and comfort, and so of course to usefulness to have it. Then as we are trying to do our own work, calico, because it can be washed seems to be needed. Enough for a dress for myself, and Mary, and for two or three aprons, I would like very much. I can also make over any other dresses that may be on hand. In a wealthy home there are many things cast off as no longer of use, that would suffice to make the humble home of the Missionary quite cheery and comfortable. Old Chintzes or Moreens, something to cover old chairs and lounges that need to be renovated so often when everything is for *use*, and used daily. Shoes for myself and children, good stout ones are next. My own size is 3½, Mary's No. 4, the other for a boy 13, large foot, a boy of four, large foot, and a little girl of eight with a long slim foot. Any clothes for them will come in play. A cap or hat for the little boy of four, who is large for his age, and has a large head. The rest of us have bonnets and also owing to the wonderful kind Providence of God, a supply of white clothing. My husband who weighs two hundred, needs very much two pairs of flannel drawers, a pair of good, substantial pants, and a pair of boots, and some pocket handkerchiefs. For the rest, anything to be used in a house, pins, needles, tapes, buttons, yarn, pocket handkerchiefs, stockings, gloves, etc., etc., the Missionary's family can use. Nothing can scarcely come amiss.

This seems a formidable list, but these are the wants of our family at present, and for the coming cold winter. God has been very good, and kind to us, and I doubt not he will remember us still. Blessed be His name.

Yours much obliged,

Mrs. Lyon

—SHELDON JACKSON CORRESPONDENCE, 1:196–97

Notes

PREFACE

1. Jackson eventually recognized the boundaries of his superintendency to include Montana, Wyoming, Utah, Colorado, New Mexico, and Arizona.

2. Robert L. Stewart, *Sheldon Jackson* (New York: Fleming H. Revell, 1908), 104. Among several theories pertaining to the origins of the association of the color blue with Presbyterian symbolism, one opinion traces the tradition back to the time in Scotland when the persecuted leaders of the new faith called their followers to forbidden services by displaying a blue flag at some secluded mountain rendezvous. See Henry P. Ford, "True Blue Presbyterians," *Journal of Presbyterian History [JPH]* 14 (March 1931): 238–39.

3. See Appendix I, "Rules for Missionaries of the Board of Home Missions."

CHAPTER 1

1. Sheldon Jackson, "The Iowa Movement for Home Missions," speech delivered at a meeting of the Synod of Iowa, 1905. Copy provided by the Reverend John Pattison, First Presbyterian Church, Cheyenne, Wyoming. Jackson's two companions, who had joined him in prayer on Prospect Hill at the Sioux City meeting, did not take missionary assignments farther west. T. H. Cleland continued to serve a congregation in Council Bluffs, Iowa, and J. C. Elliott later became pastor of a church in Ohio.

2. For a comprehensive commentary on Sheldon Jackson's genealogical antecedents and his early life, see Stewart, *Sheldon Jackson*, 17–26.

3. Ibid., 20. The complex issues pertaining to the schism of 1838 are thoroughly discussed in Earl R. MacCormac, "The Development of Presbyterian Missionary Organizations: 1790–1870," *JPH* 43 (September 1965): 149–73.

4. Stewart, *Sheldon Jackson*, 27.

5. Ibid., 28.

6. *Catalogue of the Theological Seminary of the Presbyterian Church at Princeton, New Jersey, 1855–56* (Philadelphia: C. Sherman and Sons, 1856), 15.

7. Colporteur's Commission, Presbyterian Board of Publication, April 7, 1856; Certificate as Agent of the American Systematic Beneficence Society, May 18, 1857; Jackson to "Brethren, American Systematic Beneficence Society," September 12, 1857, in *Correspondence Relating to Pioneer Presbyterian Missions West of the Mississippi and Missouri Rivers and in Alaska, 1856–1908*, 26 vols. 1:5–6. Presbyterian Historical Society [PHS], Philadelphia, Pennsylvania. 1: 5–6. Cited hereafter as Jackson Correspondence.

8. Walter Lowrie, Secretary, Board of Foreign Missions, to Jackson, December 28, 1857, Jackson Correspondence 1:8. Reasoning, perhaps, that Indian tribes were treated, in some respects, as foreign nations, in 1837 the General Assembly of the Old School branch of the church had given the care for American Indian missions to the Board of Foreign Missions.

9. Jackson to Dear Parents and Sister, January 13, 1858, Jackson Correspondence 1:10; Stewart, *Sheldon Jackson*, 38.

10. Jackson to Secretaries of the Board of Foreign Missions, October 8, 1858, Jackson Correspondence, 1:20.

11. W. David Baird, "Spencer Academy, Choctaw Nation, 1842–1900," *Chronicles of Oklahoma* 45 (Spring 1967): 25–31; Mary Jackson to My Dear Louise, October 9, 1858, Jackson Correspondence 1:22.

12. Jackson to My Dear Parents and Sister, November 10, 1858, Jackson Correspondence 1:25–26. Jackson was only a few inches over five feet in height.

13. Mary Jackson to My Dear Louise, February 11, 1859, Ibid., 46–47.

14. Memoranda of Work at Spencer Academy, 1859, ibid., 36; Stewart, *Sheldon Jackson*, 50.

15. John McDowell, president, Board of Domestic Missions, to Jackson, June 6, 1859; Mary Jackson to Dear Sister, July 27, 1859; Jackson to Dear Parents and Sister, August 2 and 13, 1859: Jackson Correspondence 1:50–55.

16. Jackson to Dear Parents and Sister, August 2, 1859; John McDowell to Jackson, September 5, 1859. Ibid., 53–54, 57; Session Records, Presbyterian Church of Hokah, Minnesota. Copy at PHS.

17. J. A. Hodge, *What Is Presbyterian Law as Defined by the Church Courts?* (Philadelphia: Presbyterian Board of Publications, 1882), 30–33, 284–87.

18. Jackson to My Dear Parents and Sister, February 13, 1860, Jackson Correspondence 1:61–62.

19. Husband to My Very Dear Wife, March 1, 1860; Jackson to the Rev. Joseph R. Wilson, August 22, 1860; M. I. Goodale to Jackson, June 2, 1862; Jackson to My Dear Christian Friends, n.d., 1865. Ibid., 66, 69–71, 97–98, A359.

20. Mary Jackson to My Dear Louise, January 24, 1861, Jackson Correspondence 1:76–77; Stewart, *Sheldon Jackson*, 66. For a useful analysis of the antebellum division in the Presbyterian Church see Clifford M. Drury, *Presbyterian Panorama* (Philadelphia: Board of Christian Education, Presbyterian Church in the United States of America, 1952), 85–90, 101–6.

21. George H. Stuart, et al., United States Christian Commission, to Jackson, July 28, 1863, ibid., 123–24. In the summer of 1863, the Army of the Cumberland was moving through southern Tennessee intent on driving the Confederate forces from Chattanooga.

22. Tracts for Civil War soldiers from the collection at PHS; Jackson to My Dear Wife, August 15, 18, and undated, 1863; W. E. Boardman, Secretary, USCC, to Jackson, November 2, 1863. Jackson Correspondence 1:129–33. The Jacksons' first child, a girl whom they had named Mary Helen, died in infancy on September 28, 1861. See Stewart, *Sheldon Jackson,* 147.

23. George Ainslie to Jackson, December 23, 1861; Charles Hageman, et al., to Jackson, March 12, 1864. Jackson Correspondence 1:89–90, 157. See also Stewart, *Sheldon Jackson,* 74–75; Edgar A. Hines, Jr., *First Presbyterian Church, Rochester, Minnesota, Centennial Celebration, 1861–1961* (Rochester, Minn.: privately published, 1961), 8, 12.

24. Mother [Jackson's mother] to My Dear Daughter, November 17, 1864, Jackson Correspondence 1:207; Stewart, *Sheldon Jackson,* 77; Augustus Kemper, paper on Sheldon Jackson, 1908, at PHS.

25. *Minutes of the General Assembly of the Presbyterian Church in the United States of America, 1865* (Philadelphia: Presbyterian Board of Publications, 1865), 741. Cited hereafter as *General Assembly Minutes.*

26. See Appendix II for a typical solicitation for clothing to supply a missionary family in Minnesota in the 1860s.

27. To "Dear Children from Your Western Missionary, Sheldon Jackson," [1865], Jackson Correspondence 1:A361.

28. Raven Fund account book in Sheldon Jackson Collection, PHS. When a friend asked Jackson how he was getting all of this money, he evasively replied that the Presbytery of Southern Minnesota simply had a private treasury of its own. Kemper, paper on Jackson, 1908, PHS.

29. Jackson to the Rev. William M. Paxton, [1867], Jackson Correspondence 1:A364–66.

30. Alfred Nevin, ed., *Encyclopaedia of the Presbyterian Church in the United States of America* (Philadelphia: Presbyterian Encyclopaedia Publishing Co., 1884), 558–59.

31. George Musgrave, "A Caution," *North-Western Presbyterian,* October 24, 1868.

32. *General Assembly Minutes,* 1869, 15–16.

33. Stewart, *Sheldon Jackson,* 90; "Resolutions Unanimously Adopted by Members of the First Presbyterian Church, Rochester, Minnesota, January 28, 1869," Jackson Correspondence 2:526–27.

34. George Musgrave to Jackson, April 23, 1869, Jackson Correspondence 2:581.

35. *Inaugural Addresses of the Presidents of the United States* (Washington, D.C.: Government Printing Office, 1969), 129–31.

36. S. M. G. Merrill to Jackson, January 14, 1869, Jackson Correspondence 2:520.

37. "Sherman to End-of-Track," October 1868, Sheldon Jackson Scrapbooks, 64 vols., 59:7–8, PHS. Cited hereafter as Jackson Scrapbooks. These scrapbook

items are often unidentifiable by author or place of publication. Dates, where not provided in the clippings, have been inserted, where possible, through knowledge of the events described. When no other information is available, references are cited only by volume and page number.

38. "Our Chicago Letter—The Board of Missions Visitation," n.d., Jackson Scrapbooks 59:21.

39. C. D. Roberts, Moderator, and T. H. Cleland, Temporary Clerk, Presbytery of Missouri River, to Jackson, May 1, 1869, Jackson Correspondence 2:576.

40. D. S. Tappan, Moderator, and J. M. Batchelder, Stated Clerk, Presbytery of Des Moines, to Jackson, April 24, 1869; R. Merrill, Moderator, and George Graham, Stated Clerk, Presbytery of Fort Dodge, to Jackson, May 8, 1869. Ibid., 575–76.

41. Sheldon Jackson, "A Story of Early Home Mission Work," *Assembly Herald* 10 (1904): 1 (copy in PHS); Jackson to George Musgrave, May 7, 1869, in Stewart, *Sheldon Jackson*, 105.

42. George Musgrave to Jackson, May 17, 1869, Jackson Correspondence 2:592.

43. John Hall, "The Future Church," in *Presbyterian Reunion Memorial Volume, 1837–1871* (New York: DeWitt C. Lent, 1870), 461–62. Hall compared the anticipated reunion to the occasion on which the English and Prussians effected a crucial junction on the field of Waterloo.

44. Ibid., 463–64.

45. When he decided to start his work along the Union Pacific, Jackson believed "there was not a Presbyterian Church for 2,000 miles toward the setting sun." Sheldon Jackson, "Pioneer Presbyterianism in the Rocky Mountain Territories, 1869–1876," Historical Sermon, November 1876, 1, at PHS. This comment could only have applied to areas directly along the railroad, as Presbyterian churches had already been established on the West Coast in California and Oregon.

46. Stewart, *Sheldon Jackson*, 96–97, 102. An article in a Presbyterian periodical announcing these appointments was headlined "The Union Pacific Railroad Occupied for Presbyterianism," Jackson Scrapbooks 59:1.

47. Stewart, *Sheldon Jackson*, 110–11; *Wyoming*, American Guide Series (New York: Oxford University Press, 1941), 185–86; "To the Rocky Mountains . . . Chicago to Cheyenne," [September 1868], Jackson Scrapbooks 59:6.

48. Sheldon Jackson, "Cheyenne, The Magic City of the Plains," July 18, 1869, Jackson Scrapbooks 59:13.

49. Sheldon Jackson, "A Voice Beyond the Mountains," July 24, 1869, Jackson Scrapbooks 59:91–92.

50. John L. Gage to Dear [T.H.] Cleland, May 18, 1869; W. F. Thompson et al. [twenty-seven signatures], June 1, 1869, Jackson Correspondence 2:594, 602.

51. Stewart, *Sheldon Jackson*, 112; "Minutes, Board of Domestic Missions," June 15, 1869, unpaginated, PHS; George Musgrave to Jackson, July 7, 1869, Jackson Correspondence 2:627.

52. For a comprehensive analysis of Jackson's understanding of his role as superintendent of missions, see Norman J. Bender, "Sheldon Jackson's Crusade to Win the West for Christ, 1869–1880," *Midwest Review* 4 (Spring 1982): 1–12. Many

years later, Jackson openly acknowledged his deliberate intention to ignore the instructions of his mission board. Commenting on the financing for his work along the Union Pacific in 1869, he admitted, "I ran a little Board of Home Missions on my own hook." Sheldon Jackson, "Autobiographical Sketch," 1897, Jackson Collection, 2, at PHS.

53. Stewart, *Sheldon Jackson*, 466.

CHAPTER 2

1. Sheldon Jackson, "Early Home Mission Work," 3.

2. Sheldon Jackson, "Cheyenne, the Magic City of the Plains," July 18, 1869, Jackson Scrapbooks 59:13; Stewart, *Sheldon Jackson*, 11–13; Session Minutes, "Historical Statement," First Presbyterian Church of Cheyenne, Wyoming, 2.

3. Hughes to Dear Brother Cleland, June 14, 1869, and Hughes to Jackson, June 24 and 30, 1869, Jackson Correspondence 2:613–14, 619–23. Jackson's pocket-sized travel journals for the years 1860, 1869, 1871, 1872, 1877, and 1881 are retained at the PHS. Regrettably, the entries therein are often brief and impersonal.

4. *Wyoming*, 247; Sheldon Jackson, "Sweetwater Mines, Rocky Mountains," [July 1869], Jackson Scrapbooks 59:14; Stewart, *Sheldon Jackson*, 114–15.

5. *Wyoming*, 319–20; Hughes to Jackson, June 30, 1869, Jackson Correspondence 2:622–23; Sheldon Jackson, "Sweetwater Mines, Rocky Mountains," 14–15.

6. Sheldon Jackson, "Synod of Colorado: An Historical Sketch," *Rocky Mountain Presbyterian*, May 1872. Cited hereafter as *RMP*. Beginning in March of 1872 Jackson published this newspaper monthly, except in 1874 when it was published weekly from his headquarters in Denver.

7. *Montana*, American Guide Series (New York: Hastings House, 1939), 160–61; Stewart, *Sheldon Jackson*, 116.

8. George G. Smith to Thomas V. Moore, 1897, as quoted in George Edwards, "Presbyterian Church History," *Contributions to the Historical Society of Montana* 6 (1907): 295. Smith stayed in Montana for two years, but he then departed because he found the cost of living greatly exceeded the allowance received from his mission board. Patricia McKinney, *Presbyterianism in Montana: Its First Hundred Years* (Helena, Mont.: privately published, 1969), 10.

9. W. A. Clark to Jackson, June 9, 1869, Jackson Correspondence 2:610; Stewart, *Sheldon Jackson*, 116, 179; Historical Narrative of the Presbytery of Wyoming in Minutes, Synod of Colorado, 1871–88, PHS, 8.

10. *Wyoming*, 240; Wm. C. Wilson, et al., to Jackson, August 8, 1869, Jackson Correspondence 3:656; Session Records, Presbyterian Church of Rawlins, Wyoming, 1; "Rawlings," n.d., Jackson Scrapbooks 59:24.

11. *Wyoming*, 196–97; Walter C. Reusser, et al., *The United Presbyterian Church of Laramie, Wyoming, 1869–1969* (Laramie: privately printed, 1969), 8–10; "Laramie—First Scene, 1869," n.d., Jackson Scrapbooks 59:45; Stewart, *Sheldon Jackson*, 118; George Musgrave to Jackson, August 9, 1869, and J. N. Hutchinson to Jackson, August 24, 1869, Jackson Correspondence 2:577–78 and 3:645.

12. Stewart, *Sheldon Jackson*, 121; Drury, *Presbyterian Panorama*, 167–68. The reunited church selected as its name the Presbyterian Church in the United States of America.

13. Charles M. Campbell to Jackson, September 23, 1869, Jackson Correspondence 3:693; Stewart, *Sheldon Jackson*, 121; *General Assembly Minutes, 1869*, 1158–59; "Synod of Colorado: An Historical Sketch," *RMP*, May 1872.

14. *Colorado*, American Guide Series (New York: Hastings House, 1941), 38, 129; Wilbur F. Stone, *History of Colorado* (Chicago: S. J. Clarke, 1918), 1:669; "Synod of Colorado, An Historical Sketch," *RMP*, May 1872; Robert L. Stewart, "The Mission of Sheldon Jackson in the Winning of the West," *JPH* 6 (June 1911): 49.

15. "Minutes of Local Attempts to Organize a Presbytery of Colorado, January 15 and 16 and February 3, 1866," PHS, 6.

16. Joseph W. Wilson, *The Presbyterian Historical Almanac and Annual Remembrance of the Church for 1867* (Philadelphia: privately printed, 1867), 43.

17. *Ninth Census of the United States: Statistics of Population* (Washington, D.C.: Government Printing Office, 1872), 95; *Rocky Mountain News* (Denver), February 18, 1870, cited hereafter as *RMN*; Sheldon Jackson, "Rocky Mountain Correspondence," March 7, 1870, Jackson Scrapbooks 38:23.

18. Sheldon Jackson, "From the Rocky Mountains," [1870], Jackson Scrapbooks 38:24–25; Jackson to My Dear Wife, February 23, 1870, Jackson Correspondence 3:813; "Synod of Colorado, An Historical Sketch," *RMP*, May 1872; Minutes, Presbytery of Colorado, February 18, 1870, PHS, 20.

19. Sheldon Jackson, "From the Rocky Mountains" and "Rocky Mountain Correspondence," [1870], Jackson Scrapbooks 38:25–28; "Synod of Colorado, An Historical Sketch," *RMP*, May 1872; *France Memorial United Presbyterian Church, Rawlins, Wyoming, Centennial Booklet, 1869–1969* (Rawlins: privately printed, 1969), 12–13; Session Records, Rawlins, 2; "The Presbyterian Church at Rawlins," [March 1870], Jackson Scrapbooks 59:35–37.

20. Minutes, Board of Domestic Missions, March 14, 1870, PHS, unpaginated; Drury, *Presbyterian Panorama*, 177; *General Assembly Minutes, 1871*, 513; Nevin, *Encyclopaedia*, 394; Thomas S. Goslin, II, "Henry Kendall and the Evangelization of a Continent," Ph.D. thesis, 76, 119, University of Pennsylvania, Philadelphia, 1948.

21. Nevin, *Encyclopaedia*, 188–89.

22. Hughes to Dear Brother Cleland, June 14, 1869, Jackson Correspondence 2:613–14.

23. "Corinne, Its Past, Present and Future," August 2, 1869, Jackson Scrapbooks 59:79.

24. Hughes to Jackson, June 28, 1869, Jackson Correspondence 2:619–20.

25. "A Voice Beyond the Mountains," July 24, 1869, Jackson Scrapbooks 59:91–92.

26. Edward E. Bayliss to Jackson, April 12 and 30 and May 17, 1870, Jackson Correspondence 3:819–20, 834, 846–48.

27. *RMN*, October 29, 1870.

28. Stewart, *Sheldon Jackson*, 147.

29. Bayliss to Jackson, October 7, 1870, Jackson Correspondence 3:924–25.

30. "First Presbyterian Church of Corinne," [November 1870], Jackson Scrapbooks 59:103–4.

31. Sheldon Jackson, "Organization of a Presbyterian Church in Salt Lake City," [November 1871], Jackson Scrapbooks 59:112.

32. "Bible Cause in Utah," April 1873, and "Territorial Church News–Utah," June 1873, *RMP*; Stewart, *Sheldon Jackson*, 206.

33. Sheldon Jackson, "A Missionary Tour Into Little Cottonwood Canon, [May 1873], Jackson Scrapbooks 61:44; Sheldon Jackson, "The Land of the Saints," n.d., Jackson Scrapbooks 61:59; Schell to Jackson, July 7, 1873, Jackson Correspondence 4:284–85.

34. Eugene V. Smalley, *History of the Northern Pacific Railroad* (1883; reprint, New York: Arno, 1975), 185–88.

35. Sheldon Jackson, "The Northern Territories: A Missionary Tour of Five Thousand Miles," Jackson Scrapbooks 38:86.

36. Ibid.

37. Ibid., 87–88.

38. Edwards, "Presbyterian Church History," 315–16; Memoranda, May 30, 1872, Jackson Correspondence 4:161; Jackson, "The Northern Territories," Jackson Scrapbooks 38:39; *First Presbyterian Church, Bozeman, Montana, Centennial Edition* (Bozeman, Mont.: privately printed, 1972), 2; R.W.H., "From Gallatin City," June 1, 1872, and untitled article, June 1872, Jackson Scrapbooks 51:13–14.

39. Stewart, *Sheldon Jackson*, 183.

40. Jackson, "The Northern Territories," Jackson Scrapbooks 38:88.

41. Edwards, "Presbyterian Church History," 375–76; Stewart, *Sheldon Jackson*, 183.

42. Edwards, "Presbyterian Church History," 317, 339; Untitled article, June 12, 1872, Jackson Scrapbooks 51:16.

43. Jackson, "The Northern Territories," Jackson Scrapbooks 38:90; Jackson Travel Journals, 1872, PHS, entries for June 21 and 22.

44. Jackson, "The Northern Territories," Jackson Scrapbooks 38:90.

45. Reverend Henry M. Field, "On the Sides of Mount Lincoln," August 20, 1872, Jackson Scrapbooks 38:104; *Colorado*, 406. Jackson organized other churches in Colorado at this time, in Colorado Springs (July 21), Caribou (July 28), Middle Boulder, later known as Nederland (July 28), Canon City (August 18), and Fort Collins (August 25).

46. A. P. White to Jackson, September 1, 1875, and William Curtis to Jackson, September 28, 1875, Jackson Correspondence 6:699–700, 720; Stewart, *Sheldon Jackson*, 232–33; *General Assembly Minutes, 1875*, 506.

47. Jackson to My Dear Friends [family in Denver], April 8, 1876, Jackson Correspondence 6:899.

48. *Arizona*, American Guide Series (New York: Hastings House, 1956), 257–58.

49. "An Arizona Notice," *RMP*, June 1876.

50. "Arizona," n.d., Jackson Scrapbooks 53:402; Stewart, *Sheldon Jackson*, 233.

Donor of the organ, and selected as elder of the new congregation, was John P. Clum, who was serving at the time as agent to the Apache Indians on the San Carlos Reservation in Arizona. An interesting account of Clum's colorful career appears in Woodworth Clum, *Apache Agent* (Lincoln: University of Nebraska Press, 1978).

51. John P. Clum, et al., "Petition for the Establishment of a Presbyterian Church in Tucson, Arizona," April 8, 1876, Jackson Correspondence 6:828; "Arizona," n.d., Jackson Scrapbooks 53:402.

52. Stewart, *Sheldon Jackson*, 235.

53. The organization service for the Santa Fe church was held on January 13, 1867, although the action to take this step was approved a week earlier, on January 6.

54. George Darley, a missionary in Colorado at this time, tried to organize a church at Silverton in southwestern Colorado in 1877, but, as his son recalled, he failed "because he found only one Presbyterian and he was not willing to be organized." Interview with Marshall Darley, May 16, 1969.

55. "Minutes of the Presbytery of Montana, February 13–17, 1880," as quoted in G. J. Slosser, ed., *They Seek a Country: The American Presbyterians* (New York: Macmillan, 1955), 185–86.

56. R. B. Abbott, "Extracts From the History of the Presbytery of Winona," 1888, Jackson Correspondence 2:645A.

57. Jackson, "Pioneer Presbyterianism," 4.

58. Jackson as quoted in Stewart, *Sheldon Jackson*, 135.

CHAPTER 3

1. "Hunting for a Church," *RMP*, July 1876.

2. Jackson Scrapbooks [1879] 34:96.

3. William Meyer to Jackson, July 3, 1879, Jackson Correspondence 9:250.

4. "Domestic Missions—Corinne, Utah," [1869], Jackson Scrapbooks 59:82; "Evanston—Wyoming, Territory" [n.d.], ibid., 42–43. The writer from Corinne recalled how attendance for the Sunday services averaged about thirty, unless, as actually occurred, a circus was held on the Sabbath across the street, when the attendance was only three or four.

5. "The Presbyterian Church in the San Luis Valley," n.d., Jackson Scrapbooks 41:118; Session Records, "Register of Pastors," Del Norte Presbyterian Church, 1; Isaac Beardsley, *Echoes from Peak and Plain* (Cincinnati, Ohio: Curts and Jennings, 1898), 471–72.

6. George Darley to Dear Brother Loder, February 18, 1883, George Darley Scrapbook, Adams State College, Alamosa, Colorado, 8; George Darley, Pastor's Register, May 9, 1878, Darley Collection, Archives, University of Colorado at Boulder Libraries.

7. Bayard Taylor, *Colorado: A Summer Trip, 1866* (New York: G. P. Putnam and Son, 1867), 56.

8. "Stuart Presbyterian Church of Denver, Colorado," June 8, 1871, Jackson Scrapbooks 38:67.

9. "The Stewert [*sic*] Reunion Dedication Services," *RMP,* April 1872.

10. "First Church in Lake City," [1876], Jackson Scrapbooks 41:120. When a meeting was called to organize a choir at the church in Corinne, Utah, a musically gifted lady from the congregation was willing to lead the singers. One gentleman departed angrily from the gathering, however, stating that "he was not going to sing under any woman." E. Bayliss to Jackson, October 7, 1870, Jackson Correspondence 3:925.

11. J. Schenck to Jackson, September 11, 1869, Jackson Correspondence 3:683–84.

12. Edwards, "Presbyterian Church History," 382.

13. Finks to Jackson, February 9, 1874, Jackson Correspondence 5:371; Delos Finks, "Fairplay, Colorado," Historical Sermons, 1876, PHS, 3–4. Jackson requested that Presbyterian missionaries in Colorado in 1876 prepare sermons on the history of their churches to commemorate the national centennial. Cited hereafter as Historical Sermons.

14. "Historical Sketch," Session Records, Lake City, Colorado, 7; Finks to Jackson, July 2, 1873, Jackson Correspondence 4:283.

15. Edwards, "Presbyterian Church History," 370.

16. E. P. Wells to Jackson, September 11, 1869, Jackson Correspondence 3:683.

17. Duncan McMillan, "Who Will Furnish A Bell For Utah?" *RMP,* March 1876.

18. Mrs. J. M. Ginn to Jackson, May 22, 1874, Jackson Correspondence 5:426–27.

19. W. E. Hamilton to Jackson, November 7, 1876, ibid., 6:939–40.

20. "Buckskin Versus Broadcloth," *RMP,* February 1877.

21. J. L. Merritt to Jackson, November 10, 1875, Jackson Correspondence 6:749.

22. Philip H. Tooley to Jackson, April 2, 1874, ibid., 5:389.

23. Samuel Gillespie to Jackson, September 8, 1874, ibid., 5:492.

24. Gillespie to Jackson, December 1, 1874, ibid., 5:540.

25. "Manners in Church," *RMP,* June 10, 1874.

26. J. A. Merrill, "Arizona," [1877], Jackson Scrapbooks 34:82.

27. Josiah Welch to Jackson, January 16 and December 16, 1872, Jackson Correspondence 4:137, 201.

28. W. E. Hamilton, "Home Missions and Orthodoxy," *RMP,* May 1875.

29. Edwards, "Presbyterian Church History," 369–70.

30. "Farewell," *RMP,* June 1873.

31. R. M. Carson to Jackson, June 14, 1875, Jackson Correspondence 6:662.

32. George Darley, "What We Owe the Old Folks," "The Family," "Special Sermon on Hard Times," and "Manliness," sermons in the Darley Collection, Archives, University of Colorado at Boulder Libraries. Darley's favorite example of the manly man was Abraham Lincoln.

33. George Darley, "The Twentieth Century Prodigal," unpublished manuscript, ibid., chapter 1, page 2.

34. George Darley, "Gone Away," unpublished manuscript, ibid., chapter 1, page 5; 3, 1; and 5, 1–2.

35. Ibid., Chapter 6, 3, 5, 6–7, 9, 20–21.

36. George Darley, "The Roman Catholic Church and Our Public Schools" and "America," sermons, ibid.

37. J. G. Lowrie, "Domestic Missions—Colorado," January 24, 1871, Jackson Scrapbooks 38:43–44.

38. D. E. Finks to Jackson, January 18, 1875, Jackson Correspondence 5:562.

39. *General Assembly Minutes, 1873*, 613.

40. E. S. Mills, Jr., to A. Darley, February 6, 1877, Jackson Correspondence 7:23. When the pastor of the Presbyterian church in Santa Fe, New Mexico, learned of an effort to bring a Methodist missionary to that city, he told Jackson, "If he can get hold of the brainless, emotional, capricious element, which is essentially un-Presbyterian and Methodistical, I shall rejoice." George Smith to Jackson, October 21, 1878, ibid., 8:273–74.

41. A. T. Blachly to Jackson, January 6, 1874, and W. A. Ross to Jackson, November 7, 1874, ibid., 5:360–61, 528.

42. Cited in Colin B. Goodykoontz, *Home Missions on the American Frontier* (Caldwell, Idaho: Caxton, 1939), 151; *General Assembly Minutes, 1873*, 613.

43. *Home Missionary*, 1874, 162, as cited in Goodykoontz, *Home Missions*, 352.

44. "Longmont, Colorado," *RMP*, May 13, 1874; Session Records, Longmont, Colorado, Presbyterian Church, December 6, 1874, 9; William Teitsworth to Jackson, January 27 and June 29, 1875, Jackson Correspondence 5:568 and 6:675–76.

45. William E. Teitsworth, "Longmont, Colorado," Historical Sermons, 1876, PHS, 7–8. Alex Darley made his position on these matters quite clear. "Shortly I'll have expurgated my Del Norte church of enough to start a Cong. cesspool," the volatile missionary asserted. "May the devil take Unionism, for Christ won't have it." Darley to Jackson, September 1, 1878, Jackson Correspondence 8:219.

46. Kendall to Jackson, October 5, 1874, Jackson Correspondence 5:511; "Comity," *RMP*, March 1875; *General Assembly Minutes, 1877*, 637; Alvin Bailey, "The Strategy of Sheldon Jackson in Opening the West for National Missions, 1860–1880," Ph.D. thesis, Yale University, 1948, 433.

47. "New Presbyterian Church," [1870], Jackson Scrapbooks 59:33–34. Writing about the completion of his little church building in Alta, Utah, James Schell boasted, "We feel proud of it and think it might compare favorably for beauty, use and situation with the famous temple of Solomon." J. P. Schell, "Church Dedication—Alta," *RMP*, November 1873.

CHAPTER 4

1. "Missionary Superintendents," *RMP*, November 1876.

2. Henry Kendall, "Presbyterian Evangelists—Synodical Missionaries," ibid.

3. Sheldon Jackson, "The Preachers Which the Times and the Country Demand," n.d., Jackson Scrapbooks 38:33.

4. Minutes, Board of Home Missions, Presbyterian Church in the United States of America, PHS, June 22 and November 29, 1870, 1–4, 20; Placard, etc., in Jackson Scrapbooks 64:69.

5. Jackson to Henry J. Van Dyke, February 14, 1879, Jackson Correspondence 8:93–94; Minutes, Pueblo [Colorado] Presbytery, typed copy, 97, October 13, 1883.

6. Session Records, Lake City, Colorado, June 18, 1876, and December 20, 1881, 10–13, 32.

7. Session Records, Rosita, Colorado Presbyterian Church, May 25, 1879, 23.

8. Robert L. Stewart, "Golden and Black Hawk, Colorado," Historical Sermon, 1876, PHS, 4.

9. Alex Darley to Jackson, January 25, 1876, Jackson Correspondence 6:786.

10. Session Records, Idaho Springs, Colorado, Presbyterian Church, May 7, 1879, and January 31 and May 13, 1880, 7, 9–10; Session Records, Valmont, Colorado, Presbyterian Church, preface.

11. "Presbytery of Colorado," *RMP*, April 8, 1874.

12. R. L. Stewart to Jackson, April 10, 1874, Jackson Correspondence 4:250–51. The Presbytery of Colorado, in its official ruling on this case, cited various directives of the church to show how the actions of the Black Hawk session were, quite simply, improper. "Church Rules," *RMP*, May 27, 1874.

13. "Missionary Superintendent," *RMP*, November 1873.

14. "Presbytery of Colorado," October 8, 1880, Jackson Scrapbooks 40:22.

15. See chapter 3.

16. John Stewart to Jackson, October 7 and 22, 1873, and Philip H. Tooley to Jackson, April 2, 1874, Jackson Correspondence 4:322, 326–27 and 5:389. When a former pastor of the Evanston church learned about the rental of the church to the Mormons, he told Jackson, "I would rather have heard that the building had been burned to ashes. I believe it would be better to rent it for a hog pen than to rent it to Mormons." Frederick Welty to Jackson, September 28, 1874, ibid., 5:506.

17. J. Trumbull Backus to Jackson, April 6, 1874, ibid., 5:393.

18. "Presbytery of Wyoming," *RMP*, June 3, 1874.

19. *General Assembly Minutes, 1871*, 546–47, and *1880*, 239; Hodge, *What is Presbyterian Law?*, 231; Minutes, Synod of Colorado, 1871–88, September 4, 1871, PHS, 20–21.

20. "Synod of Colorado," *RMP*, October 1872.

21. "Presbytery of Colorado," *RMP*, December 1877.

22. George Darley, "Thirty-five Years of Presbyterianism in Colorado," undated manuscript in Darley Collection, Archives, University of Colorado at Boulder Libraries.

23. James H. White, *The First Hundred Years of Central Presbyterian Church, 1860–1960* (Denver: Great Western Stockman, 1960), 17–24; Jackson to My Dear Wife, February 23, 1870, Jackson Correspondence 3:813.

24. "Presbytery of Colorado," *RMP*, October 1872; A. R. Day, "Synod of Colorado—Historical Sketch," *RMP*, May 1872; *General Assembly Minutes, 1871*, 720.

25. *RMN*, September 18 and 29, 1872.

26. Minutes, Board of Home Missions, June 17 and September 23, 1873, 139–40, 147.

27. Sheldon Jackson, "The Consolidation of the Two Presbyterian Churches of Denver," [n.d.], Jackson Scrapbooks 41:1–2.

28. "Denver," *RMP*, April 15, 1874.

29. "Change of Names," *RMP*, November 18, 1874. The minutes of the Board of Home Missions noted the legal action pertaining to the two churches as "amicably settled" after various papers were signed for discontinuance of the suit in the Denver courts. Minutes, Board of Home Missions, June 16, 1874, 182.

30. "Action of the St. Paul's Congregational Church of Denver, Colorado," *RMP*, April 1875. In this notice, the Congregationalists acknowledged that the Presbyterians "have fairly won the field."

31. "News From the Churches," *RMP*, April 1875; Nevin, *Encyclopaedia*, 444–45.

32. T. E. Bliss to Jackson, May 18, 1875, Jackson Correspondence 5:648.

33. Bliss to Jackson, January 3, 1876, ibid., 6:779–80.

34. Willis Lord cited ill health as the reason for his resignation, and the pastor of the Seventeenth Street Church left to seek another assignment in the East. "Religious News," *RMP*, August 1876; White, *Central Presbyterian Church*, 25.

35. Robert Thompson to Jackson, March 19, 1874, and T. C. Easton to Jackson, June 24, 1874, Jackson Correspondence 5:381, 441.

36. Easton to Jackson, June 24, 1874, and Thompson to Jackson, June 26, 1874, ibid., 441, 444–45.

37. Jackson to Thompson, July 3, 1874, ibid., 445–46.

38. M. Gifford to Jackson, October 24, 1875; R. G. Thompson to Jackson, February 22, 1876; and Jackson to Thompson, n.d., ibid., 6:738–39, 808–12; "Presbytery of Colorado," *RMP*, January 1877.

39. James Russel as quoted in Edwards, "Presbyterian Church History," 305.

40. Petition for Presbytery of Montana, n.d., Jackson Correspondence 4:157; *General Assembly Minutes, 1872*, 87–88.

41. Edwards, "Presbyterian Church History," 303–4; "Montana," *RMP*, August 1872.

42. Edwards, "Presbyterian Church History," 304–5; "Minutes of the Presbytery of Montana, February 21, 1873," *RMP*, April 1873.

43. Will Frackelton to Jackson, March 31, 1873, Jackson Correspondence 4:244.

44. The church at Willow Creek had a short history. Within a year of its organization, the one elder in the little congregation had moved away to enroll in a theological seminary and the other six members soon after moved elsewhere. Edwards, "Presbyterian Church History," 305.

45. Lyman Crittenden to Jackson, March 9, 1873, Jackson Correspondence 4:239–40.

46. William Rommel to Jackson, December 3, 1873, ibid., 5:344.

47. James Russel to Jackson, May 4, 1874, ibid., 415–16.

48. Jackson to Russel, June 22, 1874, ibid., 416–19.

49. Russel to Jackson, July 13, 1874, ibid., 455–56.

50. Stewart, *Sheldon Jackson*, 190.

51. Kendall to Jackson, April 19, 1877, Jackson Correspondence 7:54.

52. John MacAllister to Jackson, June 27, 1877, ibid., 82.

53. Kendall to Jackson, July 16, 1877, ibid., 92; Jackson to MacAllister, n.d., ibid., 82; *RMP*, November 11, 1877.

54. *RMP*, April 1878.

CHAPTER 5

1. Josiah Strong, *Our Country, Its Possible Future and Its Present Crisis* (1885; reprint, New York: Baker and Taylor, 1891), 265.

2. Jackson to *New York Evangelist*, January 1, 1871, Jackson Correspondence 4:1.

3. Henry Kendall to Jackson, November 29, 1871, ibid., 108; *General Assembly Minutes, 1871*, 645–46, and *1872*, 16–17.

4. Kirk H. Porter and Donald B. Johnson, *National Party Platforms, 1840–1964* (Urbana: University of Illinois Press, 1966), 46–48.

5. "Board of Home Missions," *RMP*, November 1873.

6. Jackson to W. Y. Brown, November 18, 1873, Jackson Correspondence 5:337.

7. Cyrus Dickson to Jackson, July 13 and August 13, 1874, ibid., 455, 476; *General Assembly Minutes, 1874*, 39; "Home Missions—The Debt," *RMP*, December 23, 1874.

8. *General Assembly Minutes, 1875*, 487–89.

9. *RMP*, January 1876, and "Hard Times," *RMP*, March 1876.

10. *Inaugural Addresses*, 138; *General Assembly Minutes, 1877*, 587; *1878*, 166; *1879*, 677. Hayes won the election when he finally received twenty disputed electoral votes.

11. A. Darley to Jackson, May 7 and 27, 1875, Jackson Correspondence 5:639–41, 652.

12. Josiah Welch, "Reply to Theological Student," *RMP*, November 1875.

13. John Annin to Jackson, October 31, 1874, Jackson Correspondence 5:523.

14. "Paying the Minister," *RMP*, July 1872.

15. W. Teitsworth to Jackson, June 9, 1875, Jackson Correspondence 6:659.

16. H. R. Wilson to Jackson, September 18, 1869, Jackson Correspondence 3:689; "Bridges' Ready Made Houses," n.d., and "Our Chicago Letter, The Church on the Pacific R.R.," June 24, 1869, Jackson Scrapbooks 38:16 and 59:18.

17. H. P. Peck to Dear Brother Cleland, November 20, 1869, and Lyman Bridges to Jackson, December 4, 1869, ibid., 3:722, 732.

18. Bridges to Jackson, June 17, 1870, and Jackson to John Wilson, Board of Church Erection, n.d., ibid., 3:878, 4:143A; Session Records, July 17, 1870, Cheyenne Presbyterian Church, 2; Raven Fund Account Book, PHS, entries for March, May, and September of 1870.

19. Jackson to John Wilson, n.d., and Wilson to Jackson, April 20, 1872, Jackson Correspondence 4:143A, 154.

20. "Christian Parents, What Will You Do About It?" *RMP*, October 1876.

21. "A Plea For Home Missions," *RMP*, September 1873.

22. "Home Missions," *RMP*, July 29, 1874.

23. B. Crary, "Frontier Missions," *RMP*, August 26, 1874.

24. F. C. M., "The Assembly Excursion," *RMP*, June 24, 1874. One widely read commentator, who visited the mining camps of Colorado in the 1860s, reported, "One often heard sunburnt miners, while resting upon their spades, discussing Shakespeare, the classics, religion, and political economy." Albert D. Richardson, *Beyond the Mississippi, 1857–1867* (Hartford, Conn.: American Publishing, 1867), 199–200.

25. *RMP,* November 1878.

26. Rev. R. Irwin, "Commissioner's Excursion," n.d., Jackson Scrapbooks 38:50. The Kansas Pacific Railroad reached Denver in August of 1870. This direct route offered an alternative to the inconvenience of changing from the Union Pacific in Cheyenne to the Denver Pacific, the connecting line between Cheyenne and Denver.

27. "Colorado—The Presbyterian Excursionists," June 5, 1871, and J. G. Monfort, "Editorial Correspondence," June 5, 1871, Jackson Scrapbooks 38:54–55, 57; Jackson Travel Journals, 1871, PHS, entry for June 3.

28. "Colorado—The Presbyterian Excursionists," June 5, 1871, Jackson Scrapbooks 38:54–56.

29. Ibid., 62; "Going Home," n.d., ibid., 56.

30. "General Assembly Excursion," *RMP,* May 20, 1874, and "The Assembly Excursion," *RMP,* June 24, and July 1 and 8, 1874.

31. "Home Mission Address to the Churches," *RMP,* July 1, 1874, and "Home Missions," *RMP,* July 29, 1874.

32. "Denver and Rio Grande Railway," *RMP,* July 1, 1874.

33. "A New Departure," *RMP,* July 1873.

34. "Presbyterian Church—Dedication Service," [February 1872], Jackson Scrapbooks 59:42, 46.

35. Union Pacific Railroad, *RMP,* September 1873. A thorough evaluation of the scandals associated with construction of the Union Pacific Railroad is provided in Maury Klein, *Union Pacific: Birth of a Railroad, 1862–1893* (Garden City, N.Y.: Doubleday, 1987), 285–305. In his scrapbooks, Jackson retained a clipping of an article that severely criticized his position on the Union Pacific case. "When the religious press endorses a steal of $40,000,000," the writer declared, and "denounces efforts made for its recovery, the least that can be said is that they occupy a very low plane of morality, and entertain very loose ideas of the responsibilities of public men." Jackson Scrapbooks, n.d., 41:29.

36. "Montana," May 27, 1872, Jackson Scrapbooks 51:18.

37. Sheldon Jackson, "Railways and Civilization," *RMP,* April 1876; Smalley, *History of the Northern Pacific Railroad,* 196, 205; Stewart, *Sheldon Jackson,* 191–92.

38. Sheldon Jackson, "The Home Field," [1871], Jackson Scrapbooks 38:38–41.

39. Jackson Travel Journals, 1872, PHS, entry for November 17; "Home Missions," [1872], Jackson Scrapbooks 38:121.

40. "Home Missions in the General Assembly," *RMP,* July 1875.

41. Ibid.

42. George M. Darley, *Pioneering in the San Juan* (New York: Fleming H. Revell, 1899), 107–12.

43. "The Witherspoon Statue," *RMP,* April 1875; Salary figures compiled from minutes of the Board of Home Missions, 1870–80. Jackson attended the great exposition in Philadelphia, and he gained free admission to the grounds with a press ticket that showed him representing *The Presbyterian,* Denver, Colorado. Sheldon Jackson Collection, Speer Library, Princeton Theological Seminary, Princeton, New Jersey, File D.

44. "Home Mission Items," *RMP*, April 1875.

45. J[ulia] M. Graham to Jackson, January 1, 1873, Jackson Correspondence 4:208.

CHAPTER 6

1. Porter and Johnson, *National Party Platforms*, 47.

2. An excellent analysis of the role of women in the early years of the Presbyterian Church in the United States is included in Lois A. Boyd and R. Douglas Brackenridge, *Presbyterian Women in America: Two Centuries of a Quest for Status* (Westport, Conn.: Greenwood, 1983), 3–14.

3. "News from the Churches," *RMP*, December 1872.

4. Mrs. D. Willson in Edwards, "Presbyterian Church History," 327–28.

5. Patricia McKinney, *First Presbyterian Church, Helena, Montana* (Helena: privately printed, 1947), 19; Edwards, "Presbyterian Church History," 362.

6. Edwards, "Presbyterian Church History," 368–69.

7. Kendall to Jackson, September 7, 1872, and Cornelia Martin to Jackson, August 1, 1870, July 28, 1872, and June 9, 1883, Jackson Correspondence 4:170–71, 167; 3:900–902; and 13:140–41; Report of Santa Fe Association, Auburn, [1872], Jackson Scrapbooks 53:118.

8. Julia M. Graham to Jackson, July 8, 1872, Jackson Correspondence 4:164–65; Jackson Travel Journals, 1872, PHS, entries for September 25–27.

9. "Territorial Church News," *RMP*, January 1873; Stewart, *Sheldon Jackson*, 262; Historical sketch preceding annual reports of *The New Mexico, Arizona, and Colorado Missionary Association* bound as *Our Mission Field* in the Sheldon Jackson Collection, PHS, unpaginated.

10. "The Ladies Board of Missions of the Presbyterian Church," *RMP*, February 1873.

11. *RMP*, September, October, and December 1873; Stewart, *Sheldon Jackson*, 264–65. The president of the society organized in the 17th Street Church in Denver was Mrs. Sheldon Jackson.

12. "Woman's Work For Jesus," *RMP*, January 28, 1874.

13. *General Assembly Minutes, 1874*, 32; "Shall Women Pray and Speak?" *RMP*, June 17, 1874.

14. "Shall Women Pray and Speak?" *RMP*, June 17, 1874.

15. *General Assembly Minutes, 1874*, 66.

16. "Woman's Work For Woman," *RMP*, August 26, 1874.

17. *General Assembly Minutes, 1875*, 487–89, 594.

18. Kendall to Jackson, August 30, 1875, and "Home Mission Meetings to be Addressed by Dr. Sheldon Jackson," September 30, 1875, ibid., 697–98, 723.

19. Stewart, *Sheldon Jackson*, 270; Minutes, Board of Home Missions, January 25, 1876, 259.

20. *General Assembly Minutes, 1876*, 144–45; Stewart, *Sheldon Jackson*, 267.

21. *General Assembly Minutes, 1876*, 31.

22. Ibid., *1877*, 633.

23. H. Kendall and Cyrus Dickson, "Appeal," [1877], Jackson Scrapbooks 62:19; "Woman's Work for Home Missions at the General Assembly," *RMP*, July 1877.

24. "Progress," *RMP*, March 1878.

25. Mrs. R. T. Haines, "To the Christian Women Within the Bounds of the Synod of New Jersey," *RMP*, April 1878.

26. F. E. H. Haines to Jackson, February 23, 1878, Jackson Correspondence 7:270; Janet H. Penfield acknowledges the work of Mrs. Haines on these issues in "Women in the Presbyterian Church—an Historical Overview," *JPH* 55 (Summer 1977): 112–13.

27. Mrs. J. P. E. Kumler to Jackson, May 1878, Jackson Correspondence 8:61.

28. Melissa P. Dodge to My Dear Mrs. Paxton, May 15, 1878, ibid., 8:66.

29. Julia M. Wright, "The Need of Thorough Organization in Woman's Home Mission Work," *RMP*, September 1878.

30. Minutes of the preliminary meeting held by Presbyterian Women in the First Presbyterian Church, Pittsburgh, Pa., May 24, 1878, for the consideration of the formation of a national organization of the Presbyterian Women of the United States in the interests of Home Missions, Jackson Correspondence 8:72–74.

31. Mrs. S. F. Scovel, "Woman's Executive Committee of Home Missions," *RMP*, June 1879. A comprehensive account of steps taken to organize the new board appears in Boyd and Brackenridge, *Presbyterian Women in America*, 15–29. See also Stewart, *Sheldon Jackson*, 256–75.

32. *General Assembly Minutes, 1878*, 110.

33. F. E. H. Haines to Jackson, June 27, 1878, and Jackson to Mrs. Haines, My Dear Sister, July 4, 1878, Jackson Correspondence 8:75–79.

34. Kendall to Jackson, July 11, 1878, Jackson Correspondence 8:123.

35. Mrs. S. F. Scovel, "Woman's Executive Committee of Home Missions," *RMP*, June 1879; F. E. H. Haines to Jackson, July 12, 1878, Jackson Correspondence 8:80.

36. Julia McNair Wright to Jackson, August 1, 1878, Jackson Correspondence 8:82–83.

37. Minutes, Board of Home Missions, October 7, 1878, 414–16; Mrs. S. F. Scovel, "Woman's Executive Committee of Home Missions," *RMP*, June 1879.

38. Mrs. S. F. Scovel, "Woman's Executive Committee of Home Missions," *RMP*, June 1879; F. E. H. Haines, "Woman's Executive Committee of Home Missions of the Presbyterian Church," December 21, 1878, in *RMP*, February 1879.

39. "*General Assembly Minutes, 1879*, 593; "Our Annual Meeting" and "Action of the General Assembly," *RMP*, June 1879.

40. F. E. H. Haines to Jackson, December 26, 1878, Jackson Correspondence 9:51.

41. H. Kendall, "Woman's Work for Woman," n.d., Jackson Scrapbooks 62:22–24.

42. Stewart, *Sheldon Jackson*, 279.

43. Ibid., 280.

44. In her perceptive study on the development of the position of women in the Presbyterian Church, Elizabeth Verdesi acknowledged the importance of Jackson's

position in securing support from women for home mission work. She concluded, however, that Jackson was not an advocate of a broadly defined feminist movement at the time. Elizabeth H. Verdesi, *In But Still Out: Women in the Church* (Philadelphia: Westminster, 1975), 48, 53–54.

45. "Our Work For The Present Year," August 1880, Jackson Scrapbooks 62:46–49.

46. The Rev. J. M. Stevenson, "The Religious Future of the Rocky Mountains," *RMP,* January 28, 1874.

CHAPTER 7

1. The Rev. J. M. Stevenson, "The Religious Future of the Rocky Mountains," *RMP,* January 28, 1874.

2. The Rev. T. E. Bliss, "Matters Presbyterian," May 10, 1878, Jackson Scrapbooks 40:32–33.

3. John H. Fisher provides a thoughtful analysis of Presbyterian interest in education in the nineteenth century in his "Primary and Secondary Education and the Presbyterian Church in the United States of America," *JPH* 24 (March 1946): 13–43.

4. Stewart, *Sheldon Jackson,* 78–79.

5. M. P. B., "How Shall We Educate?" *RMP,* March 1872.

6. "American Railway Literary Union," *RMP,* March 1872.

7. "A Brave Girl," ibid.

8. Advertising prospectus for the *Rocky Mountain Presbyterian,* n.d., Jackson Correspondence 4:132.

9. Wilson, *Presbyterian Historical Almanac,* 259. For a thorough examination of the development of Sabbath schools in the United States, see Anne M. Boylan, *Sunday School: The Formation of an American Institution, 1790–1880* (New Haven: Yale University Press, 1988.

10. "Sunday School Institute," June 10, 1871, Jackson Scrapbooks 38:37–38; *RMN,* June 11, 1871.

11. "The Bible School," *RMP,* July 1872.

12. "What Makes Boys Bad?" ibid., September 1878.

13. J. D. Hewett to Jackson, January 28, 1878, Jackson Correspondence 7:254.

14. Delos Finks to Jackson, December 15, 1873, ibid., 5:348; "Narrative of the State of Religion in the Presbytery of Colorado," *RMP,* July 1, 1874.

15. *RMP,* September 1876.

16. Samuel L. Gillespie, "Corinne, Utah," Historical Sermon, 1876, PHS, 13–14.

17. Lyman Crittenden to Jackson, December 10, 1872, Jackson Correspondence 4:202; Mary Ellen Scott, archivist, Pittsburgh Theological Seminary, to author, December 6, 1977.

18. Lyman Crittenden to Jackson, December 20, 1872, Jackson Correspondence 4:202–3; Mary Crittenden, "The Gallatin Female Seminary," [1877], Jackson Scrapbooks 51:65. The competing school in Helena was St. Vincent's Academy, a Catholic school for girls.

19. Lyman Crittenden and Mary Crittenden [1873], Jackson Scrapbooks 51:42–43; C. W. Martin to Jackson, January 16, 1873, Jackson Correspondence 4:213.

20. J. R. Russell, "Montana Territory," n.d., *RMP*, November 1876.

21. L. B. Crittenden, "Montana Letter," October 9, 1873, *RMP*, December 1873.

22. "Territorial Church News," *RMP*, November 1873.

23. Crittenden to Jackson, September 9, 1873, Jackson Correspondence 4:310–11.

24. Cornelia Martin to Jackson, May 12, 1874, and L. B. Crittenden to Jackson, April 21, 1874, ibid., 5:421–22, 406–8. Regarding the sad situation at the Gallatin City church, Crittenden announced, "Elder Dick is never at home, or his home is in the mountains, and there are besides only two aged females left."

25. L. B. Crittenden to Jackson, October 22, 1874, ibid., 5:518–19; Mary Crittenden, "The Gallatin Female Seminary," [1877], Jackson Scrapbooks 51:67; McKinney, *Presbyterianism in Montana*, 55; "Religious News," *RMP*, August 5, 1874.

26. L. B. Crittenden to Jackson, December 20, 1872, Jackson Correspondence 4:202.

27. *Our Mission Field*, [1875], 9; Edwards, *Presbyterian Church History*, 335; Mary Crittenden to Jackson, January 25, 1875, Jackson Correspondence 5:565–66.

28. Mary Crittenden in Edwards, *Presbyterian Church History*, 335–36.

29. W. C. Rommel to the Rev. Drs. Kendall and Dickson, April 12, 1876, Jackson Correspondence 6:830.

30. "Religious News," *RMP*, May and June 1876; Editorial comment, *RMP*, September 1876.

31. Mary Crittenden, "Gallatin Valley Female Seminary," *RMP*, October 1877; Edwards *Presbyterian Church History*, 338; C. L. Richards to Jackson, October 9, 1878, Jackson Correspondence 8:259–60. For an account of other late nineteenth-century Presbyterian academies founded in Montana following Sheldon Jackson's departure, see Norman J. Bender, "'The Very Atmosphere is Charged With Unbelief. . . .'—Presbyterians and Higher Education in Montana 1869–1900," *Montana, The Magazine of Western History* 28 (April 1978): 16–25.

32. "Rocky Mountain Correspondence," March 7, 1870, Jackson Scrapbooks 38:23; *Colorado*, 365; Carl Abbott, *Colorado: A History of the Centennial State* (Boulder: Colorado Associated University Press, 1976), 146.

33. "Evans University," n.d., Jackson Scrapbooks 41:14.

34. Stone, *History of Colorado*, 613, 624.

35. "Presbyterian College," *RMP*, July 1, 1874; "Articles of Incorporation of Evans University," Jackson Correspondence 5:468–70; W. T. Wylie, "The College at Evans, Colorado," *RMP*, September 16, 1874.

36. W. E. Hamilton to Jackson, July 20, 1874, Jackson Correspondence 5:459.

37. James Lowrie to Jackson, July 21, 1874, ibid., 5:461.

38. W. T. Wylie to Jackson, July 20, 1874, J. F. Stewart to Jackson, July 28, 1874, and E. M. Rollo to Jackson, September 2 and 14, 1874, Jackson Correspondence 5:458, 466–67, 491, and 498.

39. Stewart to Jackson, August 17, 1874, ibid., 5:476.

40. Minutes of the Synod of Colorado, September 22, 1874, 33.

41. J. L. Gage to Jackson, April 30, 1875, Jackson Correspondence 5:634.

42. J. Merrill to Jackson, February 7, 1877, and A. Darley to Jackson, February 22, 1876, ibid., 7:18–19 and 6:807.

43. "Old Papers," *RMP*, October 1875; "The Presbyterian Church in the San Luis Valley," [1876], and Alex M. Darley, "The Miners of the San Juan and Their Thanks for Books Given," August 30, 1876, Jackson Scrapbooks 41:118 and 130–31.

44. Stewart, *Sheldon Jackson*, 100. Efforts to "uplift" Chinese and Afro–Americans in Jackson's mission field were not particularly notable, perhaps because of their relatively small numbers. The Central Presbyterian Church in Denver did, however, take pride in its school, organized originally as a Sabbath school, for Chinese residents. White, *Central Presbyterian Church*, 51. A visitor to the Central Church in 1877 thought that he perceived the reason for the interest of the Chinese in this school. "John C. [Chinaman] comes," the observer explained, "that he might learn how to make more money in increased facilities of communication with his customers." "St. Louis Letter," May 12, 1877, Jackson Scrapbooks 41:145.

45. Ibid., 194.

CHAPTER 8

1. Nevin, *Encyclopaedia*, 213; Frank Ellinwood, "Utah and the Next Vexed Question" and "Among the Mormons," [1869], Jackson Scrapbooks 59:83–88.

2. Ellinwood, "Utah and the Next Vexed Question" and "Among the Mormons," Jackson Scrapbooks 59:83–88.

3. Ibid.

4. Edward Bayliss to Jackson, April 13 and 30, 1870, Jackson Correspondence 3:819, 834.

5. Bayliss to Jackson, May 17, 1870, ibid., 847–48.

6. Bayliss to Jackson, December 5, 1870, and January 3, 1871, ibid., 3:951 and 4:3–4; Edward E. Bayliss, "To Sunday-School Children," [1870], Sheldon Jackson Scrapbooks, Westminster College, Salt Lake City, Utah, 1:88.

7. E. E. Bayliss, "Rocky Mountain Academy," [1871], Jackson Scrapbooks, Westminster College, 1:88; Henry Kendall to Bayliss, January 20, 1871, Jackson Correspondence 4:13. In the opinion of the pastor of the church in Cheyenne, Wyoming, "A Presbyterian College in Corinne for the next twenty years will be a thing about as intangible as real estate in moonshine." William Kephart to Jackson, January 31, 1871, Jackson Correspondence 4:17.

8. "The Rocky Mountain Female Academy," Jackson Scrapbooks, Westminster College, 1:88; Samuel L. Gillespie, "Corinne, Utah," Historical Sermon, 1876, PHS, 11; Session Records, Corinne, Utah, Presbyterian Church, 8.

9. D. J. McMillan to Jackson, March 17, 1875, Jackson Correspondence 5:604. Coronation was a name used for a popular hymn that began with the line "All Hail the Power of Jesus' Name." An interesting account of Duncan McMillan's colorful life appears in Florence McMillan, *The Rev. Duncan James McMillan, 1846–1939— A Tribute* (New York: McAuliffe-Booth, 1939).

10. Duncan J. McMillan, et al., "Addresses Celebrating the 25th Anniversary of Westminster College." *The Utah Westminster* (Salt Lake City), special edition, October 1922, 6, Westminster College, Salt Lake City, Utah; Duncan McMillan, "Early Beginnings of Wasatch Academy," n.d., Wasatch Academy, Mt. Pleasant, Utah, 10–11; "News From The Churches," *RMP*, September 1875.

11. Sheldon Jackson, "Persecutions on a Home Mission Field," *RMP*, April 1876.

12. Sheldon Jackson, "An Appeal to Christian Women," *RMP*, April 1875.

13. McMillan to Jackson, May 1, 1875, Jackson Correspondence 5:635.

14. Andrew Madsen, "The Personal History of Andrew Madsen and the Early History of Sanpete County and Mt. Pleasant, Utah," n.d., Western History Department, Marriott Library, University of Utah, Salt Lake City, 81–82.

15. Sherman H. Doyle, *Presbyterian Home Missions* (Philadelphia: Presbyterian Board of Publications and Sabbath School Work, 1902), 162; Lewis G. Webster, "A History of Westminster College of Salt Lake City, 1875–1969," M.S. thesis, Utah State University, Logan, 1970, 9.

16. Welch to Jackson, April 3, 1875, Jackson Correspondence 5:613.

17. John Coyner, "History of the Salt Lake Collegiate Institute From Its Organization, April 12, 1875 to May 5, 1885," 10, Westminster College, Salt Lake City, Utah.

18. Ibid., 11–12; "Salt Lake Collegiate Institute," *RMP*, September 1875.

19. "First Annual Circular of the Salt Lake Collegiate Institute," June 8, 1876, 2–3, Westminster College.

20. J. M. Coyner, "Utah-Educational Matters," September 1875; *RMP*, October 1875.

21. John Coyner, "History of the Salt Lake Collegiate Institute," 12, 23; Coyner, "Utah," *RMP*, March 1876.

22. Coyner to Jackson, December 22, 1876, and January 9 and May 11, 1877, Jackson Correspondence 6:968 and 7:2–3, 60; J. M. Coyner, "Salt Lake Collegiate Institute," *RMP*, April 1877.

23. "Presbytery of Utah," *RMP*, April 1877.

24. Catalogue of the Salt Lake Collegiate Institute, privately printed, 1877, 14–15, Westminster College, Salt Lake City, Utah; John Coyner, "History of the Salt Lake Collegiate Institute," 16, 20; Minutes, Board of Home Missions, December 18, 1877, 355, and December 24, 1877, 362.

25. Much has been written about the early development of Presbyterian churches and schools in Utah. Particularly useful works are Carl Wankier, "History of Presbyterian Schools in Utah," M.S. thesis, University of Utah, Salt Lake City, 1968; George K. Davies, "A History of the Presbyterian Church in Utah," Ph.D. dissertation, University of Pittsburgh, 1942; and Thomas E. Lyon, "Evangelical Protestant Missionary Activities in Mormon Dominated Areas, 1865–1900," Ph.D. thesis, University of Utah, Salt Lake City, 1962.

26. *Utah*, American Guide Series (New York, Hastings House, 1941), 205, 362; G. M. Anderson to Jackson, June 5, 1876, Jackson Correspondence 6:842–43.

27. George W. Gallagher to Jackson, April 1 and 15, 1878. Jackson Correspondence 8:3, 20.

28. Gallagher to Jackson, July 9, 1878, ibid., 8:115; Theodore D. and Marian E. Martin, "Presbyterian Work in Utah, 1869–1969," 343, manuscript at Westminster College, Salt Lake City, Utah.

29. Gallagher to Jackson, July 9, 1878, Jackson Correspondence 8:116.

30. "An Appeal from the Presbytery of Utah," *RMP*, November 1878; "Ogden Educational Institute," [1878], Jackson Scrapbooks 61:132–33.

31. *The Church Review* (Salt Lake City, Utah), 10, historical edition, December 29, 1895, Westminster College, Salt Lake City. Josiah Welch died in 1877 from what one of his friends described as "Bright's disease of the kidneys." "The Late Rev. Josiah Welch," [1877], Jackson Scrapbooks 61:67.

32. J. P. Schell, "Church Dedication—Alta," *RMP*, November 1873.

33. Stewart, *Sheldon Jackson*, 207; J. P. Schell to Jackson, March 23, 1874, Josiah Welch to Jackson, August 12, 1874, and R. G. McNiece to Jackson, August 5, 1878, Jackson Correspondence 5:383, 474, and 8:175.

34. Sarah Yates, *A Centennial History of the Community Presbyterian Church of Brigham City, Utah, 1878–1978* (Brigham City, Utah: privately printed, 1978), 1; Samuel Gillespie to Jackson, July 31, 1874, Jackson Correspondence 5:468; *Utah*, 277.

35. Gillespie to Jackson, September 24, 1877, November 20, 1877, January 22, 1878, and July 20, 1878, Jackson Correspondence 7:133, 182, and 248, and 8:146; Yates, *History of Brigham City Church*, 2; Wallace Stegner, *Mormon Country* (New York: Bonanza, 1942), 255–56.

36. "Presbyterianism in Utah," *RMP*, April 1877.

37. Kendall to Jackson, March 4 and September 28, 1878, Jackson Correspondence 7:279 and 8:255.

38. McMillan to Jackson, April 4 and May 2, 1878, ibid., 8:4, 36.

39. Sheldon Jackson, "Persecutions on a Home Mission Field," *RMP*, April 1876.

40. "A Sample Presbyterian Bait," *Deseret News* (Salt Lake City), June 13, 1879, in *Journal History*, 2 (bound extracts from newspapers and periodicals at the church historian's office), Church of Jesus Christ of Latter-day Saints, Salt Lake City, Utah.

41. Sheldon Jackson, "Organization of a Presbyterian Church in Utah," [November 1871], Jackson Scrapbooks 59:112–13.

42. Mrs. C. M. Hawley, et al., "To The Ladies of the Presbyterian Church on Behalf of Salt Lake City," [December 1871], Jackson Scrapbooks 61:3.

43. "One of the Deluded Women," to the editor, *Deseret News*, (Salt Lake City), December 14, 1871, ibid., 61:16.

44. *Evening News* (Salt Lake City), December 13, 1871, Jackson Scrapbooks 61:17–18.

45. Sheldon Jackson to "Ladies of the Presbyterian Churches of Brooklyn, New York," [1877], Jackson Correspondence 7:301.

46. Ibid., 302–4.

47. Mrs. Wm. Brooks to Jackson, May 8, 1877, ibid., 58.

48. Duncan McMillan to Jackson, March 18, 1879, ibid., 9:146.

49. R. G. McNiece, "Thanksgiving Sermon—God's Wondrous Works in Utah," 47 of a scrapbook compiled by Emil Nyman, archives of Westminster College, Salt Lake City, Utah.

50. Sheldon Jackson to "Ladies of the Presbyterian Churches of Brooklyn, New York," [1877], Jackson Correspondence 7:302.

51. "The Heathen at Home," [n.d.], Jackson Scrapbooks 61:72.

52. "Report of the Assembly's Standing Committee on Home Missions," *RMP,* July 1, 1874.

Chapter 9

1. Fred Israel, ed., *Major Peace Treaties of Modern History, 1648–1967* (New York: Chelsea House/McGraw Hill, 1967), 2:739.

2. William Kephart to Jackson, February 17, 1872, Jackson Correspondence 4:140–42. Kephart also distributed antislavery tracts while he was in New Mexico. Lawrence R. Murphy has examined this aspect of his activities in his *Antislavery in the Southwest: William G. Kephart's Mission to New Mexico, 1850–53* (El Paso: Texas Western Press, 1978). Bishop Jean Baptiste Lamy's early experiences in New Mexico are well documented in Paul Horgan, *Lamy of Santa Fe: His Life and Times* (New York: Farrar, Straus, and Giroux, 1975).

3. *The Annual of Washington and Jefferson College, Washington, Pennsylvania* (Buffalo, N.Y.: Gies, 1889), 99–100; Edith J. Agnew and Ruth K. Barber, "The Unique Presbyterian School System of New Mexico," *JPH* 49 (Fall 1971): 202. Eveline Alexander's experiences in New Mexico at the time are revealed in Sandra L. Myres, ed., *Cavalry Wife: The Diary of Eveline Alexander, 1866–1867* (College Station: Texas A & M University Press, 1977).

4. "Minutes of the Presbytery of Santa Fe, 1868" in *JPH* 33 (September 1955): 199.

5. Ibid., 206.

6. Minutes, Board of Domestic Missions, July 12, 1869; *Necrological Reports and Annual Proceedings of Princeton Theological Seminary* (Princeton, N.J.: C. S. Robinson, 1891, 1899, 1909, 1919), 3:287–88.

7. Ruth K. Barber and Edith J. Agnew, *Sowers Went Forth: The Story of Presbyterian Missions in New Mexico and Southern Colorado* (Albuquerque: Menaul Historical Library, 1981), 17–20; Session Records, First Presbyterian Church, Las Vegas, New Mexico, 1; "Memorial Sketch of the Reverend José Ynes Perea, 1837–1910," *La Aurora* (Las Vegas, N.M.), November 15, 1910.

8. Kendall to Jackson, July 14, 1870, Jackson Correspondence 3:893–94.

9. John Irvine to Jackson, April 25, 1870, Jackson Correspondence 3:831.

10. An objective history of the Penitente Brotherhood is found in Marta Weigle, *Brothers of Light, Brothers of Blood: The Penitentes of The Southwest* (Albuquerque: University of New Mexico Press, 1976).

11. Kendall to Jackson, September 22, 1870, Jackson Correspondence 3:919.

12. McFarland to Jackson, December 20, 1870, Jackson Correspondence 3:955; *Santa Fe New Mexican,* November 19 and 21, 1870. The term "Mexican" was widely used at the time to refer to Americans of Mexican or Spanish descent in the Southwest.

13. Cyrus Dickson to Jackson, November 22, 1870, Jackson Correspondence 3:942; Charter of the Santa Fe University, Industrial and Agricultural College,

December 6, 1870, file L–1, American Indian Correspondence [AIC], PHS; *Santa Fe New Mexican*, December 15, 1870.

14. Kendall to Jackson, January 3, 1872, Jackson Correspondence 4:133.

15. Sheldon Jackson, "Home Missions: A Trip Along the Frontier," [1872], Jackson Scrapbooks 38:113–14.

16. Ibid., 117.

17. James Roberts to Jackson, July 14 and 16, 1873, Jackson Correspondence 4:285, 289. For a complete account of the experiences of James Roberts as a missionary to the Navajos, see Norman J. Bender, *New Hope for the Indians: The Grant Peace Policy and the Navajos in the 1870s* (Albuquerque: University of New Mexico Press, 1989).

18. Roberts to Jackson, July 14 and 16, 1873, Jackson Correspondence 4:285, 289; "Taos, New Mexico," *RMP*, April 1, 1874; "Organization," *RMP*, January 1875.

19. M. E. Roberts to Jackson, July 2, 1874, and James Roberts to Jackson, July 16, 1873, Jackson Correspondence 5:448 and 4:290.

20. C. W. Martin to Jackson, June 26, 1875, ibid., 6:672.

21. "Religious News," *RMP*, March 1875.

22. Sheldon Jackson, "A Missionary Tour Through New Mexico," *RMP*, October 1875.

23. Melancthon Hughes to Jackson, April 9, 1873, Jackson Correspondence 4:247; *RMP*, June, October, and December 1873. Before he left Santa Fe, David McFarland performed a marriage ceremony on March 1, 1873, for William Antrim and Catherine McCarty. Among those listed in the church records as witnesses was Henry McCarty, son of Catherine by a previous marriage. This young man later achieved considerable notoriety as an outlaw in New Mexico under several aliases, but he was best known as Billy the Kid. Katherine W. Sellers, Scrapbooks, First Presbyterian Church, Santa Fe, New Mexico, 1976, vol. 2, unpaginated.

24. Mrs. M. E. Roberts to Jackson, July 2, 1874, Jackson Correspondence 5:448.

25. Sheldon Jackson, "A Missionary Tour Through New Mexico," *RMP*, November 1875; T. D. Allen, *Not Ordered By Men* (Santa Fe, N.M.: Rydal, 1967), 50, 53.

26. Sheldon Jackson, "Missionary Tour Through New Mexico," *RMP*, December 1875.

27. Sheldon Jackson, "A Ride Of Two Thousand Miles Through New Mexico", *RMP*, January 1876.

28. Jackson, "Ride of Two Thousand Miles," *RMP*, January 1876.

29. John Annin, "Las Vegas, New Mexico," historical sermon, 1876, PHS, 24.

30. "Presbytery of Santa Fe," *RMP*, December 1877; "Memorial Sketch of the Reverend José Ynes Perea, 1837–1910," *La Aurora*, (Las Vegas, New Mexico), November 15, 1910. Mark Banker's "Missionary to His Own People: José Ynes Perea and Hispanic Presbyterianism in New Mexico" provides a good account of José Perea's colorful career, in Carl Guarneri and David Alvarez, eds., *Religion and Society in the American West* (Lanham, Md.: University Press of America, 1987), 79–104.

31. Perea to Jackson, December 8, 1879, Jackson Correspondence 9:305; José Perea, "Los Corrales, New Mexico," *RMP*, July 1879.

32. "Presbyterianism in New Mexico," *RMP*, March 1877; Minutes, Board of Home Missions, December 24, 1877, 362.

33. Kendall to Jackson, June 22, 1877, ibid., 7:76–77.

34. Alex Darley to Jackson, June 26, 1877, ibid., 7:81. For a perceptive synthesis of Alex Darley's anti-Catholicism crusade in southern Colorado, see R. Douglas Brackenridge and Francisco O. García-Treto, *Iglesia Presbiteriana: A History of Presbyterians and Mexican Americans in the Southwest* (San Antonio: Trinity University Press, 1974).

35. James Roberts to Jackson, July 28, 1879, Jackson Correspondence 9:253; "History of the Church at Sinisero [Cenicero], New Mexico," *RMP*, April 1878. The article in the *Rocky Mountain Presbyterian* placed Cenicero in New Mexico, but it was actually just a few miles across the border into southern Colorado.

36. Unidentified article, October 21, 1878, in Alexander Darley, Scrapbook, 17, Darley Collection, Archives, University of Colorado at Boulder Libraries.

37. Kendall to Jackson, December 17, 1879, Jackson Correspondence 9:320. An excellent account of the experiences of Anna Ross, a teacher who accepted employment in one of the Presbyterian schools, can be found in D. Reid Ross, "The War For Souls in the San Luis Valley," *American Presbyterians* 65 (Spring 1987), 29–37.

38. Julia M. Wright, "Children's Letters," *RMP*, September 1876.

39. Ibid.

40. "Ought New Mexico Be Admitted to the Union?," *RMP*, April 1876.

41. "New Mexico and the *Rocky Mountain Presbyterian*—Pious Lies and Religious Abuse," Jackson Scrapbooks, [1877], 53:350–51.

42. Ibid. The article in question by William H. Rideing entitled "New Mexico: Its People and Customs" appeared in the March 1877 edition of the *Rocky Mountain Presbyterian*.

43. Doyle, *Presbyterian Home Missions*, 208; Robert M. Craig, *Our Mexicans* (New York: Board of Home Missions of the Presbyterian Church in the United States of America, 1904), 24. Randi Jones Walker provides an informative table of terms used to describe New Mexicans at that time in *Protestantism in the Sangre de Cristos, 1850–1920* (Albuquerque: University of New Mexico Press, 1991), 20.

44. Jackson was surely pleased when the board of the National Anti-Papal League unanimously elected him as an honorary member. George P. Edgar, acting secretary, National Anti-Papal League, April 7, 1879, Jackson Correspondence 9:184.

45. B. B. Border to Jackson, December 15, 1879, ibid., 9:315; *RMP*, August 1879; Minutes, Board of Home Missions, January 13, 1880, 488.

46. José Perea to Jackson, January 27, 1880, Jackson Correspondence 10:28. An illuminating account of the problems encountered by one of the Presbyterian traveling evangelists in New Mexico can be found in Gabino Rendón, as told to Edith Agnew, *Hand On My Shoulder* (New York: Board of National Missions, United Presbyterian Church in the U.S.A., 1963).

47. Minutes, 362, Board of Home Missions, December 24, 1877; 362; "Presbytery of Colorado," *RMP*, November 1878; J. D. Kerr to Jackson, February 2, 1880, Jackson Correspondence 10:34.

48. *General Assembly Minutes, 1880*, 132–33.

CHAPTER 10

1. Doyle, *Presbyterian Home Missions,* 74.

2. Sheldon Jackson, "From The Rocky Mountains," [1870], Jackson Scrapbooks 38:26.

3. G. L. S., "From Colorado," [1870], ibid., 38:18.

4. *General Assembly Minutes, 1870,* 37. For a thorough discussion of the intent and results of the so-called Grant Peace Policy, see Francis P. Prucha, *American Indian Policy in Crisis: Christian Reformers and the Indian, 1865–1900* (Norman: University of Oklahoma Press, 1976).

5. "New Hope For The Indians," *Record of the Presbyterian Church in the United States of America* 21 (October 1870): 227.

6. Sheldon Jackson, "Home Missions: A Trip Along the Frontier," [1872], Jackson Scrapbooks 38:116–18.

7. Ibid., 117. An interesting account of the history of the Pueblo Indians appears in Joe S. Sando, *The Pueblo Indians* (San Francisco: Indian Historian Press, 1976).

8. Jackson Scrapbooks 53:75–76, February 3, 1873.

9. John Lowrie to General O. O. Howard, February 17, 1873, Board of Foreign Mission [BFM], letterpress copies of letters sent, PHS, RG31–43–2, 294; Edward P. Smith, Commissioner of Indian Affairs to John O. Cole, May 22, 1873, Records of the Bureau of Indian Affairs, Record Group 75, Office of Indian Affairs, [OIA], letters sent, 1824–82, Microcopy M21, Roll 112; Edwin C. Lewis to L. Edwin Dudley, Superintendent of Indian Affairs, Santa Fe, New Mexico, September 25, 1873, AIC, file M, document 255.

10. Edward P. Smith to Benjamin Thomas, September 17, 1874, OIA, M21, Roll 120; Edwin Lewis to Smith, November 30, 1874, Records of the Bureau of Indian Affairs, Record Group 75, OIA, letters received, 1824–80, New Mexico Superintendency, 1849–80, Microcopy M234, Roll 563. An admirable study of Thomas's interesting life in New Mexico is Reba N. Benge, "Benjamin M. Thomas: Career in the Southwest, 1870–1892," Ph.D. dissertation, University of New Mexico, Albuquerque, 1979.

11. B. M. Thomas to J. C. Lowrie, corresponding secretary, Board of Foreign Missions, May 7, 1875, AIC, file o(2), document 190; Sheldon Jackson, "A Missionary Tour Through New Mexico," *RMP,* November and December 1875. For a thoughtful commentary on the Presbyterian association with the pueblo schools, see Mark T. Banker, "Presbyterians and Pueblos: A Protestant Response to the Indian Question, 1872–1892," *JPH* 60 (Spring 1982): 23–40. Jackson called the circular building at the Taos Pueblo an "Estufa" (hot-house, or steam room). These structures, common to many of the ancient Indian villages in the Southwest, are customarily referred to today as kivas. In his examination of the relationship of the Pueblo Indians to the Aztecs, Benjamin Read found no evidence supporting a direct connection. The myth, initiated by the Spanish, was simply picked up later among the Pueblos. Benjamin M. Read, "The Last Word on 'Montezuma,'" *New Mexico Historical Review,* 1 (July 1926): 350–58.

12. Stewart, *Sheldon Jackson*, 229.

13. "Pueblo Indian Village, New Mexico," *RMP*, August 1876; the Rev. Samuel Gorman, "Interesting Reminiscences of Early Missionary Operations at Laguna Pueblo," November 1876, Jackson Scrapbooks 58:116.

14. B. M. Thomas to John Lowrie, June 28, 1875, AIC, file o(2), document 213; Edwin Lewis to E. P. Smith, August 25, 1874, and B. M. Thomas to Smith, January 13, 1876, OIA, M234, Rolls 563 and 569; J. W. Daniels to E. P. Smith, Commissioner of Indian Affairs, August 31, 1874, Records of the Bureau of Indian Affairs, Record Group 75, OIA, Reports of Inspection of the Field Jurisdiction, 1873–1900, Microcopy M1070, Roll 29.

15. John Menaul to Lowrie, January 15, 1876, AIC, file C, document 198; *Necrological Reports, Princeton Theological Seminary* 4:165–66; Mark T. Banker, "Presbyterian Missionary Activity in the Southwest: The Careers of John and James Menaul," *Journal of the West* 23 (January 1984), 55–56.

16. B. M. Thomas to John Lowrie, June 28, 1875, AIC, file o(2), document 213; John Menaul to Jackson, February 10, 1876, and Cyrus Dickson to Jackson, February 23, 1876, Jackson Correspondence 6:794–95, 812–13.

17. Sheldon Jackson, "Home Missions Among the Ancient Pueblos," *RMP*, July 1876.

18. B. M. Thomas to John Lowrie, February 5, 1877, AIC, file C, document 133.

19. William Henry Jackson, *Time Exposure: The Autobiography of William Henry Jackson* (Albuquerque: University of New Mexico Press, 1968), 244–45.

20. Sheldon Jackson Travel Journals, 1877, PHS, entries for March 22–April 5.

21. Jackson Travel Journals, 1877, PHS, April 7, 10, 11, and 22; "St. Louis Letter, May 12, 1877," Jackson Scrapbooks 41:146–47.

22. "Missionary Explorations in New Mexico and Arizona," Jackson Scrapbooks 55:17; W. H. Jackson diary, 1877, 10–11, typed transcript, Rare Books and Manuscripts Division, New York Public Library, Astor, Lenox and Tilden Foundations.

23. Sheldon Jackson Travel Journals, 1877, PHS, entry for March 31.

24. Thomas to Sheldon Jackson, March 2, 1877, Jackson Correspondence 7:29; Thomas to E. P. Smith, Commissioner of Indian Affairs, May 16, 1877, OIA, M234, Roll 571; Thomas to Jackson, July 2, 1877, miscellaneous Letters Sent by the Pueblo Indian Agency, 1874–91, Microfilm M941, Roll II, National Archives Regional Office, Federal Center, Denver, Colorado.

25. *RMP*, August 1877.

26. H. K. Palmer, "Aztec Mission at Zuni," *RMP*, January 1878; Benjamin Thomas to Palmer, October 2, 1877, Letters Sent, Pueblo Agency, M941, Roll II.

27. Mrs. H. K. Palmer, "The Journey to Zuni in an Ox Wagon," *RMP*, February 1878.

28. Mrs. Flora D. Palmer, "To the Ladies of the Presbyterian Church," April 8, 1878, Jackson Scrapbooks 55:14–16.

29. Stewart, *Sheldon Jackson*, 238.

30. Sheldon Jackson, untitled article, *RMP*, November 1877; Kendall to Jackson, June 15, 1877, Jackson Correspondence 7:71; Stewart, *Sheldon Jackson*, 239–40;

William Vandever to E. P. Smith, October 8, 1877, OIA, M234, Roll 572; John Menaul, "Laguna Aztec Mission," [1877], Jackson Scrapbooks 55:16–17.

31. J. M. Shields, "Home Mission Letter to Children," June 4 and August 8, 1878, Jackson Scrapbooks 57:22–24; Alice Blake, "Spanish Speaking Missions in New Mexico," manuscript, 234, PHS; "Historical Sketch of Jemez Mission and Church," September 7, 1878, Jackson Correspondence 8:233. Joe Sando has provided an interesting study of the Jemez Pueblo in his *Nee Hemish: A History of Jemez Pueblo* (Albuquerque: University of New Mexico Press, 1982.)

32. J. M. Roberts, moderator, and J. A. Annin, stated clerk, Presbytery of Santa Fe, to John Lowrie, secretary, Board of Foreign Missions, November 10, 1877, Jackson Correspondence 7:173.

33. James Roberts to John Lowrie, December 31, 1877, AIC, file G, document 315.

34. Lowrie to Ben Thomas, February 24, 1877, BFM, Letters Sent, K–1, 341.

35. *General Assembly Minutes, 1877*, 521–22.

36. Minutes, Board of Home Missions, April 8, 1878, 375–77.

37. *RMP*, October 1878.

38. "Laguna Pueblo—Presbyterian Church Organized," [1878], Jackson Scrapbooks 57:27; *RMP*, October 1878; Sheldon Jackson, "Through The Ancient Province Of Tiguex To Hah-Koo-Kee-Ah," *RMP*, December 1878.

39. "Dr. H. K. Palmer," *RMP*, July 1878; Henry Palmer, "Zuni Mission, New Mexico," *RMP*, March 1878; Henry Palmer, "Among The Aztecs," *RMP*, May 1878; John Menaul to Henry Kendall, April 18, 1878, Jackson Correspondence 8:23.

40. Sheldon Jackson, "The Ancient Cities of Cibola, No. 2," *RMP*, January 1879.

41. Sheldon Jackson, "Through The Ancient Province Of Tiguex To Hah-Koo-Kee-Ah," *RMP*, December 1878.

42. Sheldon Jackson, "The Ancient Cities of Cibola, No. 2," *RMP*, January 1879; "The Children's Church Building Stock Company," *RMP*, October 1878.

43. Report of A. L. Earle, March, 1879, in *Board of Indian Commissioners, Eleventh Annual Report for 1879* (Washington, D.C., 1880), 56.

44. For a comprehensive examination of Taylor Ealy's work at Lincoln, New Mexico, and the Zuni Pueblo, see Norman J. Bender, *Missionaries, Outlaws, and Indians: Taylor F. Ealy at Lincoln and Zuni, 1878–1881* (Albuquerque: University of New Mexico Press, 1984).

45. J. M. Shields to Jackson, November [n.d.], 1878, Jackson Correspondence 8:288–90.

46. Shields to Jackson, July 28, 1879, Jackson Correspondence 9:253–54; "Missionary Weddings," *RMP*, December 1879.

47. J. V. Lauderdale to Jackson, January 21, 1877, Jackson Correspondence 7:6.

48. Joseph Wasson, "The Southwest in 1880," *New Mexico Historical Review* 5 (July 1930): 277–78. A copy of several pages from a catechism printed by Menaul shows that the usual catechetical questions were studied. The Indian children discovered, for example, that their first parents were two people named Adam and Eve. "Catechism," Jackson Scrapbooks 58:73.

49. J. M. Shields to Jackson, April 19, 1880, Jackson Correspondence 10:123;

RMP, May 1880; Jackson to Carl Schurz, secretary of the interior, March 1, 1880, Records of the Bureau of Indian Affairs, OIA, M234, Roll 579. A useful examination of the origins of the famous Carlisle School is found in Robert L. Brunhouse, "The Founding of the Carlisle Indian School," *Pennsylvania History* 6 (April 1939): 72-85.

50. Stewart, *Sheldon Jackson*, 243-45.

51. Sheldon Jackson, "Gathering Indian Children for Carlisle and Hampton," *RMP*, March and April 1881.

52. J. S. Shearer to Jackson, December 28, 1881, Jackson Correspondence 11:356; E. Conklin, "New Mexico's Indians," n.d., Jackson Scrapbooks 58:46; Lillie G. McKinney, "History of Albuquerque Indian School," *New Mexico Historical Review*, 20 (April 1945): 113. The Presbyterian Church still supports a highly regarded secondary school for Indian and Hispanic students in Albuquerque. The Menaul School was named for John Menaul's brother James who came to Albuquerque to take charge of the Presbyterian church organized in that city in 1880.

53. John M. Hamilton, "History of the Presbyterian Work among the Pima and Papago Indians of Arizona," 22-30. M.A. thesis, University of Arizona, 1948. After several relocations, the school started by Charles Cook functions today in Tempe, Arizona, as the Cook College and Theological School, offering courses for Indian students.

54. W. Conklin, "New Mexico's Indians," [1881], Jackson Scrapbooks 58:46.

55. Granville Stuart with Paul C. Phillips, *Forty Years on the Frontier* (Cleveland, Ohio: Arthur A. Clark, 1925), 2:75.

56. *RMP*, September 1877.

57. Stewart, *Sheldon Jackson*, 296.

CHAPTER 11

1. "Annual Narrative of the State of Religion," *RMP*, July 1878.

2. Henry Kendall and Cyrus Dickson to the secretary of the interior, December 10, 1877, Jackson Correspondence 7:191-92.

3. Stewart, *Sheldon Jackson*, 294-98.

4. Sheldon Jackson, "Statement of Pecuniary Relations Between Rev. Aaron L. Lindsley and Mrs. Amanda McFarland," n.d., ibid., 7:221; H. Kendall to Jackson, April 19, 1877, ibid., 7:54-55. At the bottom of Kendall's letter, Jackson wrote, "The above letter resulted in the opening of Alaska to gospel work."

5. Jackson to Dear Brother Condit, July 12, 1878, ibid., 8:303; *RMP*, May 1878.

6. Sheldon Jackson, "The Northwest" and "Home Mission Sketches from the Northwest," *RMP*, November and December 1877; *Annual of Washington and Jefferson College*, 100; Charles A. Anderson, "Letters of Amanda R. McFarland," *JPH* 34 (June 1956): 83.

7. Stewart, *Sheldon Jackson*, 290-92.

8. Sheldon Jackson, "Alaska," *RMP*, February 1878; Jackson to Henry J. Van Dyke, February 14, 1879, Jackson Correspondence 9:95. An admirable account of the extraordinary career of the young missionary appointed to Sitka can be found in Ted C.

Hinckley, *Alaskan John G. Brady: Missionary, Businessman, Judge and Governor, 1878–1918* (Columbus, Ohio: Ohio State University Press with Miami University, 1982).

9. "Fort Wrangell, Alaska," *RMP,* October 1879; Jackson to Henry J. Van Dyke, February 14, 1879, Jackson Correspondence 9:95.

10. Amanda McFarland, "Alaska" and "Fort Wrangell, Alaska," *RMP,* January and March 1880; "Organization of the First Presbyterian Church in Alaska," *RMP,* October 1879.

11. Sheldon Jackson, *Alaska and Missions on the North Pacific Coast* (New York: Dodd, Mead, 1880).

12. R. W. and Sadie H. Hall to Jackson, December 15, 1879, Jackson Correspondence 9:313–14.

13. George G. Smith, Presbytery of Montana, to Drs. Kendall and Dickson, secretaries of the Board of Home Missions, February 21, 1880, ibid., 10:48–50.

14. Stewart, *Sheldon Jackson,* 327; *Presbyterian Home Missions* (formerly *Rocky Mountain Presbyterian*), July 1881; J. M. Coyner, "The Utah Column," *RMP,* November 1880; "Commission," October 1, 1881, Jackson Scrapbooks 64:111. McMillan moved on to serve as president of the College of Montana, which opened at Deer Lodge in 1883. In 1890 he was honored with an appointment as secretary of the Board of Home Missions, *General Assembly Minutes,* 1890, 212.

15. Stewart, *Sheldon Jackson,* 335–36.

16. Minutes, Board of Home Missions, December 27, 1881.

17. Stewart, *Sheldon Jackson,* 329; Minutes, Board of Home Missions, November 22, 1881, 26.

18. Stewart, *Sheldon Jackson,* 36–38; Hinckley, *Alaskan John G. Brady,* 38, 47, 58–59; Sheldon Jackson, *The Presbyterian Church in Alaska: An Official Sketch of Its Rise and Progress, 1877–1884* (Washington, D.C.: Thomas McGill, 1886), in Jackson Correspondence 13:411.

19. Minutes, Board of Home Missions, January 24, 1882, 38.

20. Ibid., January 23, 1883, 103; Ted C. Hinckley, "Sheldon Jackson: Gilded Age Apostle," *Journal of the West* 23 (January 1984):21.

21. Stewart, *Sheldon Jackson,* 339.

22. Ted C. Hinckley has provided a thorough account of Jackson's activities as a lobbyist in Washington, D.C., in his "Sheldon Jackson, Presbyterian Lobbyist for the Great Land of Alaska," *JPH* 40 (March 1962):3–23.

23. Ted C. Hinckley, "Sheldon Jackson and Benjamin Harrison: Presbyterians and the Administration of Alaska," *Pacific Northwest Quarterly* 54 (April 1963):69–70.

24. T. W. Bicknell to Jackson, December 3, 1884, Jackson Correspondence 13:434; Stewart, *Sheldon Jackson,* 342–44; Minutes, Board of Home Missions, June 10, 1884, 201; Presbytery of Alaska: Minutes of the First Meeting, September 14–15, 1884, Jackson Correspondence 13:415–19.

25. Stewart, *Sheldon Jackson,* 346–47; "Appointment as Special Agent for Alaska," April 11, 1885, Jackson Scrapbooks 64:139.

26. Stewart, *Sheldon Jackson,* 352–54; Ted C. Hinckley, *The Americanization of Alaska, 1867–1897* (Palo Alto, Calif.: Pacific, 1972), 166–67.

27. Henry Kendall to Jackson, December 20, 1886, Jackson Correspondence 14:249–50.

28. Stewart, *Sheldon Jackson*, 380–81, 386.

29. Sheldon Jackson, Annual Report, 1890, ibid., 387.

30. Karl Ward, "A Study of the Introduction of Reindeer into Alaska," *JPH* 33 (December 1955): 235–36, and *JPH* 34 (December 1956): 245–47.

31. Stewart, *Sheldon Jackson*, 440–41.

32. Ibid., 442–48.

33. Ibid., 448.

34. Ibid., 456.

35. Frank C. Churchill, "Reports on the Condition of Educational and School Service and the Management of Reindeer Service in the District of Alaska," *Senate Executive Documents*, 59th Congress, 1:483 (Washington: Government Printing Office, June 12, 1906), 12–13, 65, 116–17.

36. Jackson to George Darley, January 9, 1909 inside front cover of Robert L. Stewart, *Sheldon Jackson*, Archives, University of Colorado at Boulder Libraries; Hinckley, *Alaskan John G. Brady*, 354–56.

37. A. K. Baird to Jackson, November 26, 1881, Jackson Correspondence 11:320; Clarence G. Reynolds, "Last Chapter of Sheldon Jackson's Life," *Home Mission Monthly* 23 (July 1909):212–13.

CONCLUSION

1. C. L. Richards, "Montana Letter," *RMP*, April 1880; McKinney, *Presbyterianism in Montana*, 14; Mary Ellen Scott to author, December 6, 1877; Smalley, *History of the Northern Pacific Railroad*, 396. The Presbyterian Church sponsored two more schools in Montana late in the nineteenth century, the Bozeman Academy (1887–1892) and the College of Montana at Deer Lodge (1883–1900). Bender, "The Very Atmosphere is Charged with Unbelief," 21, 23–24.

2. "Historical Sketch" and "Ministers Dismissed," Minutes of the Presbytery of Pueblo (typed copy), 5, 175; Delos Edwin Finks, *The Auburn Seminary Record*, 296 (n.d., n.p.) in biographical files H5 at PHS; M. H. MacLeod, *Historical Sketch of the Presbytery of Pueblo*, 81.

3. Alex Darley to Jackson, March 8, 1880, and J. J. Gilchrist to Jackson, October 27, 1881, Jackson Correspondence 10:64 and 11:279.

4. Annie G. Darley, "The Literature of Salvation Among the Spanish Speaking People of the Southwest," n.d., Alexander Darley Scrapbook, unpaginated, Darley Collection, University of Colorado.

5. "The Late Rev. Alexander Darley," *Daily Bulletin* (Manila, P.I.), 1912, ibid. In his condemnation of Penitente rituals, Darley gave himself the title "Apostle of the Colorado Mexicans." Alexander M. Darley, *The Passionists of the Southwest or the Holy Brotherhood—A Revelation of the Penitentes* (Pueblo, Colorado; privately printed, 1893). When asked why Alex Darley went to the Philipines in 1907, his nephew replied, "Maybe he was looking for some more Catholics to whip." Marshall Darley, interview with author, May 16, 1969.

6. George Darley, *Pioneering in the San Juan*, 45; George Darley to Jackson, March 9, 1880, and February 15, 1881, Jackson Correspondence 10:67 and 11:53–54; *RMP,* July 1881; "Rev. G. M. Darley, Pioneer Pastor, is Buried Today," *Denver Times,* February 23, 1917. A compelling story of the life and ministry of a graduate of the College of the Southwest can be found in Gabino Rendón, as told to Edith Agnew, *Hand on My Shoulder* (New York: Board of National Missions, The United Presbyterian Church in the U.S.A., 1963). For a brief history of the College of the Southwest, see Norman J. Bender, "A College Where One Ought to Be," *The Colorado Magazine* 49 (Summer 1972): 196–218.

7. J. M. Coyner, "The Utah Column" and "Utah Presbytery," *RMP,* April 1880; *General Assembly Minutes,* 1890, 212; Donald T. McMillan, n.d., "A Genealogical Record of the McMillan Family," Wasatch Academy, Mt. Pleasant, Utah. The Wasatch Academy, founded by McMillan in 1875, still operates under this name in Mt. Pleasant.

8. "Sheldon Jackson on Mormonism," address at General Assembly, 1902, in biographical files H5 at PHS; Resolutions of the Board of Home Missions of the Presbyterian Church, December 8, 1899, Jackson Correspondence 19:122–24. Westminster College is a thriving school in Salt Lake City at present with joint sponsorship by several Protestant denominations. Andrew E. Murray, *The Skyline Synod,* 105.

9. Mark T. Banker, "Presbyterian Missionary Activity in the Southwest," 59–60 and *Presbyterian Missions and Cultural Interaction in the Far Southwest, 1850–1950,* 58; "John Menaul," *Necrological Reports, Princeton Theological Seminary* 4:165–66; "Necrology—John Milton Shields," *General Assembly Minutes, 1916,* 298; Bender, *Missionarys, Outlaws and Indians,* 138, 157, 166.

10. Benge, "Benjamin Thomas," vi, vii, 251, and paper presented at annual meeting of the Historical Society of New Mexico, April 1991, copy to author; Drury, *Presbyterian Panorama,* 191.

11. "Historical Sketch of the United States Indian School, Albuquerque, New Mexico," n.d., R. W. D. Bryan Collection, Library, University of New Mexico, Albuquerque, 3–5; Barber and Agnew, *Sowers Went Forth,* 44–45; Banker, "Presbyterian Missionary Activity in the Southwest," 58–59; Hamilton, "History of the Presbyterian Work Among the Pima and Papago Indians," 37; *Catalogue, Cook Christian Training School* (Tempe, Arizona: privately printed, 1969), 9.

12. "John Alexander Annin," *Necrological Reports, Princeton Theological Seminary* 4:287–88; Rendón, *Hand On My Shoulder,* 43; Mary Maude Roberts Mercereau, "Story of the Life of Some Home Missionaries in the Early Days," May 9, 1941, manuscript in the library, Menaul School, Albuquerque, New Mexico, 8.

13. John Shields to Jackson, April 19, 1880, Jackson Correspondence 10:123; Minutes, Board of Home Missions, October 4, 1880, 532.

14. "Memorial Sketch of the Reverend José Ynes Perea, 1837–1910," *La Aurora* (Las Vegas, New Mexico), November 15, 1910.

15. "Rev. Henry Kendall, D.D.," *Home Missionary Hero Series, Number 10* (New York: Board of Home Missions, 1902), 8.

16. Walter Prescott Webb, *The Great Plains* (New York: Grosset and Dunlap, 1931), 8; and *The Great Frontier* (Austin: University of Texas Press, 1952), 91.

17. Earl Pomeroy, "Toward a Reorientation of Western History: Continuity and Environment," *Mississippi Valley Historical Review* 41 (March 1955), 581, 593; Louis B. Wright, *Culture on the Moving Frontier* (Bloomington: Indiana University Press, 1955), 168; Peter G. Mode, *The Frontier Spirit in American Christianity* (New York: Macmillan, 1923), 143.

18. Webb, *The Great Frontier,* 91.

19. Stewart, *Sheldon Jackson,* 155; Robert G. Athearn, *The Coloradans* (Albuquerque: University of New Mexico Press, 1976), 103–5.

20. George Darley reported a particularly successful series of temperance lectures at his church in Lake City, Colorado. "The saloons are closing," he told Jackson. "No business. Some of the saloon keepers do not think as much of me as they did." Darley to Jackson, December 27, 1877, Jackson Correspondence 7:204–5.

21. Robert E. Morris, ed., *Collections of the Wyoming Historical Society* (Cheyenne: Wyoming Historical Society, 1897), 272–73; Dorothea R. Muller, "Church Building and Community Making on the Frontier, A Case Study: Josiah Strong, Home Missionary in Cheyenne, 1871–73," *Western Historical Quarterly* 10 (April 1979): 200, 208, 211; *RMP,* June 1873.

22. Stuart, *Forty Years on the Frontier,* 1:251–52.

23. Goodykoontz, *Home Missions,* 420. Several writers have addressed the significance of Presbyterian schools among the "exceptional populations" in the late nineteenth century. George K. Davies examined the meaningful role of Presbyterian missionaries in securing a free public school system in Utah in his doctoral dissertation "A History of the Presbyterian Church in Utah," University of Pittsburgh, 1942. Sarah Deutsch considered the value placed on education by many Hispanic families and the resulting attendance of large numbers of their children in Presbyterian schools in her book *No Separate Refuge: Culture, Class and Gender on an Anglo-Hispanic Frontier in the American Southwest, 1880–1940* (New York: Oxford University Press, 1987). Ruth K. Barber and Edith J. Agnew provided a provocative history of the so-called "plaza schools" conducted by the Presbyterian Church for Hispanic students in small rural communities in New Mexico and southern Colorado in *Sowers Went Forth* (Albuquerque: Menaul Historical Society, 1981). Mark T. Banker discussed Presbyterian involvement with schools for Hispanic and Indian students in the Southwest in his excellent study *Presbyterian Missions and Cultural Interaction in the Far Southwest, 1850–1950* (Urbana: University of Illinois Press, 1993).

24. Hinckley, "Sheldon Jackson and Benjamin Harrison," 70–74. Hinckley regarded Jackson's position on the liquor issue as a regrettable blunder.

25. Churchill, "Reports," 12, 22; Hinckley, *Alaskan John G. Brady,* 241.

26. Churchill, "Reports," 13.

27. Stewart, *Sheldon Jackson,* 363–66.

28. Ted Hinckley, "The Presbyterian Leadership in Pioneer Alaska," *Journal of American History* 42 (March 1966): 745–46.

29. Stewart, *Sheldon Jackson*, 391.

30. Churchill, "Reports," 34, 65.

31. Dorothy Jean Ray, "Sheldon Jackson and the Reindeer Industry of Alaska," *JPH* 43 (June 1965), 71–99. J. Arthur Lazell provides a succinct analysis of the long term reproduction and survival rate of the Alaskan reindeer in his *Alaskan Apostle: The Life Story of Sheldon Jackson* (New York: Harper and Brothers, 1960), 195–96.

32. Jackson, *Alaska and Missions*, 123.

33. Michael C. Coleman, *Presbyterian Attitudes toward American Indians, 1837–1893* (Jackson: University Press of Mississippi, 1985), 139–65.

34. Andrew Murray suggests that Jackson's work has been so romanticized that legend and reality are inseparable. Andrew E. Murray, *The Skyline Synod: Presbyterianism in Colorado and Utah* (Denver, Colo.: Golden Bell, 1971), 53. Ferenc Szasz concluded that the portrayal of western missionaries as heroes represents a difficult task, since the subjects generally personified society's conventional traits. Ferenc Morton Szasz, *The Protestant Clergy in the Great Plains and the Mountain West, 1869–1915* (Albuquerque: University of New Mexico Press, 1988), 214.

35. Drury, *Presbyterian Panorama*, 191.

36. Ted Hinckley, "Sheldon Jackson as Preserver of Alaska's Native Culture," *Pacific Historical Review* 33 (November 1964): 416–17.

37. H. H. Young, Hanover, Indiana, to Jackson, June 19, 1874, Jackson Correspondence 5:440; "Who's Who in Presbyterian Missions," n.d., n.p., and "Sheldon Jackson: Autobiographical Sketch," 1897, in biographical files H5 at PHS.

38. Stewart, *Sheldon Jackson*, 148.

39. Ted Hinckley, "Publicist of the Forgotten Frontier," *Journal of the West* 4 (January 1965): 27.

Bibliography

Government Documents

Board of Indian Commissioners. *Eleventh Annual Report for 1879.* Washington, D.C., 1880.

Churchill, Frank C. "Reports on the Condition of Educational and School Service and the Management of Reindeer Service in the District of Alaska." *Senate Executive Documents*, 59th Congress, 1:483. Washington, D.C.: Government Printing Office, June, 12, 1906.

Miscellaneous Letters Sent by the Pueblo Indian Agency, 1874–1891, Microfilm M941, National Archives Regional Office, Federal Center, Denver, Colorado.

Ninth Census of the United States: Statistics of Population. Washington, D.C.: Government Printing Office, 1872.

Records of the Bureau of Indian Affairs, Record Group 75. Office of Indian Affairs, Letters Sent, 1824–1882, Microcopy M21.

———. Letters Received, 1824–1880, New Mexico Superintendency, 1849–1880, Microcopy M234.

———.Reports of Inspection of the Field Jurisdiction, 1873–1900, Microcopy M1070.

Session Records of Presbyterian Churches

Del Norte, Colorado
Idaho Springs, Colorado
Lake City, Colorado
Longmont (Central), Colorado
Rosita, Colorado
Valmont, Colorado
Hokah, Minnesota

Las Vegas, New Mexico
Corinne, Utah
Cheyenne (First), Wyoming
Rawlins, Wyoming

OTHER PRESBYTERIAN MINUTES AND RECORDS

Board of Foreign Missions, Letterpress Copies of Letters Sent, PHS.
Minutes, Board of Domestic Missions, PHS.
Minutes, Board of Home Missions, PHS.
Minutes of the First Meeting, Presbytery of Alaska, September 14–15, 1884, PHS.
Minutes of the General Assembly of the Presbyterian Church in the United States of America. Philadelphia: Presbyterian Board of Publications, published annually.
"Minutes of Local Attempts to Organize a Presbytery of Colorado, January 15 and 16 and February 3, 1866." Presbyterian Historical Society [PHS], Philadelphia, Pennsylvania.
Minutes, Presbytery of Colorado, 1870–1878, PHS.
Minutes, Pueblo [Colorado] Presbytery, 1880–1891. Typed copy at Faith Presbyterian Church, Colorado Springs, Colorado.
"Minutes of the Presbytery of Santa Fe, 1868." *Journal of Presbyterian History* 33 (September 1955): 199–206.
Minutes, Synod of Colorado, 1871–1888, PHS.

CHURCH HISTORIES

First Presbyterian Church, Bozeman, Montana, Centennial Edition. Bozeman: privately printed, 1972.
France Memorial United Presbyterian Church, Rawlins, Wyoming, Centennial Booklet, 1869–1969. Rawlins: privately printed, 1969.
Hines, Edgar A., Jr. *First Presbyterian Church, Rochester, Minnesota, Centennial Celebration, 1861–1961.* Rochester: privately printed, 1961.
MacLeod, M. H. *Historical Sketch of the Presbytery of Pueblo.* Pueblo, Colo.: privately printed, 1906.
McKinney, Patricia. *First Presbyterian Church, Helena, Montana.* Helena: privately printed, 1947.
———. *Presbyterianism in Montana: Its First Hundred Years.* Helena: privately printed, 1969.
Morton, Katharine A., and Dubois, William R. *A Century of Service: First Presbyterian Church, Cheyenne, Wyoming, 1869–1969.* Cheyenne: privately printed, 1969.
Reusser, Walter C., et al. *The United Presbyterian Church of Laramie, Wyoming, 1869–1969.* Laramie: privately printed, 1969.

White, James H. *The First Hundred Years of Central Presbyterian Church, 1860–1960.* Denver, Colo.: Great Western Stockman, 1960.

Yates, Sarah. *A Centennial History of the Community Presbyterian Church of Brigham City, Utah, 1878–1978.* Brigham City: privately printed, 1978.

SPEECHES AND SERMONS

Jackson, Sheldon. "The Iowa Movement for Home Missions." Speech delivered at a meeting of the Synod of Iowa, 1905. Copy provided by the Reverend John Pattison, First Presbyterian Church, Cheyenne, Wyoming.

Historical Sermons, 1876, PHS.

Annin, John. "Las Vegas, New Mexico."

Finks, Delos. "Fairplay, Colorado."

Gillespie, Samuel L. "Corinne, Utah."

Jackson, Sheldon. "Pioneer Presbyterian in the Rocky Mountain Territories, 1869–1876."

Stewart, Robert L. "Golden and Black Hawk, Colorado."

Teitsworth, William E. "Longmont, Colorado."

DISSERTATIONS AND THESES

Bailey, Alvin K. "The Strategy of Sheldon Jackson in Opening the West for National Missions, 1860–1880." Ph.D. thesis, Yale University, New Haven, 1948.

Benge, Reba N. "Benjamin M. Thomas: Career in the Southwest, 1870–1892." Ph.D. dissertation, University of New Mexico, Albuquerque, 1979.

Davies, George K. "A History of the Presbyterian Church in Utah." Ph.D. dissertation, University of Pittsburgh, 1942.

Goslin, Thomas S., II. "Henry Kendall and the Evangelization of a Continent." Ph.D. thesis, University of Pennsylvania, Philadelphia, 1948.

Hamilton, John M. "History of the Presbyterian Work among the Pima and Papago Indians of Arizona." M.A. thesis, University of Arizona, Tucson, 1948.

Lyon, Thomas E. "Evangelical Protestant Missionary Activities in Mormon Dominated Areas, 1865–1900." Ph.D. thesis, University of Utah, Salt Lake City, 1962.

Wankier, Carl. "History of Presbyterian Schools in Utah." M.S. thesis, University of Utah, Salt Lake City, 1968.

Webster, Lewis G. "A History of Westminster College of Salt Lake City, 1875–1969." M.S. thesis, Utah State University, Logan, 1970.

NEWSPAPERS

Church Review (Salt Lake City, Utah), historical edition, December 29, 1895.

La Aurora (Las Vegas, New Mexico), November 15, 1910.

North–Western Presbyterian (Chicago), October 24, 1868.

Rocky Mountain News (Denver), 1870–1880.
Rocky Mountain Presbyterian (Denver), 1872–1880.
Santa Fe New Mexican, November 19 and 21, and December 15, 1870.
Utah Westminster (Salt Lake City), special edition, October 1922.

CORRESPONDENCE AND INTERVIEWS

American Indian Correspondence, PHS.
Sheldon Jackson. Correspondence Relating to Pioneer Presbyterian Missions
      West of the Mississippi and Missouri Rivers and in Alaska, 1856–1908, 26
      volumes, PHS.
Mary Ellen Scott, Archivist, Pittsburgh Theological Seminary, Pittsburgh, to
      author, December 6, 1977.
Interview with Marshall Darley, Monte Vista, Colo., May 16, 1969.

BOOKS

Abbott, Carl. *Colorado: A History of the Centennial State.* Boulder: Colorado
      Associated University Press, 1976.
Allen, T. D. *Not Ordered by Men.* Santa Fe, N.M.: Rydal, 1967.
Annual of Washington and Jefferson College, Washington, Pennsylvania. Buffalo,
      N.Y.: Gies, 1889.
Arizona. American Guide Series. New York: Hastings House, 1956.
Athearn, Robert G. *The Coloradans.* Albuquerque: University of New Mexico
      Press, 1976.
Banker, Mark T. "Missionary to His Own People: José Ynes Perea and Hispanic
      Presbyterianism in New Mexico." In *Religion and Society in the American
      West*, edited by Carl Guarneri and David Alvarez. Lanham, Md.:
      University Press of America, 1987.
————. *Presbyterian Missions and Cultural Interaction in the Far Southwest,
      1850–1950.* Urbana: University of Illinois Press, 1993.
Barber, Ruth, and Edith Agnew. *Sowers Went Forth:* The Story of Presbyterian
      Missions in New Mexico and Southern Colorado. Albuquerque: Menaul
      Historical Library, 1981.
Beardsley, Isaac. *Echoes from Peak and Plain.* Cincinnati, Ohio: Curts and
      Jennings, 1898.
Bender, Norman J. *Missionaries, Outlaws and Indians: Taylor F. Ealy at Lincoln and
      Zuni, 1878–1881.* Albuquerque: University of New Mexico Press, 1984.
————. *New Hope for the Indians: The Grant Peace Policy and the Navajos in the
      1870s.* Albuquerque: University of New Mexico Press, 1989.
Boyd, Lois A., and R. Douglas Brackenridge. *Presbyterian Women in America: Two
      Centuries of a Quest for Status.* Westport, Conn.: Greenwood, 1983.
Boylan, Anne M. *Sunday School: The Formation of an American Institution,
      1790–1880.* New Haven: Yale University Press, 1988.

Brackenridge, R. Douglas, and Francisco O. García–Treto. *Iglesia Presbiteriana: A History of Presbyterians and Mexican Americans in the Southwest.* San Antonio, Tex.: Trinity University Press, 1974.

Clum, Woodworth. *Apache Agent.* Lincoln: University of Nebraska Press, 1978.

Coleman, Michael C. *Presbyterian Missionary Attitudes toward American Indians, 1837–1893.* Jackson: University Press of Mississippi, 1985.

Colorado. American Guide Series. New York: Hastings House, 1941.

Craig, Robert M. *Our Mexicans.* New York: Board of Home Missions of the Presbyterian Church in the United States of America, 1904.

Darley, George M. *Pioneering in the San Juan.* New York: Fleming H. Revell, 1899.

DeTocqueville, Alexis. *Democracy in America.* Translated by George Lawrence and edited by J. P. Mayer. New York: Anchor Doubleday, 1969.

Deutsch, Sarah. *No Separate Refuge: Class and Gender on an Anglo–Hispanic Frontier in the American Southwest, 1880–1940.* New York: Oxford University Press, 1987.

Doyle, Sherman H. *Presbyterian Home Missions.* Philadelphia: Presbyterian Board of Publications and Sabbath School Work, 1902.

Drury, Clifford M. *Presbyterian Panorama.* Philadelphia: Board of Christian Education, Presbyterian Church in the United States of America, 1952.

Goodykoontz, Colin B. *Home Missions on the American Frontier.* Caldwell, Idaho: Caxton, 1939.

Hall, John. "The Future Church." In *Presbyterian Reunion Memorial Volume, 1837–1871.* New York: DeWitt C. Lent, 1870.

Hinckley, Ted C. *Alaskan John G. Brady: Missionary, Businessman, Judge and Governor, 1878–1918.* Columbus: Ohio State University Press with Miami University, 1982.

———. *The Americanization of Alaska, 1867–1897.* Palo Alto, Calif.: Pacific, 1972.

Hodge, J. A. *What is Presbyterian Law as Defined by the Church Courts?* Philadelphia: Presbyterian Board of Publications, 1882.

Horgan, Paul. *Lamy of Santa Fe: His Life and Times.* New York: Farrar, Straus and Giroux, 1975.

Inaugural Addresses of the Presidents of the United States. Washington, D.C.: Government Printing Office, 1969.

Israel, Fred, ed. *Major Peace Treaties of Modern History, 1648–1967.* 4 vols. New York: Chelsea House/McGraw Hill, 1967.

Jackson, Sheldon. *Alaska and Missions on the North Pacific Coast.* New York: Dodd, Mead, 1880.

———. *The Presbyterian Church in Alaska: An Official Sketch of Its Rise and Progress, 1877–1884.* Washington, D.C.: Thomas McGill, 1886. PHS.

Jackson, William Henry. *Time Exposure: The Autobiography of William Henry Jackson.* Albuquerque: University of New Mexico Press, 1968.

Klein, Maury. *Union Pacific: Birth of a Railroad, 1862–1893.* Garden City, N.Y.: Doubleday, 1987.

Lazell, J. Arthur. *Alaskan Apostle: The Life Story of Sheldon Jackson.* New York: Harper and Brothers, 1960.

McMillan, Florence. *The Rev. Duncan James McMillan, 1846–1939—A Tribute.* New York: McAuliffe–Booth, 1939.

Mode, Peter G. *The Frontier Spirit in American Christianity.* New York: Macmillan, 1923.

Montana. American Guide Series. New York: Hastings House, 1939.

Morris, Robert E., ed. *Collections of the Wyoming Historical Society.* Vol. 1. Cheyenne: Wyoming Historical Society, 1897.

Murphy, Lawrence R. *Antislavery in the Southwest: William G. Kephart's Mission to New Mexico, 1850–1853.* El Paso: Texas Western Press, 1978.

Murray, Andrew E. *The Skyline Synod: Presbyterianism in Colorado and Utah.* Denver: Golden Bell, 1971.

Myres, Sandra L., ed. *Cavalry Wife: The Diary of Eveline Alexander, 1866–1867.* College Station: Texas A & M University Press, 1977.

Necrological Reports and Annual Proceedings of Princeton Theological Seminary. 4 vols. Princeton, N.J.: C. S. Robinson, 1891, 1899, 1909, 1919.

Nevin, Alfred, ed. *Encyclopaedia of the Presbyterian Church in the United States of America.* Philadelphia: Presbyterian Encyclopaedia Publishing, 1884.

Porter, Kirk H., and Donald B. Johnson. *National Party Platforms, 1840–1964.* Urbana: University of Illinois Press, 1966.

Prucha, Francis P. *American Indian Policy in Crisis: Christian Reformers and the Indian, 1865–1900.* Norman: University of Oklahoma Press, 1976.

Rendón, Gabino, as told to Edith Agnew. *Hand on My Shoulder.* New York: Board of National Missions, the United Presbyterian Church in the U.S.A., 1963.

Richardson, Albert D. *Beyond the Mississippi, 1857–1867.* Hartford, Conn.: American Publishing, 1867.

Sando, Joe S. *Nee Hemish: A History of Jemez Pueblo.* Albuquerque: University of New Mexico Press, 1982.

———. *The Pueblo Indians.* San Francisco: Indian Historian Press, 1976.

Slosser, G. J., ed. *They Seek a Country: The American Presbyterians.* New York: Macmillan, 1955.

Smalley, Eugene V. *History of the Northern Pacific Railroad.* 1883. Reprint. New York: Arno, 1975.

Stegner, Wallace. *Mormon Country.* New York: Bonanza, 1942.

Stewart, Robert L. *Sheldon Jackson.* New York: Fleming H. Revell, 1908.

Stone, Wilbur F. *History of Colorado.* 4 vols. Chicago: S. J. Clarke, 1918.

Strong, Josiah. *Our Country, Its Possible Future and Its Present Crisis.* 1885. Reprint. New York: Baker and Taylor, 1891.

Stuart, Granville, with Paul C. Phillips. *Forty Years on the Frontier.* 2 vols. Cleveland, Ohio: Arthur A. Clark, 1925.

Szasz, Ferenc Morton. *The Protestant Clergy in the Great Plains and the Mountain West, 1865–1915.* Albuquerque: University of New Mexico Press, 1988.

Taylor, Bayard. *Colorado: A Summer Trip, 1866.* New York: G. P. Putnam and Son, 1867.

Utah. American Guide Series. New York: Hastings House, 1941.

Verdesi, Elizabeth H. *In But Still Out: Women in the Church.* Philadelphia: Westminster, 1975.

Walker, Randi Jones. *Protestantism in the Sangre de Cristos, 1850–1920.* Albuquerque: University of New Mexico Press, 1991.

Webb, Walter P. *The Great Frontier.* Austin: University of Texas Press, 1952.

———. *The Great Plains.* New York: Grosset and Dunlap, 1931.

Weigle, Marta. *Brothers of Light, Brothers of Blood: The Penitentes of the Southwest.* Albuquerque: University of New Mexico Press, 1976.

Wilson, Joseph W. *The Presbyterian Historical Almanac and Annual Remembrance of the Church for 1867.* Philadelphia: privately printed, 1867.

Wright, Louis B. *Culture on the Moving Frontier.* Bloomington: Indiana University Press, 1955.

Wyoming. American Guide Series. New York: Oxford University Press, 1941.

ARTICLES

Agnew, Edith J., and Ruth K. Barber. "The Unique Presbyterian School System of New Mexico." *Journal of Presbyterian History* 49 (Fall 1971): 197–221.

Anderson, Charles A. "Letters of Amanda R. McFarland." *Journal of the Presbyterian Historical Society* 34 (June 1956): 83–102.

Baird, W. David. "Spencer Academy, Choctaw Nation, 1842–1900." *Chronicles of Oklahoma* 45 (Spring 1967): 25–31.

Banker, Mark T. "Presbyterian Missionary Activity in the Southwest: The Careers of John and James Menaul." *Journal of the West* 23 (January 1984): 55–61.

———. "Presbyterians and Pueblos: A Protestant Response to the Indian Question, 1872–1892." *Journal of Presbyterian History* 60 (Spring 1982): 23–40.

Bender, Norman J. "A College Where One Ought To Be." *Colorado Magazine* 49 (Summer 1972): 196–218.

———. "Sheldon Jackson's Crusade to Win the West for Christ, 1869–1880." *Midwest Review* 4 (Spring 1982): 1–12.

———. "'The Very Atmosphere is Charged With Unbelief. . . .'—Presbyterians and Higher Education in Montana, 1869–1900." *Montana* 28 (April 1978): 16–25.

Brunhouse, Robert L. "The Founding of the Carlisle Indian School." *Pennsylvania History* 6 (April 1939): 72–85.

Edwards, George. "Presbyterian Church History." *Contributions to the Historical Society of Montana* 6:1907.

Fisher, John H. "Primary and Secondary Education and the Presbyterian Church in the United States of America." *Journal of the Presbyterian Historical Society* 24 (March 1946): 13–43.

Ford, Henry P. "True Blue Presbyterians." *Journal of Presbyterian History* 14 (March 1931): 238–39.

Hinckley, Ted C. "The Presbyterian Leadership in Pioneer Alaska." *Journal of American History* 42 (March 1966): 742–56.

———. "Publicist of the Forgotten Frontier." *Journal of the West* 4 (January 1965): 27–40.

———. "Sheldon Jackson and Benjamin Harrison: Presbyterians and the Administration of Alaska." *Pacific Northwest Quarterly* 54 (April 1963): 66–74.

———. "Sheldon Jackson as Preserver of Alaska's Native Culture." *Pacific Historical Review* 33 (November 1964): 411–24.

———. "Sheldon Jackson: Gilded Age Apostle." *Journal of the West* 23 (January 1984): 16–25.

———. "Sheldon Jackson, Presbyterian Lobbyist for the Great Land of Alaska." *Journal of Presbyterian History* 40 (March 1962): 3–23.

Jackson, Sheldon. "A Story of Early Home Mission Work." *Assembly Herald* 10 (1904): 1.

MacCormac, Earl R. "The Development of Presbyterian Missionary Organizations, 1790–1870." *Journal of Presbyterian History* 43 (September 1965): 149–73.

McKinney, Lillie G. "History of Albuquerque Indian School." *New Mexico Historical Review* 20 (April 1945): 109–38.

Muller, Dorothea R. "Church Building and Community Making on the Frontier, A Case Study: Josiah Strong, Home Missionary in Cheyenne, 1871–73." *Western Historical Quarterly* 10 (April 1979): 191–216.

"New Hope for the Indians." *Record of the Presbyterian Church in the United States of America* 21 (October 1870): 227.

Penfield, Janet H. "Women in the Presbyterian Church—An Historical Overview." *Journal of Presbyterian History*, 55 (Summer 1977): 107–23.

Pomeroy, Earl. "Toward a Reorientation of Western History: Continuity and Environment." *Mississippi Valley Historical Review* 41 (March 1955): 579–600.

Ray, Dorothy Jean. "Sheldon Jackson and the Reindeer Industry of Alaska." *Journal of Presbyterian History* 43 (June 1965): 71–99.

Read, Benjamin M. "The Last Word on 'Montezuma.'" *New Mexico Historical Review* 1 (July 1926): 350–58.

Reynolds, Clarence G. "Last Chapter of Sheldon Jackson's Life." *Home Mission Monthly* 23 (July 1909): 212–13.

Ross, D. Reid. "The War for Souls in the San Luis Valley." *American Presbyterians* 65 (Spring 1987): 29–37.

Stewart, Robert L. "The Mission of Sheldon Jackson in the Winning of the West." *Journal of Presbyterian History* 6 (June 1911): 49–68.

Ward, Karl. "A Study of the Introduction of Reindeer into Alaska." *Journal of Presbyterian History* 33 (December 1955): 229–37; *JPH* 34 (December 1956): 245–56.

Wasson, Joseph. "The Southwest in 1880." *New Mexico Historical Review* 5 (July 1930): 263–87.

MISCELLANEOUS

Sheldon Jackson Collection, Presbyterian Historical Society.
    Annual reports of the New Mexico, Arizona, and Colorado Missionary
        Association, bound as *Our Mission Field.*
    Raven Fund Account Book.
    Scrapbooks, 64 volumes.
    Travel Journals, 1860, 1869, 1871, 1872, 1877, and 1881.
Darley Collection, Archives, University of Colorado at Boulder Libraries.
    Alexander Darley, Scrapbook.
    George Darley, Pastor's Register.
    George Darley, Sermons.
    George Darley, "Thirty-five Years of Presbyterianism in Colorado," "The
        Twentieth Century Prodigal," and "Gone Away," unpublished
        manuscripts.

Catalogues.

Cook Christian Training School, Tempe, Arizona, 1969.
Princeton Theological Seminary, Princeton, New Jersey, 1855–1856.
    Philadelphia: C. Sherman and Sons, 1856.
Salt Lake Collegiate Institute (catalogue), Salt Lake City, Utah, 1877.
Salt Lake Collegiate Institute (circular), Salt Lake City, Utah, 1876.

Manuscripts.

Blake, Alice. "Spanish Speaking Missions in New Mexico," PHS, Philadelphia.
Coyner, J. M. "History of the Salt Lake Collegiate Institute from Its
    Organization, April 12, 1875." Westminster College, Salt Lake City,
    Utah.
Kemper, Augustus. Paper on Sheldon Jackson, 1908, PHS.
McMillan, Duncan. "Early Beginnings of Wasatch Academy," Wasatch
    Academy, Mt. Pleasant, Utah.
Madsen, Andrew. "The Personal History of Andrew Madsen and the Early
    History of Sanpete County and Mt. Pleasant, Utah." University of Utah,
    Salt Lake City, Utah.
Martin, Theodore D. and Marian E. "Presbyterian Work in Utah, 1869–1969."
    Westminster College, Salt Lake City, Utah.

Scrapbooks.

Emil Nyman, random clippings, Westminster College, Salt Lake City, Utah.
First Presbyterian Church, Santa Fe, New Mexico.
George Darley Collection, Adams State College, Alamosa, Colorado.
"Journal History," random clippings, church historian's office, Church of Jesus
    Christ of Latter-Day Saints, Salt Lake City, Utah.
Sheldon Jackson, 3 vols., Westminster College, Salt Lake City, Utah.

Other.

Sheldon Jackson, "Autobiographical Sketch," 1897. Sheldon Jackson
    biographical file, PHS.
Sheldon Jackson Collection, Speer Library, Princeton Theological Seminary,
    Princeton, New Jersey.
Sheldon Jackson, "Who's Who in Presbyterian Missions." Sheldon Jackson
    biographical file, PHS.
Tracts for Civil War Soldiers, PHS.
William Henry Jackson Diaries, Rare Books and Manuscripts Division, New
    York Public Library, Astor, Lenox and Tilden Foundations.

Index

Abstainers League, 140

Adult education, 123

Alaska, 183–92; Fort Wrangell, 182; Haines, 187; missions, 104, 124, 182, 188; Point Barrow, 189; politics, 191; Sitka, 185, 187, 188, 189; Skagway, 191; temperance, 201; territorial status, 188; Yukon Valley, 190

Alaska and Missions on the North Pacific Coast (1880), 185–86

Alaska, Presbytery of, 188

American Bible Society, 32

American Home Missionary Society, 4–5, 17

American Missionary Association, 150

American Railway Literary Union, 113

American Systematic Beneficence Society of Philadelphia, 5–6

Annin, John, 152–54, 157, 164, 197

Anti-Hispanic propaganda, 94

Apache Indians, 180, 181. *See also* Southern Apache Agency

Arizona: First Presbyterian Church of Tucson, 37; Fort Defiance, 152, 156, 168–69, 171, 173; Prescott, 123; Tucson, 36–37, 197

Army garrisons, 158–59

Arthur, Chester (President), 188

Baptism, 59

Baptist Church: Alaska schools, 202; Baptist Mission Committee, 15; missions in New Mexico, 170

Bayliss, Edward E., 30–31, 136–37

Bells, church, 44

Bent, Mrs. Charles, 155

Bible schools, 57, 114. *See also* Sabbath schools

Board of Domestic Missions: appoints Jackson district missionary, 19–20; Civil War affects, 9; conflicts, 13–14, 19–20; Iowa as base for mission efforts, 4; misunderstandings, 16; opposes Jackson's fund-raising, 13–14; recruits David McFarland, 151; reduces mission allotments, 13. *See also* Board of Home Missions

Board of Foreign Missions: Indians, 152, 166; Jackson applies, 6;